Penn State Season Records - Paterno from 1950 through 2011

Year	Coach	Record	Champs	Bowl col 2
1950	Rip Engle	5-3-1		
1951	Rip Engle	7–2–1		
1952	Rip Engle	7–2–1		
1953	Rip Engle	6-3		
1954	Rip Engle	7-2		
1955	Rip Engle	5-4		
1956	Rip Engle	6-2		
1957	Rip Engle	6-3		
1958	Rip Engle	6–3-1		
1959	Rip Engle	9-2		Won Liberty
1960	Rip Engle	7-3		Won Liberty
1961	Rip Engle	8-3		Won Gator
1962	Rip Engle	9-2		Won Gator
1963	Rip Engle	7-3		
1964	Rip Engle	6-4		
1965	Rip Engle	5-5		
1966	Joe Paterno	5-5		
1967	Joe Paterno	8-2-1		Tied Gator
1968	Joe Paterno	11-0		Won Orange
1969	Joe Paterno	11-0		Won Orange
1970	Joe Paterno	7-3		
1971	Joe Paterno	11-1		Won Cotton
1972	Joe Paterno	10-2		Lost Sugar
1973	Joe Paterno	12-0		Won Orange
1974	Joe Paterno	10-2		Won Cotton
1975	Joe Paterno	9-3		Lost Sugar
1976	Joe Paterno	7-5		Lost Gator
1977	Joe Paterno	11–1		Won Fiesta
1978	Joe Paterno	11-1		Lost Sugar
1979	Joe Paterno	8–4		Won Liberty
1980	Joe Paterno	10-2		Won Fiesta
1981	Joe Paterno	10-2		Won Fiesta
1982	Joe Paterno	11-1	Champs	Won Sugar
1983	Joe Paterno	8-4-1		Won Aloha
1984	Joe Paterno	6–5		
1985	Joe Paterno	11-1		Lost Orange
1986	Joe Paterno	12-0	Champs	Won Fiesta
1987	Joe Paterno	8–4		Lost Citrus
1988	Joe Paterno	5-6		Won Fiesta
1989	Joe Paterno	8-3		Won Holiday
1990	Joe Paterno	9–3		Lost Champs
1991	Joe Paterno	11-2		Won Fiesta
1992	Joe Paterno	7-5		Lost Champs
1993	Joe Paterno	10-2		Won Citrus
1994	Joe Paterno	12-0		Won Rose
1995	Joe Paterno	9–3		Won Outback
1996	Joe Paterno	11-2		Won Fiesta
1997	Joe Paterno	9-3		Lost Citrus.
1998	Joe Paterno	9-3		Won Outback
1999	Joe Paterno	10-3		Won Alamo

Year	Coach	Record		Bowl
2000	Joe Paterno	5-7		
2001	Joe Paterno	5-6		
2002	Joe Paterno	9-4		Lost Cap "1"
2003	Joe Paterno	3-9		
2004	Joe Paterno	4-7		
2005	Joe Paterno	11-1		Won Orange
2006	Joe Paterno	9-4		Won Outback
2007	Joe Paterno	9-4		Won Alamo
2008	Joe Paterno	11-2		Lost Rose
2009	Joe Paterno	11-2		Won Cap "1"
2010	Joe Paterno	7-6		
2011	Joe Paterno	8-1		

Total PSU Wins   867
Total PSU Wins when retired   828
Total Paterno Wins as head coach 409
Total Paterno Wins @ PSU   513
Through August 2017

JoePa
409 Victories:
Say No More!

The winningest Division IA college football coach ever.

This book is written for those of us who love Penn State Football and who never doubted JoePa, or have gotten over the false accusations about Joe Paterno. It recounts his inning legacy – each of the 409 games are in this book. Joseph Vincent Paterno is the winningest coach in major College Football. He was not only a great man but he was an outstanding football coach. There are many malevolent people in life. We meet them every day. Joe Paterno was not one of them!

As I researched my first book about Great Moments in Penn State Football, I had to discuss the Sandusky scandal and end that book with the state of the team with the current coach and administration. This book does not address the scandals in any way. Joe Paterno is the winningest Division I coach ever, period. For those of us who care a lot, 409 isn't just about football. It's about great success with honor.

I admit that I am a Paterno fan. Reading through Joe Paterno's coaching record, which constitutes better than 60% of Penn State's winning record overall, it is tough to not have him as your # 1 coach of all time. He coached the best players and the best teams of all time. His teams played against the best and he passed an endurance test, coaching into his eighties. Nobody ever expected a Joe Paterno team to lose. I rest my case.

You will not be able to put this book down.

Brian Kelly

Copyright © April 2017   Brian W. Kelly
Editor: Brian P. Kelly
JoePa 409 Victories: Say No More!
Author   Brian W. Kelly

All rights reserved: No part of this book may be reproduced or transmitted in any form, or by any means, electronic or mechanical, including photocopying, recording, scanning, faxing, or by any information storage and retrieval system, without permission from the publisher, LETS GO PUBLISH, in writing.

Disclaimer: Though judicious care was taken throughout the writing and the publication of this work that the information contained herein is accurate, there is no expressed or implied warranty that all information in this book is 100% correct. Therefore, neither LETS GO PUBLISH, nor the author accepts liability for any use of this work.

Trademarks: A number of products and names referenced in this book are trade names and trademarks of their respective companies.

Referenced Material: *Standard Disclaimer: The information in this book has been obtained through personal and third party observations, interviews, and copious research. Where unique information has been provided, or extracted from other sources, those sources are acknowledged within the text of the book itself or in the References area in the front matter. Thus, there are no formal footnotes nor is there a bibliography section. Any picture that does not have a source was taken from various sites on the Internet with no credit attached. If resource owners would like credit in the next printing, please email publisher.*

Published by: ....LETS GO PUBLISH!
Editor in Chief ....Brian P. Kelly
Email: ....info@letsgopublish.com
Web site .... www.letsgopublish.com

Library of Congress Copyright Information Pending
Book Cover Design by **Brian W. Kelly using a cover designer**
Editor—**Brian P. Kelly**

ISBN Information: The International Standard Book Number (ISBN) is a unique machine-readable identification number, which marks any book unmistakably. The ISBN is the clear standard in the book industry. 159 countries and territories are officially ISBN members. The Official ISBN for this book is

978-0-9988111-1-6

The price for this work is:...........   **$ 12.99 USD**

10   9   8   7   6   5   4   3   2   1

Release Date: April 2017

LETS GO PUBLISH!

Dedication

*This book is dedicated to my beautiful wife, Patricia, and our three wonderful children—
Brian, Michael, and Kathleen.
Additionally, I recognize the great help from two furry friends, Angel Ben, and Buddy Kelly.*

Acknowledgments:

I appreciate all the help that I received in putting this book together, along with the 66 other books from the past.

My printed acknowledgments were once so large that book readers needed to navigate too many pages to get to page one of the text. To permit me more flexibility, I put my acknowledgment list online at www.letsgopublish.com. The list of acknowledgments continues to grow. Believe it or not, it once cost about a dollar more to print each book.

Thank you all on the big list in the sky and God bless you all for your help.

Please check out www.letsgopublish.com to read the latest version of my heartfelt acknowledgments updated for this book. Thank you all!

In this book, I received some extra special help from many avid Penn State supporters including Bruce Ikeda, Dennis Grimes, Gerry Rodski, Wily Ky Eyely, Angel Irene McKeown Kelly, Angel Edward Joseph Kelly Sr., Angel Edward Joseph Kelly Jr., Ann Flannery, Angel James Flannery Sr., Mary Daniels, Bill Daniels, Robert Gary Daniels, Angel Sarah Janice Daniels, Angel Punkie Daniels, Joe Kelly, Diane Kelly, Brian P. Kelly, Mike P. Kelly, Katie P. Kelly, Angel Irene & Ralph Jachimiak, George & Madelyn Elias, Angel Ben Kelly, and Budmund (Buddy) Arthur Kelly.

References

I learned how to write creatively in Grade School at St. Boniface. I even enjoyed reading some of my own stuff.

At Meyers High School and King's College and Wilkes-University, I learned how to research, write bibliographies and footnote every non-original thought I might have had. I learned to hate ibid, and op. cit., and I hated assuring that I had all citations written down in the proper sequence. Having to pay attention to details took my desire to write creatively and diminished it with busy work.

I know it is necessary for the world to stop plagiarism so authors and publishers can get paid properly, but for an honest writer, it sure is annoying. I wrote many proposals while with IBM and whenever I needed to cite something, I cited it in place, because my readers, IT Managers, could care less about tracing the vagaries of citations. I always hated to use stilted footnotes, or produce a lengthy, perfectly formatted bibliography. I bet most bibliographies are flawed because even the experts on such drivel do not like the tedium.

I wrote 109 books before this book and several hundred articles published by many magazines and newspapers and I only cite when an idea is not mine or when I am quoting, and again, I choose to cite in place, and the reader does not have to trace strange numbers through strange footnotes and back to bibliography elements that may not be readily accessible or available.

Yet, I would be kidding you, if in a book about the great coaches in Penn State Football, I tried to bluff my way into trying to make you think that I knew everything before I began to write anything in this book. I spent as much time researching as writing. I might even call myself an expert of sorts now for all the facts that I have uncovered.

Without any pain on your part you can read this book from cover to cover to enjoy the stories about the many great moments in Penn State Football.

It took me about two months to write this book. If I were to have made sure a thought that I had was not a thought somebody else ever had, this book never would have been completed or the citations pages would exceed the prose.

I used PSU Season summaries from whatever source I could to get the scores of all the games. I verified facts when possible. There are many web sites that have great information and facts. Ironically most internet stories are the same exact stories. While I was writing the book, I wrote down a bunch of Internet references that I show you below and when you finish reading this book, you may click and enjoy them.

My favorite source has been the **Penn State Student Magazine** called the Collegian, which has been published almost from day one under various names by the university.

http://www.collegian.psu.edu/

About

July 1, 2013

"The dual mission of Collegian Inc. is to publish a quality campus newspaper and to provide a rewarding educational experience for the student staff members."

While I was writing this book, because I was not sure that my citations within the text would be enough, and I was not producing a bibliography, I copied URLs into some of the book text of areas from the Internet in those cases in which I had read articles or had downloaded material and had brought articles or pieces of articles into this book. Hopefully, this will satisfy any request for additional information. If there is anything which needs a specific citation, I would be pleased to change the text.

Preface:

This book is all about Joe Paterno, aka, JoePa, and his impact on the Pennsylvania State University with 409 wins as a head coach and 104 wins as an assistant coach under Rip Engle for a total of 513 wins for Penn State University. Nobody else's record in major football can compare to the coaching record of Joe Paterno at one of the most heralded football institutions in the United States.

Like many Pennsylvanians, I learned to love Penn State as a kid. I especially love Penn State football from the days of Rip Engle when I was coached by my older brother Ed (RIP) about the PSU nuances to eventually the takeover of the program by the one and only Joe Paterno.

People like me, who love Penn State, will not be able to apply any other emotion to this book but a lot of love for the institution and for the winningest coach of all time Joe Paterno, who literally took PSU into the modern era and made it one of the greatest college football superpowers of all time. Yes, it was a humble Italian boy from Brooklyn with an accent for life. Thank Joe Paterno for most of that.

You will love this book. If you have never cared much about Penn State, and you read this book, you may develop a deep affinity for the Blue and White that you will have to explain to you friends. You may find yourself dreaming in blue and white from this day forward.

James Franklin is now the head coach of the Nittany Lions. Franklin is a great coach and I wish him well. Joe Paterno had been Penn State everything for 46 years plus 16 as an assistant. Looking at the records of coaches before and after Joseph Paterno, he is clearly in a league by himself. If you take Paterno's record and superimpose it upon any great NCAA program, Penn State's record will dominate, though the Nittany Lions did not receive proper accolades for most of its history.

Season after season from pre-teen to current age status, I rooted for the Joe Paterno-led Nittany Lions to be National Champions. They had five undefeated seasons along the way in which they were not declared the champs. Looking at those seasons, two of which were back to back, it is hard to believe.

To the faithful, they were the champs in those years. Who knows why they were not selected? In 1982 and 1986, the pundits could not deny them. PSU was finally awarded the big one—the National Championship. They surely had earned it.

This book walks you through the entire Joe Paterno head coach journey. You will read about each of JoePa's 409 head coach victories. Each one—all 409.

Even before PSU's first official game, the Lions had played an unofficial game in which they were victorious in 1881. We tell you about it early in the book. Then, after a summary of the Paterno years, and one of his great speeches, we get right to the first season without a coach in 1887. Think about the struggle of forming an intercollegiate football team without even having a coach.

Few of PSU's seventeen coaches to this day took the helm for more than five years but eventually, coaches like Hugo Bezdek, Bob Higgins and Rip Engle—and finally Joe Paterno came along and each put twelve or more years in their tenure and together, they put PSU on the football map. Joe Paterno cemented Penn State onto the map with an unbelievable 62-year showing. He did it all for Penn State. It is undeniable. He could have coached anywhere.

Penn State is a long-time football power

During the last twenty-five years, the Penn State football team competed in the Big Ten Conference, in the NCAA Division I Football Bowl Subdivision. Coach Joe Paterno worked on the arrangements for PSU to join the Big Ten in 1993 after playing as an independent college football team from its founding through the 1992 season.

I predict that you are going to love this book because it is the perfect read for anybody who loves Penn State, Penn State Football, and Joe Paterno and who wants to know more about the games played by the most revered football coach and program of all time.

Few sports books are a must-read but Brian Kelly's *JoePa 409 Victories: Say No More!* will quickly appear at the top of Americas most enjoyable must-read books about sports. Enjoy!

Who is Brian W. Kelly?

Brian W. Kelly is one of the leading authors in America with this, his 110th published book. Brian is an outspoken and eloquent expert on a variety of topics and he has also written several hundred articles on topics of interest to Americans.

Most of his early works involved high technology. Later, Brian wrote a number of patriotic books and most recently he has been writing human interest books such as The Wine Diet and Thank you, IBM. His books are always well received.

Brian's books are highlighted at www.letsgopublish.com. You can view them at amazon.com/author/brianwkelly, and this takes you to Amazon or Kindle, and other booksellers where you may purchase any of Brian's books.

The best!

Sincerely,

Brian P. Kelly, Editor in Chief
I am Brian Kelly's eldest son.

Table of Contents

Chapter 1 Introduction to the Winningest PSU Coach of all Time 1

Chapter 2 Coach Paterno's Acceptance Speech from the Stagg Award 9

Chapter 3 — Penn State Football's Highlights from 1950 to 2011 25

Chapter 4 The Rip Engle / Joe Paterno Era 57

Chapter 5 Joe Paterno Era from 1966 to 1974 69

Chapter 6 The Joe Paterno Era from 1975 to 1983 95

Chapter 7 Joe Paterno Era from 1984 to 1992 119

Chapter 8 Joe Paterno Era from 1993 to 2001 135

Chapter 9 The Joe Paterno Era From 2002 to 2011 165

Chapter 10 Joe Paterno: The Fine Man, The Great Coach, & The Legend . 199

Chapter 11 Words about Joe Paterno from Penn Live 205

Chapter 12 Please Tell Me More about Coach Joseph V. Paterno. 207

LETS GO PUBLISH! Books by Brian W. Kelly 224

About the Author

Brian Kelly retired as an Assistant Professor in the Business Information Technology (BIT) Program at Marywood University, where he also served as the IBM i and Midrange Systems Technical Advisor to the IT Faculty. Kelly designed, developed, and taught many college and professional courses. He continues as a contributing technical editor to a number of technical industry magazines, including "The Four Hundred" and "Four Hundred Guru," published by IT Jungle.

Kelly is a former IBM Senior Systems Engineer. His specialty was problem solving for customers as well as implementing advanced operating systems and software on his client's machines. Brian is the author of 110 books and hundreds of magazine articles. He has been a frequent speaker at technical conferences throughout the United States.

Brian was a candidate for the US Congress from Pennsylvania in 2010 and he ran for Mayor in his home town in 2015. He loves Joe Paterno's style Penn State Football and has been a fan all his life.

Chapter 1 Introduction to the Winningest PSU Coach of all Time

PSU football celebrates 131 Years in 2017!

This book celebrates Joe Paterno as Penn State Football's greatest coach of all time in all sports, but especially football. People like me, who love the JoePa legacy and who love Penn State Football, will love this book without a doubt.

Joe Paterno Getting Ready to Lead Out the Team

When Joe Paterno stopped coaching in 2011 after his almost 46 years as a head-coach, he had 409 victories. At the time, Penn State had 826 victories. At the time, Penn State had been playing football for 125 years. Therefore, Joe Paterno in his 46 years out of PSU's 125 years had amassed almost half of the institution's wins.

Joe Paterno also served sixteen years from 1950 to 1965 as Rip Engle's Assistant Coach/ Therefore in 2011, when his coaching was over, Joe Paterno had coached 62 years out of 125 at Penn State. Joe Paterno was part of Penn State at the time for almost half of all of the Nittany Lion seasons that ever were.

During this time from 1950 to 1965 as an assistant coach, along with Head Coach Rip Engle, Joe Paterno brought in another 104 victories. Therefore, it can be said without a word of lie that Joe Paterno was responsible in whole or in part for 513 victories of the 826 victories that Penn State had amassed in its 125 years as of 2011.

One must ask oneself, what coach in the history of coaches has ever had that great a positive impact on any college team--especially a Division I superpower class A football team such as Penn State. Joe Paterno is the winningest coach of all time at all levels and his record of coaching makes him the greatest coach who ever lived. That's how I see it and I am sticking to it.

Joe Paterno did not say that "Winning isn't everything; it's the only thing." This quote is attributed to the professional football coach Vince Lombardi. Paterno wanted to win because nobody feels good about losing. This proverb stresses the importance of reaching a goal no matter what effort is required.

How you play the game most often determines whether you win or lose. Joe Paterno knew that. It's not whether you win or lose, it's how you play the game…but eventually you have to win some or you're doing something wrong. One of JoePa's favorite sayings was: "The will to win is important, but the will to prepare is vital." You've got to work for your wins folks. That's the Joe Paterno way.

We begin the rest of the Penn State football story in Chapter 2 with the founding of the Penn State institution and we continue in subsequent chapters, right into the founding of the PSU football program in 1887.

In defining the format of the book, we chose to use a timetable that is based on a historical chronology. Within this framework, we discuss the great moments in Penn State football history, and there are many great moments. No book can claim to be able to capture them all, as it would be a never-ending story, but we sure try.

We Are... Penn State!

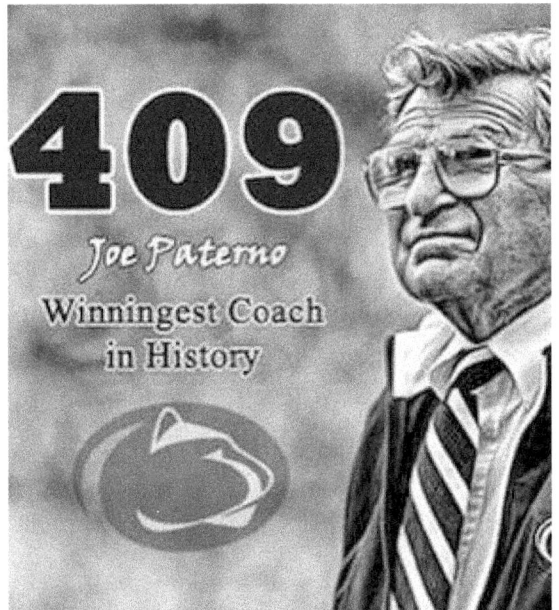

"We Are...Penn State!" These words are what you hear loud and proud during the whole game. As one side of Beaver Stadium exclaims "WE ARE," the other side responds "PENN STATE!"

Some say that this chant, which has become the emblem that embodies Penn State, began in 1948 when the Penn State football team was set to play against the Southern Methodist University at the Cotton Bowl.

Before game day, SMU wanted to meet with PSU to protest a player issue. Penn State Guard and Team Captain Steve Suhey came to the defense of his teammates proclaiming, "We are Penn State. There will be no meetings." Today, the slogan is everywhere in the Penn State community as a sign of strength and pride. Joe Paterno for 62 years was Penn State.

Penn State is a long-time football power

One hundred thirty years is a long time to be playing football. The Penn State Nittany Lions football team was established in 1887. This great and storied football powerhouse represents the Pennsylvania State University in college football. The moniker *Nittany Lions* comes from the notion of the Nittany Mountain Lions, which were once thought to have roamed Mount Nittany, the famous local landmark. Soon, we'll tell you more about the Nittany Lion.

Today, the Penn State football team competes in the Big Ten Conference, in the NCAA Division I Football Bowl Subdivision. Coach Joe Paterno worked on the arrangements for PSU to join the Big Ten in 1993 after playing as an Independent college football team from its founding through the 1992 season.

Joe Paterno gets peer recognition

In September 2001, Joe Paterno was selected to be the 2002 recipient of the American Football Coaches Association's (AFCA) Amos Alonzo Stagg Award. This is a major award for any college coach "whose services have been outstanding in the advancement of the best interests of football." Coach Paterno received the award at the Sears/AFCA Awards Luncheon on January 8 during its Convention in San Antonio, Texas. It was always a big deal and for Joe Paterno, it was a big deal to be awarded top recognition by his coaching peers.

Amos Alonzo Stagg was one of the best-ever in Football and in many ways, along with Walter Camp is responsible for the game of American College Football as played in the United States today.

"Stagg made tremendous contributions to college football and impacted the lives of thousands of people." At the time of the announcement, Coach Paterno said. "He [Stagg] was one of the truly outstanding coaches in the game. I'm honored to be receiving this award in recognition of his legacy of achievement."

Joseph Paterno is the third coach from Penn State ties to receive the AFCA's most prestigious award. Richard Harlow, who coached at Penn State from 1915-17, received the award in 1949 and Rip Engle, who coached at Penn State from 1950-65, and was Paterno's coach at Brown University and who was the man who hired Paterno as an assistant coach at Penn State, received the award in 1969.

Paterno is also the first active coach to receive the award since 1982, when Grambling's Eddie Robinson was honored.

This honor was given to Joe Paterno in his 36th season as head coach and his 52nd year as a member of the Penn State coaching staff. At the time, Paterno was the nation's leading active Division I head coach in terms of wins. He owned a 322-92-3 record, with a winning percentage of .776. At the time in 2001, his 322 wins was the fourth-best all-time in NCAA football history.

Paterno is a 1950 graduate of Brown University. In 2001, Paterno trailed only Bear Bryant in all-time Division I-A wins. The coach had already directed Penn State to five unbeaten seasons (1968-69-73-86-94), two national championships (1982, 1986) and he was also the bowl win leader with a 20-9-1 postseason record. Ironically, Paterno at the time was second only to Stagg (41) in years coached at one school. But, that would be eclipsed shortly.

Joe Paterno at the time was just one of eight coaches in NCAA history ever to record 300 wins (five of the coaches are in Division I-A), reaching the milestone faster than anyone (380 games). Coach Paterno was the only Division I-A coach with 300 wins at one school – Penn State University.

From 1950 to 2002 at the time he was given this award, Joe Paterno had been instrumental in Penn State's 426-140-7 record, with its .750 winning percentage -- the nation's best over the past 52 seasons. This great coach guided the Nittany Lions to 18 top-10 finishes in the AFCA Coaches' Poll since 1966.

With ten years left in his career at the time. Joe Paterno had already become the only four-time winner of the AFCA's Division I-A National Coach of the Year Award (1968-78-82-86). He was the only man to win the award in three different decades at any level.

Paterno also won a record 10 AFCA District/Regional Coach of the Year Awards (1967-68-71-72-73-77-78-82-85-94). In 1986, JoePa became the first football coach to be named Sports Illustrated's Sportsman of the Year.

Along with these accomplishments, by 2002, Paterno had posted 11 or more wins in a season 12 times, coached 31 first team All-America selections, sent more than 250 players to the NFL (including 25 first round draft picks), been selected as the first active coach to receive the National Football Foundation's Distinguished American Award, coached players who have won all of the major college awards - Heisman, Maxwell, Lombardi, O'Brien, Outland, Butkus and Biletnikoff and coached 14 Hall of Fame Scholar Athletes, two NFL Hall of Fame players and five College Football

Hall of Fame honorees. A sixth College Hall of Fame enshrinee, Glenn Ressler, was inducted in December 2001. Paterno achieved many more awards since this 2002 award.

Off the field, in giving him this prestigious award, his coaching peers – the best of the best-- recognized Joe Paterno as a man who remained true to the ideal that a university is an educational institution first and foremost.

Paterno's 1999 team was noted for having three first-team All-Americas and the first two players selected in the NFL Draft. It is less well known that it also included his 21st first-team Academic All-America and 17th NCAA Postgraduate Scholarship winner.

Paterno's 2000 Penn State squad had 14 Academic All-Big Ten honorees on the roster.

Paterno and his wife, Sue, have also have been recognized for their philanthropy. The couple's $3.5 million gift to Penn State in 1998 endowed faculty positions and scholarships and supported two university building projects. The Paterno's have contributed a total of more than $4 million to Penn State. What a generous man who remained humble all his life.

Joe Paterno was a man's man. Like everybody else in life, there was a time when he did not have an illustrious coaching career. He had to get his start just like all great people. In fact, Paterno began his coaching career by accepting a part-time coaching position during his last semester at Brown University in 1950, under his old coach, Rip Engle. His dad wanted him to be a lawyer and he would have been a good one. So, while waiting to begin law school at Boston University in the fall, he did some coaching at Brown.

Then, Rip Engle accepted the head coaching position at Penn State and he asked the recently graduated Paterno to accompany him to State College, Pa. There would be no Law School for JoePa, and his dad was not very happy about that but everybody must follow his own dream.

After 16 years as an assistant with Engle, Joe Paterno was named the head coach at Penn State in 1966. It was just one day after

Engle's retirement. There was no doubt who was going to get the job.

The Stagg Award was very special to Joe Paterno as he understood why he got it and he understood the good will that came with it.

As described above, the Amos Alonzo Stagg Award is given to the "individual, group or institution whose services have been outstanding in the advancement of the best interests of football." Its purpose is "to perpetuate the example and influence of Amos Alonzo Stagg."

Stagg was instrumental in forming the AFCA in the 1920's and the award is named honors him for this and many other achievements in his football career. Stagg is recognized as one of the great innovators and motivating forces in the early development of the game of football. The plaque given to each recipient is a replica of the one given to Stagg at the 1939 AFCA Convention in tribute to his 50 years of service to football. Let me say a few things about Mr. Stagg so we understand how prestigious it was for Coach Paterno to receive this award.

Amos Alonzo Stagg

Amos Alonzo Stagg began his coaching career at the School of Christian Workers, which now is known as Springfield College (located in Massachusetts), right after he graduated from Yale University in 1888. Stagg coached football for a long time as head coach at Chicago (1892-1932) and then the College of the Pacific (1933-1946). Like Joe Paterno's 46 head coaching seasons with Penn State, Stagg's 41 seasons at Chicago represents one of the longest head coaching tenures in the history of the college game.

Among the innovations credited to Stagg while the rules of American College Football were evolving. was the tackling dummy, the huddle, the reverse play, man in motion, knit pants, numbering plays and players, and the awarding of letters. Stagg himself was a long-time AFCA member, being honored as the Association's 1943 Coach of the Year.

According to NCAA records, Stagg's 57-year record as a college head coach is 314-199-35. He was 84 years old when he ended his coaching career at Pacific in 1946. He died in 1965 at the age of 103. Like Joe Paterno, Amos Alonzo Stagg was quite a man.

Chapter 2 Coach Paterno's Acceptance Speech from the Stagg Award

JoePa Comfortable with the Mike after his 409th Win

I had the great pleasure to hear Coach Paterno speak to a group of IBM Systems Engineers at a conference held at The Hershey Convention Center in the 1980's. Joe Paterno was inspiring, engaging, interesting and he was quite humorous. He was a legend already at this time at Hershey but he graciously took the time to shake everybody's hand after his speech.

On January 8, 2002, in San Antonio, Coach Paterno gave the following speech as he was being presented with the Amos Alonzo Stagg Award at the AFCA conference.

My plan is to present the speech here in its entirety as hosted by the PSU Sports Information Department. Thank you GOPSUSPORTS.COM. http://www.gopsusports.com/sports/m-footbl/spec-rel/011802aaa.html. JoePa was 75 years old at the time that he delivered this speech and he still coached for ten more years and won a lot more games, including # 409. Enjoy!

Joe Paterno loved giving speeches. He loved to talk. Here it is direct from the lips of the winningest coach in America: Joe Paterno:

"Thanks everybody.

You know, it's amazing to come into this auditorium and the AFCA convention. The first one I ever went to was in Texas – in Dallas, Texas – in January of 1951. We got in the car, I think we had a hundred bucks between the three of us that the university gave us. We all stayed together – we drove to the hotel in downtown Dallas – I don't think that hotel is there anymore – and when we got there, it was about ten o'clock at night, and we couldn't get our room – most of the coaches there couldn't move in until the next day – and when we got into the hotel, we walk into the lobby, and here's this guy – he's got about 25 to 30 coaches around, and he's giving a clinic.

He was talking about an off-tackle. He said, "we do this, this and that," and he had all these guys listening. I was just a kid out of college – 23 years old – first job I ever had, and someone says, "That's Woody Hayes." Woody had just had an undefeated football team at Miami of Ohio. At three in the morning, Woody stopped talking, and that was a four-hour clinic.

And we probably had 250-300 coaches at that AFCA meeting in 1951. To see this crowd and to see what's happened is just amazing.

I hope I could say a couple of things to you. So many things have happened to me through the years that have been fun. I was telling some of you guys that were at the luncheon, that at the third or fourth convention that I went to, and I can't remember where it was, I remember getting in the elevator, and Paul Bryant got on, Frank Leahy got on, Bud Wilkinson got on – all on the same elevator I was on. I was going to get off at the fourth floor, but I wasn't going to get off that damn elevator until they all got off.

They got off at the 12th floor – I went all the way up with them, got off with them, I was like a little dog, following them, hoping one of them would say, 'hey, want to go have a beer or something?'

I don't know what I can say to you guys. I was saying to a couple of coaches that walked over with me, you get older and you get to a point when you start preaching too much. Some of the things that we've been able to do is because we had the right people around us, we've had the right administration.

I came to Penn State in 1950 not with any idea that I was ever going to stay in coaching. I really wanted to be a lawyer. I started coaching. I was going to try to save a couple bucks – my salary was 3,600 bucks when I got started, which wasn't bad, really – there were a lot of pretty girls at Penn State – so anyway, I got caught up in the whole thing of coaching, and you know, I had never coached, I had just graduated in May of 1950, when Rip had taken the job. For some reason or another he asked me if I wanted to coach, because he was only allowed to take one coach with him.

The conditions of his contract – if he had a contract – the conditions of his hiring were such that he could only hire one guy. So, he asked me to come. Bill Doolittle, who was a great coach at one of the Michigan schools, was a backfield coach – he tried to get Bill to come, but Bill decided to stay at Brown. He tried to get another guy to come but he couldn't, so he asked me to coach. So, I come down to State College, and I get a kick of reading about "cultural shock."

I came from Brooklyn, and Providence, to State College. It was a whole different thing, and when I started to coach, I said to Rip, "how do I coach," I mean, "what's it take? Is there a course, something like that, 'coaching football?'" Rip handed me film – he said, "I'm going to give you three reels of film everyday" – in those days we had 16mm film – "and I want you to chart every single play on both sides of the football." Seriously, I used to have this chart, I'd take everyone – the ball would be snapped, I'd draw exactly where he went, and I had lines all over it. Like I said, both sides of the football. When I was done, he'd give me three more reels. I did that all summer. I finally started to realize what the game is all about. And I came back, and he said, "What do you think? Are you going to be alright?" and I said, "you know, I may be the best coach ever."

Today, if I said to a young coach, 'I want you to take every single play and diagram what 22 guys did on every single play, and I want lines – it would be a waste of time. We have a video thing now, pops up – the video guy is the most important guy on the staff now – and he can pop up things and you don't even know what's going on.

It's been a fun game for me, it's really been great, yet, when I think back to the years, the things that have influenced me most are people – you know, it's hard to stay in one place for 52 years, no matter what – there's got to be some overriding influence that keeps you there and to me it's got to be people. I worked on a staff that was absolutely fantastic – all the guys that put up with me…I was a know-it-all, we'd get into meetings and I'd be screaming and shouting.

I was fortunate to live with a guy by the name of Jim O'Hora, who was a defensive line coach at Penn State for a while. Jim had just built a house and he needed someone to help pay the rent, so he said, would you like to live with me? After 11 years, Jim called me in he said, "you know, Joe, when my dad came over from Ireland, my cousins used to come over, and they needed a place to stay." Jim was from up near Scranton – Dunmore, in the coal region. Jim said, "So my cousins would come over, and they'd be here three or four months, and my dad would say, 'Sean, you've been here three months, it's about time you find yourself a lady and get on with your life.'" And Jim says, "Joe, you've been with us 11 years.

So, I said, "alright, I get the point, Jim." I got a little apartment two blocks away, two years later I'm married. I've been around great people, who have really had a great influence on me.

I guess the one thing I could say to you as far as coaching, and I go back to something I read years and years ago, that George Washington had said at one time or another, he said: "we can't ensure success, but we can deserve it." And I think that's all I ever wanted to do. All I wanted to do is work my butt off, and get people around me, and if we couldn't win, we'd never walk away thinking we didn't deserve to win.

We've had games – I don't even want to talk about it – we didn't do a good job, we didn't deserve to win, we didn't have a good effort, we weren't able to get our kids to perform the way they should have performed. You can't ensure success, but if you walk away from a football game feeling like you deserved to win, I think that's the start of everything you want to do in your program. That's basically where I started.

I've got a couple other things I want to share with you. They are not my doing, but when I was a young coach, I went up to New York, there was a great coach by the name of John Bollinger up there, and I walked in there. John had a big sign that said, "Don't bitch about the kids, they're the only ones we have." Think about that. How many times have you sat around the office bitching about this or that kid – they are the guys that have got to make good. The time you spend bitching about a kid, it's negative. You've got to understand, those are the guys that got you here.

The other thing that I saw – and this was in a high school in north New Jersey, it was a big sign that said, "Am I going to lose your friendship because I tell you the truth?" You cannot con kids. You cannot con them. If there would be any one criticism that I have had from time to time, is people are afraid to tell a kid, hey, you're not very good, and you're not very good for these reasons, and these are the things you've got to do to be good. I've often told my staff – told them a story a hundred times, I said you win with performance and you lose with potential. Jerry Claiborne said once to a kid, "Son, your potential is going to cost me my job."

I often tell this story about a guy who got a job – this guy was a pretty good salesman, all of a sudden, he's got a big job, had a great big territory and he had to do a lot of traveling. When he started traveling, all of a sudden, his wife realized they had this great new house and they were out in the country, and she started to get nervous of things going on outside. So, she said to her husband, "Jack, I've got to have a watchdog. I'm all alone out here, I need a watchdog."

He said, "honey, don't worry about it, I make a lot of money, I'll go out there and get you a watchdog." So, he goes down and walks into the pet shop and says to the guy, "Look, I've got to get a watchdog. My wife's scared." And the guy says, "I know what you're looking for. I don't have one right now, but I've got the best watchdog in the world." And the guy says, "Well, where is it?" So, he points to this little mutt, and he says, "That's the best watchdog in the world."

The guy says, "You've got to be kidding me, what makes him so good?" he said, "That dog knows karate." So, he says, "prove it." And the pet shop owner puts the dog next to a table, and says, "karate!" and the dog chops it and table splinters go everywhere. So, the guy asks how much for the dog, and the pet shop owner says give me $500 for the dog. So, he buys the watchdog, sticks it in the backseat of the station wagon, takes it back into the country, takes it back to his house, and walks in the house and says,

"Hey honey, honey I'm home." "Jack, did you get me my watchdog?"

"I got you the greatest watchdog." He was all filled up with himself with this great watchdog. She says, "Where is it?" and he says, "Right there." She says, "You expect me to be out in the country with that little mutt to protect me?" he said, "Honey, that dog knows karate." She says, "karate my ass."

Now remember, how many times do you see, we've got a guy, he's 6'3", weighs 215 pounds, he runs 4.7, he does everything – sheds blocks, he hits the sleds, he looks great. Then you scrimmage, and he doesn't even make a tackle. What happened to him? Then you've got a guy, maybe 5'9", 250, doesn't look like a football player, but he's busting his butt, he's chasing every play down, he's making plays, he's being a nuisance he's driving people nuts. Why can't you win with him? Well, 'he's too slow,' 'he's too fat,' 'he's too this or that.' The other guy…looks the part, alright – looks the part. You end up losing games.

As Jerry Claiborne said, "son, your potential is going to cost me my job." That square rear-end kid that can come off blocks, who will bust his but for you, believes in the program, wants to be good, wants to pay the price to be good – just remember the karate story.

There are some people in my life that have been heroes to me – Robert E. Lee is one of them. Now, I don't mean to play the professor, but the Civil War was all set to go this way, when McClellan was threatening Richmond down there on the river and they were going to do some things, and they appointed Lee the general of the Confederate army. Lee looked over the situation, and said the only way to win is we've got to dictate our terms. They've got to do it the way we want to do it. He was willing to take a chance. To change the game. And by doing that, he gave the confederates a chance to win.

Somewhere along the line, you've got to lay it out. In my first ten games as a coach, we were five and five. The first game of my second year, we lost to a very ordinary Navy team – we lost on the last play of the game, we should have been better than them. So, I'm 5-6 in the first 11 games I coach. I'm coming back on the bus from Annapolis, and I was thinking, "Are you good enough – you better find out." We had some really good young players, we had some sophomores – in those days, freshmen were not eligible – we had some sophomores that were good players. And I said to myself, "you better find out, Paterno."

So, what I did – we were going to play Miami in September – they had a good football team – not a great team, but good. We went down there and what I did was, because I was worried about the heat, we got very little support from anybody – we went to Pittsburgh, stayed at the hotel, worked out at Moon Township high school, got on a plane the day of the game – we played on a Saturday night – went to the hotel in Miami the day of the game, went to the game on an air-conditioned bus, but we didn't know how hot it was. We ended up beating Miami with eight sophomores that had never played a game before.

We lost only one game in the next three years. There comes a time when you know that things have got to change – that something has got to be done differently, and you've got to have the guts to do it or you're just another guy. You're not going to be the guy that you have potential to be. Like I said, we beat Miami that day, and then UCLA beat us – we lost one game in the next three years.

There comes a point when you know better – but you're afraid of what the talk shows will say, your friends or recruiting gurus, you're scared to death of what the alumni will think, you don't want to run a play because the people in the stands are going to boo when you want to run the damn ball up the gut – the overriding thought I want to get across to all of you, because I'm sure I'm talking to some people that are great, great coaches – some of you have the potential to be great coaches, and maybe thirty years from now you'll be up here telling people.

As I sat down there, I listened to Bear Bryant talk. I listened to what Bryant said. And I listened to what Wilkinson said. Bryant got up and gave one of the best clinic speeches I had ever heard. He didn't have a lot to say, but he said a couple of things. Talking about game plans – "keep your plan small. Have a plan for everything." I was an assistant coach for maybe seven or eight years, and I'm listening to Bryant, he's saying, "keep your plan small. Have a plan for everything."

1971, we're playing Texas in the Cotton Bowl. Darrel Royal was coaching down there and we're playing down there, and we've got a pretty good football team. Following Coach Bryant's advice, we had a plan for what we were going to do if we were behind or if we were ahead, and I wasn't going to do any of that stuff until I observed the way we practiced. If we practiced hard and played as well as we could play, then I was going to make a plan for that. If we hadn't practiced hard and they needed a good kick in the butt at halftime, I was going to make a plan for that.

We were playing a pretty good football game, and we had a kid by the name of John Hufnagel who is now an offensive coordinator with one of the pro teams, Indianapolis, and we were doing really well. And I was getting my speech ready for what we were going to do at halftime. I'm all set, and there's about 35 seconds to go in the half. John gets a little careless, throws a pass, intercepted; Texas gets it, kicks a field goal. Now, I forgot what I was going to talk about when I went in at halftime. Everything was all geared to, "hey, you're playing your butts off, you're doing fine, if you hang in there, we're going to be ok."

So, I get in there and I grab Dave Joyner who has become a very special orthopedic surgeon – a defensive captain, and I grab 'em, and I start to talk, and he says, 'relax, we're fine.' You know what my speech was to the squad, at halftime? "Relax, we're fine." Bryant made a point that I have never forgotten, and to this day, when I have a couple of little sheets in front of me, not so much what play we're gonna call or what we're gonna do, a plan for the things that we have to do if this happens or that happens or how can I get the squad to do what it has to do?

Bud Wilkinson was one of the great teachers of football. I went down to watch Bud Wilkinson's squad practice in the spring of 1955 – some of you weren't even born in 1955 – they had a great staff there and a lot of really good football players. As I get down the line, there is something I can say that can help some young people. Coach Wilkinson said to me, you know coaching isn't circles and X's. It is, "who the circle is, who the X is."

There are too many people who think the circles and X's win the games, not the people in the circles and the X's. The other thing is, you've got to understand that basically, coaching is teaching. The best way to coach football is to create in practice the game situations that your players are going to be exposed to. And then repeat it, and repeat it, and repeat it so they do things by rote memory. And that's all coaching is, he said. Figure out what your kids can do, and then put in practice only the things you can do as many times as necessary to get people to do it by rote memory.

I was watching Miami play – I don't know if Larry is here or not – to watch Miami play, and to see how those kids came off blocks, and to see the things they did. They did the same things against us 11 games ago. They did the same things against us in 1999. The same things they did against us in 1986. Those kids knew were the ball was, knew where the block was coming from. Basically, they are kids that have done these things over and over and over again, and Larry has done a marvelous job with this program. Butch gave him the ingredients but Larry put together a great year. Keep your plan small. Make sure you can practice everything that you do.

Wilkinson also said, one of the biggest mistakes these people make is they try to do something that they haven't practiced. I wish I had the kind of discipline that Wilkinson had, and Bryant had. If I have one coach that says we're working too hard, I cut back practice. We had, obviously, not a good beginning, then we were able to do some things well enough that we were able to win some games, once we started to get people together and play well, there was so much emotion. We went down to Virginia – and Virginia did a great job against us, but we were tired – I thought maybe we should have taken a day off to get the guys rested up.

We had so many emotional games – we just didn't have it. I think you always have to be careful – when you're playing in big games week after week, that you don't get your kids tired. I thought the other thing that was important – and I'll tell you a true story – That team I was talking about – in 1967, we go to the Gator Bowl. We jump all over Florida State early, and then we got a little careless and so forth – anyway, it ends up a tied ball game. So, I find some of the kids on the team, especially Dennis Onkotz who was a very good football player, and I said to Dennis, "how would you critique the season?" And Dennis says, "coach, you blew the ball game." I said, "What do you mean?" He said, "you worked us too hard. We didn't have anything left. We played the first half on emotion but then we got tired."

I think there's something we can all probably learn from that. Let me just talk about a couple of other things that I think are important – I won't keep you that long, I don't want to bore you. I think we all have to understand that football basically is a morale game. You play with your heart, you play with your mind. If you've got morale, then you've got a chance to win. If you've got the right kind of people, then you've got a chance to win. It is a morale game. At least, if you've got morale, then you have a chance to play as well as you can. Then you could go back to Wilkinson's quote. At least we would deserve success. No morale, no chances.

I think morale is made up of two basic things. I think it's made up of pride, I think it's made up of loyalty – let me discuss those with you. To me, I don't think pride is tough to get. My brother spent some time in the Marine corps, he got out of the Marine corps – my dad was in the infantry, hated the Marines – absolutely hated them. My brother gets out of Brown with me and decides he's going to go into the Marine Corps. My dad gets all uptight and says, "I don't want a Marine in this house." And George says, "I don't want to go into the Army, I get seasick – I don't want to go into the Navy – I can be a Marine and in two years be an officer." He says, "Pop, relax. The Marines aren't that bad. I'm not going to be one of those guys."

So, 17 weeks later, after basic training and boot camp, my brother comes home on a Saturday night. He got home at 11 o'clock on a Saturday night – it was great to see him, he looked good, he was in shape, the whole bit – came home in his uniform. My mother had pressed some clothes for him to go to church thinking he wasn't going to wear the darn uniform. He gets up in the morning and says he's going to wear his uniform. Now, my dad's eyes opened real wide – says, "Oh, he's going to wear his uniform? We've got to go to church with a Marine." So now we go to church, and in Brooklyn, my mother would cook all day Sunday, and we came home from mass and everybody in the neighborhood – the kids would come in, my mom would feed us and my dad would open a bottle of wine and we'd sit around and shoot the bull.

My dad was a great guy because if you said "black," he'd say "white." If you said "republican," he'd say "democrat." He loved to needle people, just loved to be involved, and he was just really a lot of fun to be around. So as soon as three or four of George's buddies get in there, he starts pecking away. "The Marines. Bunch of patriots, right? They kill a mosquito, they want a medal." (Laughter). My brother is sitting there, angry, and all of a sudden he jumps up and he walks over to my dad, and he says "Pop, knock it off. The Marines are the greatest fighting force ever put on the face of the Earth."

I can still see my dad, Lord have mercy – he can't stop laughing. My dad is rolling on the floor because he cannot stop laughing. He got him because when he walked into that boot camp there, they said the greatest men in the world walked through those gates. Not some of the best, not pretty good, the greatest walked through those gates.

You've got to get up at 5 o'clock in the morning. Those shoes have got to look good. You better stand straight. You're a Marine! Look at all the Marines that went before you. Look at the tradition. In 17 weeks, they got it across to that kid. Just because you have the courage in you – you're willing to pay the price to be a Marine. To be a Penn State football player! To be whatever you're involved in! That's what starts morale. If you start going down, reaching down inside of you, try to keep them comfortable. Try to make them happy.

I like to tell the story of the Catholic kid and the Protestant kid. I like these stories because I think it helps emphasize the point. Catholic kid and the Protestant kid are arguing and the Protestant kid said my dad makes more money than your dad, and the Catholic kid says my mom's better than your mom, and the Protestant kid says, yeah, but we've got a bigger car, and they go back and forth, and finally, the Catholic kid says, "well, my priest knows more than your minister."

The Protestant kid wasn't about to be outdone, so he said, "well he should. You tell him everything." (Laughter).

So, I think pride and loyalty – I don't know if we've talked about the last two years – we haven't been as good as I thought we could have been. I really felt there were some kids we played that we couldn't trust. I think we played some kids that didn't buy into our program. I'm excited about what our football team can be in the future because I think we've got two young classes that are kids who do it the way we want it done. Unfortunately, I think we had some older kids who I thought should have been leaders that really did not buy into the things I thought were necessary to have a good football team.

We were talking last night with some coaches – we had a little reception – I told them that I have had football teams with poorer personnel than this year. I've had championship teams that had less talent than this group. But they had two or three guys – the great teams – that said, "we're not going to screw around on a Wednesday night, we're going to do it the way they want it done! Because we want to win! We don't want to talk, talk, talk

– I got guys who wonder if they'll get a hundred tackles so they can be a pro. When I've had good football teams, I've had three or four or five guys. I've had guys like John Shaffer and D.J. Dozier and Shane Conlan – I didn't have to worry about the squad, because they were winners, and they had character. They were strong! You could go to war with them! And you knew it…you knew it!

You get a little older, and maybe it's my fault, maybe I don't punch enough walls or whatever I used to do. You've got to have pride and loyalty. I think you've got to sell it. Obviously, you've got to sell your program. You've got to tell your kids that. Bo Schembechler told his kids that it was a privilege to play at Michigan. I want every guy on my football team to know it's a privilege. I think all of us have to do that with all of our programs.

When we try to get someone to come to Penn State, we try to give them the right reasons to come. I often tell the guys that recruiting is like getting married. You want to make yourself look as good as you can, but you can't tell too many lies, because you've got to live together. You're going to hold hands someplace down the line. A lot of people ask me about the lousy looking uniforms that we have – but you guys, you see us on TV and you say, "Hey, Penn State is playing." And your wife says, "How do you know it's Penn State?" And you say, "Look at the lousy uniforms." (Laughter).

Don't be afraid to be different. My high school coach was a great Yankees fan. He took me to a World Series one time – we had black shoes, now everyone has black shoes. I'm thinking about wearing white shoes. (Laughter). Anyway, he took me – the Cardinals were playing the Yankees. I was sitting there in the stands with him. I was a 15-year old kid, and he said, "Now watch how the Yankees walk."

And sure enough, DiMaggio and those guys walked with a little swagger. He said, "Look at their shoes." I said they were nice – I didn't know what he was talking about. The Cardinals come out. He said, "Now take a look at the Cardinals' shoes." Every Yankee had polished shoes. They were all polished. The Cardinals had scuffed up shoes, some of them didn't have the same length in their pants, the whole bit. He said, "The Yanks…are different. The Yankees are different." You know, they had the pinstripes and the whole bit. And I think that's something that we try to do.

I've got a tough time these days - I'm fighting with them all the time about face whiskers, earrings, make kids wear a coat and tie. I used to make them wear socks to class. I used to tell them, "Wear socks to class." "Why?" "Well, you're sitting in the front row, the professor looks down, the girl next to you and the guy next to you have lousy looking, dirty feet, and you've got socks on, makes the difference between a B and a C, so don't be stupid."

Napoleon said, "If you want to be a leader you've got to have a different appearance from everybody else." There's something to it. There's got to be a standard – like hats in the house. We have a sign in the locker room, "nobody in this room comes in with a hat." You know, it's interesting. We played Alabama in the first Sugar Bowl ever played in the Superdome, in 1975. Coach Bryant was coaching at Alabama at the time.

We came out before the game, and Bryant had on a cardigan sweater and I had on a tie and jacket, and he said, "Joe, you're going to make me look bad, you're all dressed up." You know, I usually wear a jacket and a tie. I asked him, "Where's your hat?"

You know how he always wore that hat. He said, "I don't wear a hat indoors." Can you imagine that? We're playing in the Superdome and he said, "If I wore a hat my mother would get upset." They are all symbols. In and of themselves they mean nothing. If I tell a kid I don't want his earring on, it doesn't mean a thing. You're a Penn State football player. You're something…different. I want you to be different. We think that's all part of the pride and the loyalty.

I've talked about loyalty. When I was a kid, about seven years old, I had one of my uncles who was born in Italy, went to take his test to be a citizen, went with a bunch of buddies. They said, "Ok Angelo, you know you have to answer a couple of questions – the first question is, "Who discovered America?" Angelo thinks for a couple of seconds and says, "oh, Christopher Columbus!" He had people there and they were all shouting, "way to go Angelo!" "Ok, you've got two more questions, Angelo."

"Angelo. Who was first the President of the United States?" – "Oh, Judge! George Washington!" His friends were hollering and the judge had to tell them all to be quiet. "Ok, Angelo. If you answer this one, then you can become a citizen of the United States. "Angelo, who shot Abraham Lincoln?" – Now Angelo didn't know this one, he put his head down. Everybody was quiet. He looks up and says, "Judge, I don't-a-know." And with that, all his buddies shouted out, "That's right Angelo – we don't squeal on nobody!"

I'll end up here pretty quick here guys. One of the things I try to get across to the squad is we're going to try to be fair to everybody, but it's impossible. We can't get everybody the same amount of reps. There is always going to be that guy that you think if maybe you could just get a little more work with him – but it isn't easy. And I think you have to make that clear to them.

The other thing that I think is important is you've got to spend time with them. You've got to bring kids in; you've got to discuss things with them all the time. You've got to be honest with them. I go back to that saying, am I going to lose your friendship because I tell you the truth?

I think that's it. They are human beings who have aspirations, they want to do certain things, and I think you owe it to them to be fair to them. It's not easy. Discipline, I think sometimes is mislabeled as to what discipline is all about. I don't think "yes sir" or "no sir" is necessary, my guys call me Joe, some call me Coach, I don't care. I want people to have enough guts to recognize what kind of situation they are in and that if they want to be good at what they're gonna do, they're going to need discipline.

The last thing I'll say to you is the will to win is important. No question. But I'll tell you what. Until you get some people who have the will and dedication to prepare and do what it takes to win – they could have the will to win comin' out their backside. I have a guy that said, "Coach, I always wanted to be on a national championship team. He's a pain in the rear end. He'll never be on a national championship team because he doesn't understand what we're talking about all of the time.

We're in a great profession, guys. This country is going through a period of time – I'd like to think it will be quick but it's not going to be quick – it's going to be a long process. Our kids, our friends, everything we've known, and all the things that have been easy for us, are not going to be easy. It's going to be tough. We've been challenged.

We've been challenged. And if we, the people in this room and the people in our profession, can't rise to the occasion, and understand what it takes to handle those kinds of challenge – they can listen to the talk shows and the crap and all the other speeches that go on – but it's going to be us. You and I and everybody in our profession is going to have more of an impact on where this country goes more than any single group. You've got to understand that.

What we believe – our values, our virtues, our willingness to work, our willingness to do things. I'll tell you, every time I talk to kids who want to get into coaching I tell them, don't get into coaching for the money. If you're good, you'll make money. Your satisfaction will be when you can look a kid in the eye ten years from now and he looks at you and says, "thanks, coach. Thanks."

This is the city of the Alamo, maybe this country needs to look at the guys that were in that Alamo, who refused to give in, who were willing to die before they gave in. By God, we've got to stick by our profession, we've got to be willing to die for the things we think are right. We've got to teach kids what we think is right. In the long run, it will be better for them, for their families, for their country, and we're going to feel good about ourselves because we've made a contribution to them.

We've done something that goes beyond hitting someone in the rear end, and we've gone beyond how much money we've made. We've reached into peoples' – literally – souls, as nobody else can do. We have more influence on kids than anybody. So, God bless you all, it's great to be around. I've been here for 52 years, and it's been a great experience. Thank you.

Chapter 3 Penn State Football's Highlights from 1950 to 2011

Unofficial and Official Games

Information from the Penn State Football Encyclopedia by Lou Prato, a noted Penn State football historian, was used in the original compilation of this chronology by CBS. Most of this – the unmodified stuff and the stuff that is not complete, and some of which is available on the Web—was all used to put this synopsis together. Our thanks to CBS for providing a good part of this for our readers, and for Lou Prato for compiling it.

The material we used was current as of March 11, 2013,. Anything further was created by your autor who provided additional research to bring this chronology current.

This section which involves only the Paterno years, is an extremely impressive compendium of happenings in Penn State Football in the Paterno era and the Engle era when JoePa was assistant coach. It is about the great moments and even the contributing moments to Penn State's greatness during the immortal coach's years.

Like all Penn State fans, I expect you to thoroughly enjoy whipping through this 62 years' worth of Penn State Football in this most efficient way. Enjoy! Then in a number of chapters, we will look at each Paterno season in detail, game, by game, one win at a time until we hit 409. Let's begin now:

March 5, 1950 — Joe Bedenk resigns after one year as head football coach, but remains on the staff as an assistant coach.

March 31, 1950 — The Athletic Board sets 30 scholarships exclusively for football to include tuition, room and board.

April 22, 1950 — Charles A. "Rip" Engle, head coach at Brown University, is named head football coach by acting Penn State president James Milholland. May 27, 1950 — Rip Engle names Joe Paterno, his senior quarterback at Brown, to the coaching staff and assigns him to coach the quarterbacks.

October 14, 1950 — Penn State loses for the first time at night after four wins at night dating to 1941, all played in the rain, as Syracuse wins, 27-7, on a clear night away at Syracuse's Archbold Stadium.

November 11, 1950 — The first Band Day is held at Beaver Field, with nine Centre County high school bands participating as Penn State beats West Virginia, 27-0. Band Day was held annually for 25 years, with the final one taking place at the Nov. 16, 1974 game with Ohio University. Band Day was brought back for the Blue-White games from 1984-88.

December 2, 1950 — A major snow storm forces postponement of the final game of the season against Pitt at Pitt Stadium on November 25. The game is moved to Forbes Field one week later, where Penn State wins, 21-20, in what becomes known as "the Snow bowl."

December 1950 — The Athletic Board adds 15 scholarships for football, bringing the total to 45.

September 1, 1951 — The Athletic Board and Eastern Intercollegiate Athletic Conference agree to make freshmen eligible for varsity play because of the Korean War. The authorization only lasts one year before freshmen are banned again.

October 21, 1951 — Another New Beaver Field attendance record —30,321 — is set, again in a Homecoming game, against unbeaten (and eventual No. 2) Michigan State, but this time Penn State loses, 32-21.

July 1952 — Ernest "Ernie" McCoy, basketball coach at Michigan since 1948, takes over as Director of Athletics and Dean of the Physical Education Department.

September 20, 1952 — Former player and Coach Joe Bedenk watches his first game since 1917 as a spectator after stepping down as assistant coach. He sees a 20-13 win over Temple at Beaver Field.

September 27, 1952 — Junior Tony Rados surprises fans and makes national headlines by giving Penn State its greatest passing day in 12 years, completing 17-of-30 passes for 179 yards and one TD (and 2 interceptions), and out-dueling Purdue's All-American passing sensation, Dale Samuels, in leading Penn State to a surprising 20-20 tie at Beaver Field.

November 13, 1952 — Penn State goes over 100,000 in total season home attendance for the first time in history (103,751 in five games) as 15,957 at Beaver Field watch the Lions escape with a 7-6 win over underdog Rutgers.

November 22, 1952 — Penn State upsets Pitt, 17-0, to knock the Panthers from the Orange Bowl before 53,766 at Pitt Stadium. The Nittany Lions' defense, led by Jack Sherry's two interceptions, and Ted Kemmerer's punting throttles the Pitt attack, while Rados' passing sparks the Lions' offense.

October 17, 1953 — Mickey Bergstein, color man and engineer for Penn State's radio network, makes a spectacular debut as play-by-play announcer in a game against Syracuse at Beaver Field, when he takes over in the fourth quarter for regular announcer Bob Prince, who has to leave to broadcast a Steelers-Eagles NFL game in Philadelphia that night. Bergstein describes how the Nittany Lions score two touchdowns in the fourth quarter in a come-from-behind 20-14 win that ends with a full-fledged brawl at the Syracuse bench.

November 7, 1953 — Heavy snow blankets State College in a 24-hour period, forcing a major snow removal at Beaver Field for a game against Fordham. Kickoff is delayed by two hours because of the late arrival of the Penn State team, which was trapped in a Clinton County hunting camp known as "Camp-Hate-To-Leave-It." The Nittany Lions go on to win a 28-21 thriller before some 13,897 hearty fans.

November 13, 1953 — Penn State becomes The Pennsylvania State University and the next day the Nittany Lions play their first game as Penn State and come from behind from a 14-6 second-quarter deficit to whip Rutgers, 54-26, at New Brunswick.

December 1953 — The Levi Lamb Fund, named for the former Penn State star, is established at the suggestion of athletic director Ernie McCoy to assist in obtaining financial aid for athletes and the athletic department.

March 1, 1954 — J.T. White, who played on Michigan's 1948 National Champion team as well as at Ohio State as a center, joins Rip Engle's staff as an assistant coach.

September 25, 1954 — Underdog Penn State stuns preseason Big Ten Conference favorite Illinois, 14-12, in the opening game of the season played at Champaign, shocking the college football world and becoming an overnight front-runner to win the Lambert Trophy.

October 23, 1954 — Jesse Arnelle, Rosey Grier and Lenny Moore become the first African Americans to play college football in Fort Worth, Texas, but the Nittany Lions make too many mistakes and lose to Texas Christian, 20-7.

October 30, 1954 — Penn State plays its first game on national television and beats Penn, 35-13, at Franklin Field, scoring the most points in the long-time series against the Quakers. Lenny Moore rushes for 140 yards and scores three touchdowns.

September 1, 1955 — Penn State begins a year-long celebration of its Centennial Year with Navy scheduled to visit Beaver Field for the first time since 1923. A new dateline of "University Park" is established with the opening of a campus post office.

September 29, 1955 — The first game is televised from Beaver Field as CBS transmits the season-opener with Boston University to a limited region in the East. The Nittany Lions win, 35-0, as an unknown fifth-string sophomore fullback — Joe Sabol — scores two touchdowns to lead the team to victory.

November 5, 1955 — Syracuse's Jim Brown outgains PSU's Lenny Moore, 159 yards to 146, and scores all the Syracuse points on three touchdowns and two extra-point kicks, but Penn State comes back from a 20-7 deficit on the quarterbacking of Milt Plum to win a thrilling 21-20 Band Day contest in one of the greatest games ever played at New Beaver Field before a crowd of 30,321 and a CBS regional TV audience.

September 29, 1956 — The first all-Penn State alumni broadcasting team works its first game for the Nittany Lions football radio network as Mickey Bergstein ('43) moves from color commentary to play-by-play and Bob Wilson ('40) takes over color. Penn State beats Pennsylvania, 34-0, at Franklin Field in Philadelphia.

October 20, 1956 — Penn State stuns heavily-favored Ohio State, 7-6, in Columbus, winning on Milt Plum's extra point kick before the largest crowd to see a Penn State football game up to that time, numbering 82,584.

October 19, 1957 — Pete Mauthe, captain of the undefeated 1912 team, becomes the first Penn State player inducted into the College Football Hall of Fame during halftime ceremonies of the Homecoming game against Vanderbilt. The Nittany Lions squander a 13-point lead and are upset, 32-20.

October 26, 1957 — The third game of the Engle era is televised from Syracuse by CBS on a regional basis as Penn State beats the Orangemen, 21-12, behind the surprise quarterbacking of sophomore Richie Lucas, who was forced to take over for the injured starter, Al Jacks.

December 1957 — Outstanding freshman running back Robert "Red" Worrell, who was a potential varsity starter on the 1958 team, is electrocuted at his family home in Denbo, Pa., while helping his father erect a TV antenna. Athletic officials establish an award in his name to honor the most improved player after spring practice. Lineman Andy Stynchula wins the first award in 1958.

Spring 1958 — Former linebacker Dan Radakovich, one of the standouts in the 7-6 upset over Ohio State in 1956, becomes Penn State's first linebacker coach when hired as an undergraduate assistant. The next year, Radakovich continues coaching linebackers as a graduate assistant.

September 27, 1958 — Penn State ends the longest running series with one of its oldest opponents, Pennsylvania, with a 43-0 victory at Franklin Field. The series, which began in 1890, was never played outside of Philadelphia and finished with Penn State winning 18, losing 25 and tying 4. The team's first ever two-point conversion is scored when Al Jacks passes to end John Bozick after Penn State's second touchdown. Later in the game, Richie Lucas passes to Jim Schwab for a second two-point conversion.

December 19, 1959 — Penn State plays in the first Liberty Bowl and tackle Charlie Janerette becomes the first African-American to play against Alabama as the Nittany Lions beat the Crimson Tide, coached by Paul "Bear" Bryant, 7-0, in Philadelphia's Municipal Stadium.

April 1959 — The Nittany Lion Club is organized by 15 alumni who want to arouse interest in Penn State athletic affairs through contributions to the Levi Lamb Fund. Membership stipulated an annual contribution to the fund of at least $50 or at least $25 for graduates of less than 10 years. Members will receive "special consideration" on game tickets and "preferred parking" at the stadium.

November 7, 1959 — The all-time attendance record is set at New Beaver Field as 34,000 watch a memorable battle of unbeatens play with national rankings and bowl berths at stake. Syracuse edges Penn State, 20-18, despite an electrifying 100-yard kickoff return by sophomore Roger Kochman as the Nittany Lions fail to make an extra point kick and two two-point conversions.

November 14, 1959 — Penn State downs Holy Cross, 46-0, in the last game played at New Beaver Field as 20,000 spectators watch the final quarter in rain and heavy wind. The Nittany Lions end the 229th game played on the site with a record of 184-34-11.

January 2, 1960 — Dan Radakovich is hired as a fulltime assistant coach in charge of linebackers. He eventually will become known as "The Father of Linebacker U."

September 17, 1960 — Penn State opens Beaver Stadium before a less than capacity crowd of 22,559 as the Nittany Lions beat Boston

University, 20-0. Lion senior halfback Eddie Caye scored the stadium's initial touchdown at 10:25 of the first quarter.

October 3, 1960 — What later becomes known as "Tailgating" is first suggested in a front-page column by Centre Daily Times Editor Jerry Weinstein after monumental traffic jams developed before and after the Homecoming game against Illinois at Beaver Stadium on Saturday, October 1. Weinstein advocates adoption of the Ivy League tradition of pregame "picnic lunches" and says Penn State fans should add "picnic suppers" for after the game while traffic disperses.

October 8, 1960 — The "hero" defensive back makes its debut in a 27-16 victory over Army at West Point. Senior Sam Sobczak is the first player designated as "Hero."

September 29, 1961 — The Athletic Department experiments with closed-circuit television by televising Penn State's first game ever against Miami (Fla.) from the Orange Bowl Stadium to Rec Hall and Schwab Auditorium on the Penn State campus. However, paid attendance is disappointing with less than 40 percent of the seating capacity filled.

November 4, 1961 — Maryland beats Penn State for the only time in the lengthy series, 21-17, at College Park behind the passing combination of Dick Shiner and Gary Collins.

December 30, 1961 — End Dave Robinson becomes the first African-American to play in the Gator Bowl and makes the defensive "play-of-the-game" with a quarterback sack and fumble recovery that helps the Nittany Lions beat Georgia Tech, 30-15.

Spring 1962 — Penn State joins Pitt, Syracuse and West Virginia in agreeing to forbid "redshirting," a practice that withholds athletes from competition for a year so they can "mature."

October 13, 1962 — Penn State becomes the first team to play three service academies in one season, losing to Army at West Point on this date, 9-6, after beating Navy, 41-7, and Air Force, 20-6, earlier in the season at Beaver Stadium.

October 27, 1962 — Assistant coach Joe Paterno is presented a game ball by the team for the first time since he joined Rip Engle's staff in 1950, when the Nittany Lions overcome the sensational debut of sophomore quarterback Craig Morton and defeat California, 23-21, in Berkeley.

December 1962 — End Dave Robinson becomes the first African-American player in Penn State's football history to be named first-team All-American when selected by the Associated Press, the Football Writers and others.

Summer 1963 — Penn State joins Pitt, Syracuse and West Virginia in a Letter of Intent agreement for incoming freshmen football players, obligating recruits to a specific school for at least one year. The national agreement under consideration also would include the Big Ten, Southwest, Southeastern, Atlantic Coast, Big Eight and Missouri Valley conferences.

Lenny Moore was among the greatest players to wear the blue and white. In 1954, he became the first Nittany Lion to rush for more than 1,000 yards in a season, gaining 1,082 with 11 touchdowns. Moore was a dynamic runner, receiver and kick returner, accumulating 3,543 all-purpose yards from 1953-55.

Moore was selected by the Baltimore Colts in the first round of the 1956 NFL Draft and had a brilliant 12-year career with the Colts, playing in seven Pro Bowls and gaining induction into the Pro Football Hall of Fame in 1975.

Summer 1964 — Joe Paterno is named associate coach and heir-apparent to succeed Rip Engle as head coach when Engle retires.

November 7, 1964 — Penn State, with a 3-4 record, shocks unbeaten No. 2 Ohio State, 27-0, in what the Associated Press calls the "college upset of the year." The Nittany Lions' defense limits the Buckeyes to 60 net yards, while the Lions' offense totals 341 yards.

November 24, 1964 — In a closed door meeting without coaches, players vote down the opportunity to play in the Gator Bowl after overcoming a 0-3 start and ending a 6-4 season with stunning shutout victories over Ohio State and Pitt and winning the Lambert

Trophy. This will mark the last time that players are given the opportunity to vote on bowl games.

Fall 1965 — College football is changed forever with a rule change implementing unlimited substitution for the first time in the modern era.

December 4, 1965 — Rip Engle coaches his last game as Penn State beats Maryland, 19-7, at Byrd Stadium, in a game televised nationally by NBC, to finish a 5-5 season and wind up 16 years at Penn State with a 104-48-4 record and no losing seasons.

February 18, 1966 — Rip Engle officially announces his retirement as head coach, about one month from his 60th birthday (March 26).

February 19, 1966 — Associate head coach Joseph V. Paterno, 38, is named head football coach by University President Eric Walker and Director of Athletics and Dean of the Physical Education Department Ernest McCoy at an annual salary of $20,000.

September 17, 1966 — Joe Paterno wins his first game, 15-7, in the season-opener against Maryland at Beaver Stadium as sophomore middle guard Mike Reid sets a team record by scoring three safeties before a crowd of 40,911. The team presents Paterno with the game ball for only the second time in his coaching career.

September 24, 1966 — Joe Paterno suffers his first loss as then No. 1 Michigan State, led by All-Americans Bubba Smith and George Webster, whip the Nittany Lions, 42-8, before 65,763 at East Lansing.

September 29, 1967 — In what becomes the "turning point" game of Joe Paterno's career, he replaces several defensive veterans with untested sophomores, including future All American Dennis Onkotz, and tackle Steve Smear and Penn State beats Miami (Fla.), 17-8, in Orange Bowl Stadium behind the running of Bobby Campbell and pass receiving of another future All-American, Ted Kwalick. Among the 39,516 spectators on hand that night are 150 members of Penn State's first Alumni Holiday Tour.

October 7, 1967 — A new policy requires students to buy tickets (at $4 each) for home games as the University eliminates pre-paid activity fees for football. Several thousand students are among the 46,007 in attendance to watch Penn State lose, 17-15, to No. 3 UCLA. The loss is the Nittany Lions' last over the next 31 games, stretching into the 1970 season.

November 11, 1967 — A Paterno-coached team gains national recognition for the first time with a 13-8 upset over then # 3 North Carolina State after a fourth-down goal line stand in the last-minute preserves the win at Beaver Stadium.

November-December 1967 — Junior tight end Ted Kwalick becomes the first first-team All American coached by Joe Paterno when named by the Newspaper Enterprise Association and the Football Coaches. Kwalick also is the first junior to win the honor and the first underclassman selected since Bob Higgins in 1915.

December 30, 1967 — Joe Paterno gains nationwide attention in the Gator Bowl by gambling for a first down on his own 15-yard line with a 17-0 third-quarter lead. When the gamble fails, Florida State rallies for a 17-17 tie in front of a record crowd of 68,019.

December 7, 1968 — The first Joe Paterno team to have a regular-season game televised nationally beats Syracuse, 30-12, at Beaver Stadium to become the first Penn State squad to be unbeaten in the regular-season since 1947 and the first one to win 10 games.

January 1, 1969 — With Chuck Burkhardt as QB, Joe Paterno's Penn State Nittany Lions completed a perfect 11-0 season and beat Kansas, 15-14, in a thrilling Orange Bowl game after the Jayhawks are penalized for having 12 men on the field.

Though undefeated and untied, the team makes its highest ever finish in the final Associated Press poll after bowl games at No. 2 behind Ohio State, which beats previous No. 1 Southern California and Heisman Trophy winner O.J. Simpson in the Rose Bowl. July 1, 1969 — Ed Czekaj, placekicker and end on the undefeated 1947 team, becomes Athletic Director, succeeding the retiring Ernie McCoy.

September 27, 1969 — Some 2,000 seats and an enlarged press box are constructed at Beaver Stadium before a record crowd of 51,402 turns out to see Penn State beat Colorado, 27-3. Paul Johnson returns a kickoff 91 yards for a touchdown. Glenn

November 29, 1969 — Penn State completes a second straight unbeaten regular-season with its 21st straight win by beating North Carolina State, 33-8, in Raleigh as part of the second half of a ABC national television doubleheader following the Army-Navy game.

All American Charlie Pittman scores two touchdowns to stretch his career touchdown record to 31, and break Pete Mauthe's 67-year-old career scoring record with 186 points.

December 31, 1969 — Earl Bruce, long-time assistant coach, retires. January 1, 1970 — Penn State's defense, led by Outland and Maxwell Trophy winner Mike Reid, sets an Orange Bowl record with seven intercepted passes as Penn State beats Missouri, 10-3, for its second consecutive 11-0 season, tying a 30-game school unbeaten streak set by teams from 1919-22, but again finishes No. 2 in the Associated Press (and UPI) poll to Texas, which beat Notre Dame in the Cotton Bowl.

September 19, 1970 — Penn State sets a record for consecutive games won (23) and unbeaten games in a row (31) with a 55-7 pasting of Navy in the season-opener at Beaver Stadium. Senior Mike Cooper of Harrisburg becomes the first African-American to start at quarterback for Penn State and throws for two touchdowns.

The new six-station television network telecasts the first of five home games on a delayed basis at 11 p.m. The games are aired in Philadelphia, Altoona, Harrisburg, Scranton, Lancaster and York. Governor Ray Shafer helps do color commentary with Dick Scherr of WTAF (Philadelphia) and Dick Richards of WFBG (Altoona) handling play-by-play and other commentary, respectively.

September 26, 1970 — Colorado ends Penn State's consecutive game winning and unbeaten streaks by beating the Nittany Lions, 41-13, in Boulder before an ABC national television audience. September 18, 1971 — Albert Vitiello, a native of Naples, Italy, becomes the first junior college transfer to play for Penn State, the first placekicking specialist to be recruited and given a "grant-in-aid" and the first soccer-style placekicker for the Nittany Lions. He debuts by kicking eight extra points in a season-opening 56-3 win at Navy.

November 20, 1971 — Lydell Mitchell establishes an NCAA record for scoring and touchdowns and breaks Pete Mauthe's 59-year old season scoring record with 174 points and Charlie Pittman's career touchdown record with 29 by scoring three touchdowns in a 55-18 win over Pitt.

December 4, 1971 — In one of the most significant losses of the Paterno era, the Nittany Lions are upset by Tennessee, 31-11, in Knoxville, ruining another unbeaten season.

December 1971 — Tackle Dave Joyner becomes Penn State's first pure offensive interior lineman to be named a first-team All-American when selected by six organizations, including United Press International, the American Football Coaches and the Football Writers.

January 1, 1972 — Penn State rallies from a 6-3 halftime deficit to stun Texas, 30-6, in the Cotton Bowl in a game Joe Paterno said was one the Nittany Lions "had to win" more than any other in Penn State history. The victory helps quiet criticism of Penn State's football program and establishes the Lions solidly as a legitimate national power.

Spring 1972 — For the first time in history, the team elects four co-captains, choosing quarterback John Hufnagel and guard Carl Schaukowitch for offense and tackle Jim Heller and safety Greg Ducatte on defense.

September 23, 1972 — The Beaver Stadium seating capacity expands to 57,537 as 5,600 seats are added to the east side and 3,570 to the north end zone, but just 50,547 turn out to watch Penn State come from behind to beat four-touchdown underdog Navy, 21-10, in the season-opening game.

September 30, 1972 — The majorettes debut with the Blue Band as a corps of 12 coeds, led by junior Judy Shearer, before a record crowd of 58,065 at the Iowa game.

Fall 1972 — Freshman eligibility, which since the early 1900s had been allowed only in the war years of 1918, 1944-45 and 1951, is restored for Division I NCAA football teams. However, Coach Joe Paterno refuses to play freshmen until the 1973 season.

November 25, 1972 — Pitt announces it will no longer follow a mutual agreement with Penn State, Syracuse and West Virginia prohibiting "redshirting" and a maximum of 25 football grants-in-aid per year.

December 31, 1972 — Penn State plays in the first Sugar Bowl held on New Year's Eve and loses, 14-0, to second-ranked Oklahoma after star running back John Cappelletti is forced to miss the game with a virus. Oklahoma is later forced to forfeit the game to Penn State after the NCAA penalizes Oklahoma for using ineligible players.

September 1973 — Defensive tackle Randy Crowder becomes the first African-American elected captain when he is chosen as a defensive co-captain along with linebacker Ed O'Neil. Tailback John Cappelletti and center Mark Markovich are elected offensive co-captains.

September 22, 1973 — Dave Shukri and Brad Benson become the first freshmen to play varsity football since 1951 when they play in the second half of a 39-0 win at Navy.

September 19, 1973 — Women become members of the marching Blue Band as the band entertains a near record Homecoming crowd of 59,980 in the home season-opener with Iowa. The five coed pioneers include Debbie Frisbee, flag carrier; Carol Gable, alto horn; Linda Hall, clarinet; Kit Murphie, alto horn; and Susan Nowlin, drums.

December 13, 1973 — John Cappelletti becomes the first Nittany Lion to win the Heisman Trophy as college football's outstanding player and accepts the award with an emotional speech about his younger brother, stricken with leukemia, before Vice President Gerald Ford and 4,000 other dignitaries in New York.

January 1, 1974 — Penn State beats LSU, 16-9, in the Orange Bowl to become the first Nittany Lion team to win 12 games without a loss, but the squad is voted No. 5 by the Associated Press and UPI. Joe Paterno calls the team "the best I've ever coached" and votes it No. 1 in the "Paterno Poll."

July 1, 1974 — Penn State withdraws from the Eastern College Athletic Conference in a dispute over financial arrangements with its 214 member schools. Penn State balks at paying 1/5th of the ECAC's total budget, plus 10 percent of television and bowl revenues.

September 21, 1974 — In what might have been the biggest upset of a Joe Paterno team ever, 24-point underdog Navy, coached by former Paterno assistant George Welsh, beats the Nittany Lions, 7-6, in rain and wind at Beaver Stadium.

October 12, 1974 — Tight end Randy Sidler becomes the first freshman to start since 1951 when two-year regular Dan Natale is sidelined by injury in the Homecoming game against Wake Forest. Sidler catches two passes for 41 yards, but another freshman wingback, Jimmy Cefalo from Northeastern PA thrills the crowd by scoring touchdowns on a 57-yard pass from Tom Shuman and a 39-yard run.

Quarterback Chuck Burkhart directed Penn State to its first two undefeated seasons under Joe Paterno in 1968 and '69. In the 1969 Orange Bowl against Kansas (above), Burkhart ran for a three-yard touchdown with eight seconds left and Bob Campbell's two-point run gave Penn State one of its most thrilling victories in program history, 15-14, to cap an 11-0 season and No. 2 finish in the Associated Press poll.

November 16, 1974 — Penn State wins its 500th game by beating Ohio University, 35-16, at Beaver Stadium despite 85 yards in penalties and four lost fumbles as Tom Donchez scores three touchdowns.

December 31, 1975 — Penn State plays in the first Sugar Bowl held at the Louisiana Superdome and loses to Alabama, 13-6.

January 6, 1976 — Ridge Riley, creator of the alumni "Football Letter," dies of a heart attack in the kitchen of head coach Joe Paterno while interviewing Paterno for the final chapter of his soon-to-be-published book, "Road to Number One."

August 1976 — John Black takes over the alumni "Football Letter" and writes the first issue analyzing the team before fall practice.

September 18, 1976 — A record crowd of 62,503 and a regional TV audience watch as Ohio State visits Penn State for the first time in history and avenges four previous losses in five games at Columbus with 12-7 win.

November 6, 1976 — Joe Paterno wins his 100th game as a head coach as the Nittany Lions beat North Carolina State, 41-20, before 60,462 at Beaver Stadium. July 1, 1977 — Assistant coaches Jim O'Hora and Frank Patrick retire; O'Hora after 31 years and Patrick after 24 years of coaching and three as athletic academic counselor.

September 19, 1977 — The last record crowd before another Beaver Stadium expansion — a standing room only gathering of 62,554 — turns out in the second game of the season to see Penn State beat Houston, 31-4. Junior quarterback Chuck Fusina hits 15-of-23 passes for 245 yards and a TD and All American Randy Sidler makes 11 tackles and causes one fumble to lead the victory.

October 15, 1977 — Joe Paterno misses the first game of his head coaching career when his 11-year old son, David, is severely injured in a trampoline accident. Paterno spends the day in a hospital in Danville, Pa., as his team, coached by offensive coordinator Bob Phillips and defensive coordinator Jerry Sandusky, staves off a fourth-quarter comeback at Syracuse and win the game, 31-24.

September 1, 1978 — The addition of 16,000 seats to Beaver Stadium is completed after lifting the existing stadium by hydraulic jacks, constructing 20 to 40 new rows of concrete stands, eliminating the track that had encircled the field, closing the south end of the horseshoe and expanding the press box.

September 11, 1978 — A Beaver Stadium record crowd of 77,154 sees Penn State beat Rutgers, 26-10, in the home season-opener.

Matt Bahr ties his brother Chris's record of four field goals and Chuck Fusina hits Scott Fitzkee for a 53-yard touchdown pass in the first quarter to spark the win.

November 6, 1978 — In a watershed battle of unbeaten teams before another record crowd of 78,019 and a national TV audience, No. 2 Penn State defeated No. 5 Maryland, 27-3, limiting the Terps to minus-32 yards rushing, intercepting five passes (three by Pete Harris) and recording 10 quarterback sacks (three by Larry Kubin). Matt Bahr kicked two field goals and Chuck Fusina connected on a 63-yard TD pass to Tom Donovan. November 13, 1978

For the first time in history, Penn State is voted No. 1 in the polls by the Associated Press and United Press International after beating North Carolina State, 19-10, thanks to another record four field goals by Matt Bahr.

November 16, 1978 — The Nittany Lion Shrine near Recreation Hall is damaged for the first time since it was dedicated in 1942, when vandals smash off the right ear.

January 1, 1979 — No. 1 ranked Penn State plays for the National Championship for first time and loses to No. 2 Alabama, 14-7, in the Sugar Bowl when Mike Guman is stopped on fourth-and-inches at the goal line in the fourth quarter in what was the biggest play of the game.

November 3, 1979 — Miami (Fla.) upsets Penn State, 26-10, at Beaver Stadium behind the passing of surprise starting freshman quarterback Jim Kelly. The Hurricanes' new coach Howard Schnellenberger tells reporters, "This day will go down in the history of Miami football as the day we turned our football program around."

December 1, 1979 — The first Penn State punt to be blocked in 10 years occurs when Ralph Giacomarro's punt is blocked by Pitt after 629 consecutive successful kicks in a 29-14 loss to the Panthers at Beaver Stadium.

March 1, 1980 — Joe Paterno becomes Athletic Director succeeding Ed Czekaj, but Paterno remains head football coach. July 1, 1980 —

J.T. White, the last assistant coach from the Rip Engle era except for Joe Paterno, retires after 26 years of coaching the defensive ends.

September 6, 1980 — Beaver Stadium's seating capacity increases to 83,600 with the addition of 7,000 seats. An electronic scoreboard also debuts as a record crowd of 78,926 watches Penn State whip Colgate, 54-10.

October 10, 1981 — A new Hall of Fame room and Indoor Sports Complex is dedicated at Homecoming festivities as the No. 2 Nittany Lions win their fourth straight by beating Boston College, 38-7, before a record crowd of 84,473.

October 20, 1981 — Penn State is voted No. 1 for only the second time in history after beating Syracuse, 41-16, in the Nittany Lions' first appearance at the Carrier Dome. Curt Warner breaks Shorty Miller's 69-year old rushing record with 256 yards and a touchdown on 26 carries. But with Warner sidelined by injury, the Lions lose two weeks later at Miami, 17-14, and drop to No. 6 as Pitt moves up to No. 1.

November 28, 1981 — Penn State pulls off one of its finest come from behind victories, snapping back from a 14-0 second-quarter deficit to rout No. 1 Pitt, 48-14, and end the national title chances of the Sugar Bowl-bound Panthers before a national television audience and 60,260 at Pitt Stadium.

The victory was sparked by interceptions of Dan Marino passes by Roger Jackson and Mark Robinson and the passing combination of Todd Blackledge to Kenny Jackson.

January 1, 1982 — Penn State plays in the first Fiesta Bowl held on New Year's Day and beats Southern California, 26-10, holding Heisman Trophy winner Marcus Allen to 85 yards as Curt Warner gains 145 yards on 26 carries. Penn State finishes No. 3 in the Associated Press and UPI rankings.

March 1, 1982 — Associate Athletic Director Jim Tarman succeeds Joe Paterno as Athletic Director as Paterno continues as head coach of the football team.

September 11, 1982 — Penn State wins its 100th game at Beaver Stadium in a 39-31 shootout with Maryland. Todd Blackledge passes for 262 yards and four touchdowns and Maryland's Boomer Esiason throws for 276 yards and two touchdowns before a sellout crowd of 84,567.

September 25, 1982 — In one of the most thrilling games ever played at Beaver Stadium, No. 8 Penn State comes from behind with a 65-yard drive in the last 1:18 to beat No. 3 Nebraska. Todd Blackledge throws the winning two-yard touchdown pass to tight end Kirk Bowman with four seconds left on the clock before record crowd of 85,304 and a national television audience.

November 26, 1982 — Curt Warner establishes the Penn State career rushing record of 3,398 yards and Todd Blackledge sets the career touchdown passing record of 41 as they lead the Nittany Lions to a 19-10 win over once-beaten Pitt at Beaver Stadium to take a No. 2 ranking to the Sugar Bowl. Warner gains 118 yards and Blackledge throws a 31-yard TD pass to Kenny Jackson to assure the victory.

January 1, 1983 — Penn State wins its first National Championship by beating previously No. 1 Georgia, 27-23, in the Sugar Bowl. Todd Blackledge passes 47 yards to Gregg Garrity for a key fourth-quarter touchdown and Curt Warner out-duels Heisman Trophy winner Herschel Walker with 117 yards and two touchdowns.

August 29, 1983 — Penn State plays in the first Kickoff Classic at Giants Stadium in the New Jersey Meadowlands and loses to a Nebraska team that would finish the regular-season ranked No. 1.

September 9, 1983 — A new Penn State sports logo is introduced featuring a sleek, Lion head.

October 8, 1983 — Unranked Penn State upsets No. 3 Alabama, 34-28, at Beaver Stadium on two last-minute defensive plays that lead to one of the biggest controversies in Penn State history when the back judge nullifies an end zone pass reception by Alabama, ruling the receiver juggled the ball as he fell out of bounds.

November 19, 1983 — In one of most bizarre finishes in Penn State football history, Nick Gancitano kicks a 32-yard field goal to tie Pitt,

24-24, after most of the 60,283 spectators and TV viewers thought the game at Pitt Stadium had ended. The clock showed no time left after a Nittany Lion running play had been stopped, but officials said six seconds remained because of a penalty a few moments earlier.

Players had to be called back from the dressing room and the field cleared for the game to finish. It was only the second tie game in Joe Paterno's coaching career.

Spring 1983 — Running backs coach Fran Ganter is promoted to offensive coordinator to succeed Dick Anderson, who takes the head coaching position at Rutgers.

September 8, 1984 — Former offensive coordinator Dick Anderson returns to Beaver Stadium as head coach of Rutgers and in the first game of his career, his team loses to Penn State, 15-12. The "Hawaiian Wave" makes its first appearance in Beaver Stadium as 84,409 fans help the "wave" roll around the stadium several times.

Fall 1984 — Permanent lights costing $575,000 are installed at Beaver Stadium after the U.S. Supreme Court rules against the NCAA's control of televised games and permits individual colleges to make their own arrangements.

September 14, 1985 — A new home team locker room and media room open at Beaver Stadium along with additional permanent seats in the North end zone for the handicapped and the visiting band. Four circular concrete ramps to help spectators reach their seats are part of the renovation.

October 26, 1985 — Penn State wins its 600th game by beating West Virginia, 27-0, before a sellout Homecoming crowd of 85,534 and an ABC regional TV audience. John Shaffer throws two touchdown passes and the defense limits the Mountaineers to 268 yards with three interceptions, two fumble recoveries and four sacks.

November 6, 1985 — Penn State is voted No. 1 for the fourth time in program history when the UPI coaches board selects the Nittany Lions first after a 16-12 come from behind fourth quarter win over Boston College. But, in the Associated Press poll, the Lions remained No. 2 behind Florida, coached by former Penn State quarterback Galen Hall.

November 13, 1985 — Penn State moves to No. 1 in the Associated Press rankings after beating Cincinnati, 31-10, in Riverfront Stadium, while Florida lost to Georgia. January 1, 1986 — Oklahoma beat the No. 1 Nittany Lions, 25-10, in the Orange Bowl to win the National Championship as two Penn State interceptions and a fumble helped the Sooners to victory.

September 6, 1986 — Penn State played the first night game at Beaver Stadium in the season-opener against Temple that helps launch the celebration of the first 100 years of Penn State football. Quarterback John Shaffer passed for three touchdowns and ran for another in the 45-15 victory.

October 25, 1986 — The sixth-ranked Nittany Lions shocked the country with a dominating 23-3 upset win over No. 2 Alabama in Tuscaloosa behind a defense led by linebackers Shane Conlan and Trey Bauer and the running of D. J. Dozier. It was just the Crimson Tide's third loss in 25 years at Bryant-Denny Stadium. The victory pushed Penn State to No. 2 in the polls and on track to play No. 1 Miami (Fla.) for the national title.

January 2, 1987 — Penn State won its second National Championship in four years by upsetting previous No. 1 Miami, 14-10, in the Fiesta Bowl with a four-down goal line stand in the last minute of play behind a defense led by All-American Shane Conlan. The Nittany Lions flustered Heisman Trophy winner Vinny Testaverde with five sacks and five interceptions, including one by linebacker Pete Giftopoulos at the goal line on the game's last play.

September 5, 1987 — Joe Paterno picked up his 200th game in a 45-19 victory over Bowling Green in the season-opening game at Beaver Stadium and later he told the media, "I may live to be 100, but I'll never be around for another 100 victories." Gittyup Gittyup Gittyup 409!

October 1, 1988 — Tony Sacca becomes the first true freshman to start at quarterback in the Paterno and Engle eras and leads Penn State to 45-9 win over Temple at Veterans Stadium in Philadelphia.

November 19, 1988 — Penn State loses to Notre Dame, 21-3, in South Bend to finish with record of 5-6 and the Nittany Lions' first losing season in 49 years.

December 19, 1989 — Representatives of Penn State and the Big Ten Conference announce that an "invitation in principle" has been extended for Penn State to join the Big Ten. The invitation is made formal on June 4, 1990 in a 7-3 vote of the Council of 10 ruling body and Penn State accepts. Penn State via Paterno decided to throw its hat into a great football conference—the Big Ten.

December 29, 1989 — In one of the zaniest games in Penn State history, the Nittany Lions best Brigham Young in a Holiday Bowl shootout, 50-39, scoring 21 points in a wild fourth quarter that includes two spectacular plays, one by All-American linebacker Andre Collins and another by defensive back Gary Brown.

Collins scores Penn State's first ever two points off an opponent conversion attempt when he returns an interception 102 yards following a BYU touchdown. Moments later, Brown strips the ball from Cougars' quarterback Ty Detmer and runs 53 yards for another touchdown with 45 seconds remaining.

November 17, 1990 — Penn State pulls off one of the biggest upsets in program history as freshman Craig Fayak kicks a 34-yard field goal with 58 seconds left to give the 18th-ranked Nittany Lions a 24-21 victory at No. 1 Notre Dame after trailing at halftime, 21-7.

Spring 1991 — The Big Ten announces Penn State football will be fully integrated into the Big Ten for the 1993 season. Iowa becomes the first opponent on the schedule, fulfilling dates previously set with Notre Dame in 1993 and 1994. The new Big Ten schedule is expected to mark the end of games with traditional rivals Pitt and West Virginia.

September 7, 1991 — A 10,000-seat upper deck is added in the north end of Beaver Stadium and a new attendance record of 94,000 is set as Penn State beats Cincinnati, 81-0, in the home-opener. The score is the largest winning point differential in the Paterno era.

January 1, 1992 — In the most bizarre and exciting four-minute span in program history, the Nittany Lions come back from a 17-7 third-quarter deficit with 28 points in less than four minutes to defeat Tennessee, 42-17, in the Fiesta Bowl. A crowd of 71,133 helps take Penn State's total season attendance over one million for the first time, with 1,017,843 attending the Lions' 13 games.

September 12, 1992 — A new policy is implemented banning smoking inside Beaver Stadium, starting with the season-opener against Temple. For just the second time in the Paterno era, a true freshman starts at quarterback as Wally Richardson leads the Nittany Lions to 49-8 victory over Temple.

October 10, 1992 — In what is the biggest game at Beaver Stadium in several years and a clash of unbeaten teams, No. 2 Miami (Fla.) beats No. 5 Penn State, 17-14, with the help of an interception return for a TD and sends the Nittany Lions into a tailspin for the season.

January 1, 1993 — Penn State loses to Stanford, 24-3, in the Blockbuster Bowl in Joe Robbie Stadium in its final game as an independent.

September 4, 1993 — Penn State ends 106 years of independence with a 38-20 win over Minnesota in its first game as a member of the Big Ten Conference. Redshirt sophomore wideout Bobby Engram catches four touchdown passes of 29, 31, 20 and 31 yards from junior quarterback John Sacca to set an all-time touchdown receiving record. Minnesota's Tim Schade sets two Penn State opponent records, completing 34-of-66 pass attempts.

September 18, 1993 — Joe Paterno wins his 250th game as head coach and receives the game ball from the players as the Nittany Lions shut out Iowa in Iowa City, 31-0, behind a defense that sets up three touchdowns with interceptions and sacks the Hawkeye quarterback nine times for 89 yards in losses.

October 16, 1993 — Penn State plays its 1,000th game in history and loses at Beaver Stadium in the first meeting with Michigan, 21-13, for its initial defeat in the Big Ten Conference.

November 27, 1993 — The Nittany Lions rally from a 37-14 deficit late in the third quarter on the passing of Kerry Collins to Bobby

Engram to beat Michigan State, 38-37, at East Lansing and clinch third place in their first year of Big Ten conference play.

December 30, 1993 — Jim Tarman retires as Athletic Director and is succeeded by former football walk-on Tim Curley.

October 15, 1994 — Unbeaten Penn State beats Michigan, 31-24, in Ann Arbor before the largest crowd ever to see the Nittany Lions play, 106,832, and is voted No. 1 for the first time since the 1987 Fiesta Bowl victory over Miami (Fla.) in polls by both the Associated Press writers and broadcasters and the USA Today / CNN coaches.

October 29, 1994 — The Nittany Lions trounce Ohio State, 63-14, but still lose their No. 1 Associated Press ranking to previously No. 3 Nebraska. Ohio native Ki-Jana Carter scores four touchdowns and runs for 137 yards and quarterback Kerry Collins passes for 265 yards and two touchdowns as the defense limits the Buckeyes to 214 net yards, while intercepting three passes.

November 5, 1994 — The Nittany Lions lose their No. 1 USAToday/CNN ranking to Nebraska after two last-minute touchdowns by Indiana claim a 35-29 victory against the Nittany Lions in Bloomington which looked closer than it was.

November 12, 1994 — The Nittany Lions clinch their first Big Ten Championship by overcoming a 21-0 first-quarter deficit with one of the greatest clutch drives in school history, a 96-yard, 15-play march into the rain and wind late in the fourth quarter to beat Illinois, 35-31, at Champaign in a late afternoon game televised by ABC.

Ki--Jana Carter breaks away in Illinois Last-Minute Victory

The drive was engineered by passes from quarterback Kerry Collins to Bobby Engram and Kyle Brady and the running of Ki-Jana Carter and Brian Milne, who scored the winning touchdown on a two-yard plunge with 57 second left in game.

November 18, 1995 — The Centre Region was hit with a rare 18-inch snowfall three days before No. 12 Michigan came to Beaver Stadium. Volunteers, including some local inmates, gladly cleared the snow from the stands and an estimated 80,000 fans attended the "Snow Bowl." Joe Nastasi's run for a touchdown on a fake field goal late in the game sealed the Nittany Lions' 27-17 win.

November 25, 1995 — Wide receiver Bobby Engram climaxes his career and cements his standing as one of the greatest clutch players in Penn State history, scoring the winning touchdown with eight seconds left and no time outs on a four-yard flanker screen pass from Wally Richardson, ducking under two Michigan State tacklers, to give the Nittany Lions a thrilling 24-20 win over Michigan State at East Lansing. No rewards for long sentences!

January 2, 1995 — Penn State whipped Oregon, 38-20, to win the Rose Bowl, but, despite a 12-0 season, the Nittany Lions were ranked # 2 to Nebraska, which was named National Champion by the Associated Press and USAToday/CNN. The New York Times computer rankings listed Penn State No. 1 with a schedule rated the 19th toughest by the NCAA compared to Nebraska's 57th rating. But, there was no opportunity for judges and arguments.

August 25, 1996 — Penn State introduced a new logo with a Lion head looking even fiercer than the last as Penn State upset Southern California, 24-7, before a record Kickoff Classic crowd of 77,716. Tailback Curtis Enis came within 15 yards of Curt Warner's game rushing record with 241 yards and three touchdowns at Giants Stadium.

September 28, 1996 — Penn State became just the sixth school in college football history to win 700 games by beating Wisconsin, 23-20, at Madison in a last-second thriller.

October 12, 1996 — Tackle John Blick became the first true freshman to start in the interior offensive line in the Paterno era in a 31-14 Homecoming win over Purdue.

April 26, 1997 — A record crowd of 60,000 attended the annual intrasquad scrimmage [Blue – White game] at Beaver Stadium, beating the previous mark of 40,000 for the 1996 Blue-White game.

September 2, 1997 — For the first time ever, Penn State was rated No. 1 in the Associated Press preseason rankings. The USAToday / CNN coaches' poll rated the Nittany Lions No. 2 behind Washington.

September 20, 1997 — Penn State scored 50 points in the first half to tie the record of the unbeaten 1947 team in a 57-21 romp at Louisville. Nonetheless, it lost the No. 1 ranking in the bogus Associated Press poll to Florida, which beat Tennessee.

October 11, 1997 — The Nittany Lions came from behind to beat No. 7 Ohio State, 31-27, before a record crowd of 97,282 at Beaver Stadium and with that victory it moved to # 1 in the Associated Press and USAToday / CNN polls for the first time since October 23, 1994. LSU had upset previous No. 1 Florida and the Nittany Lions filled the void.

October 18, 1997 — Penn State had to come from behind to beat Minnesota, 16-15, and so it lost its # 1 ranking in both the Associated Press and USAToday / CNN polls to Nebraska, which had beaten Texas Tech. All-Americans Bobby Engram (left) and Kerry Collins celebrated Penn State's thrilling 31- 24 win at Michigan on October 15, 1994 in Penn State's first game in Ann Arbor. Engram and Collins were among five first-team All-Americans that led the Nittany Lions to Big Ten and Rose Bowl titles, becoming the first Big Ten team to finish 12-0. 175 S

September 12, 1998 — Joe Paterno got his 300th career victory on the field, becoming only the sixth coach in history to reach that milestone and the first to do it all at one college. On this day, the Nittany Lions beat Bowling Green, 48-3, before 96,291 in Beaver Stadium.

October 31, 1998 — Sophomore linebacker LaVar Arrington made one of the most spectacular defensive plays in program history, leaping over the Illinois center and guard as the ball was snapped and the stopped the runner cold just as he got the hand-off. Sports Illustrated later cited the "LaVar Leap" as college football's "defensive play of the year" as the Nittany Lions beat the Fighting Illini, 27-0.

September 30, 2000 — One week after freshman cornerback Adam Taliaferro suffered a career-ending spinal injury in a game at Ohio State, the Nittany Lions rallied to beat eventual Big Ten Champion Purdue, 22-20, in Beaver Stadium.

September 1, 2001 — Less than one year after suffering a serious spinal injury, Adam Taliaferro led the Nittany Lions onto the field against Miami (Fla.) in the first game in the newly-expanded Beaver Stadium, which had grown to a capacity of 107,282.

October 27, 2001 — Penn State rallied from a 27-9 deficit to score the final 20 points and defeat Ohio State, 29-27, giving Joe Paterno his 324th career victory on the field and moving him past Paul "Bear" Bryant and into the all-time victories lead among major college coaches. The comeback is then Penn State's greatest at home under Paterno. Quarterback Zack Mills gains a school-record 418 yards of total offense.

September 14, 2002 — The Nittany Lions buried unbeaten and No. 8 ranked Nebraska, 40-7, in a primetime meeting in front of a Beaver Stadium record crowd of 110,753.

November 16, 2002 — Senior tailback Larry Johnson rushed for a Penn State record 327 yards, scoring four touchdowns, to lead the Nittany Lions to a 58-25 win at Indiana.

November 23, 2002 — Larry Johnson rushed for 279 yards and four touchdowns against Michigan State to become the first Nittany Lion and only the ninth player in NCAA Division I-A history to gain 2,000 yards in a season. The Maxwell and Doak Walker awards winner, Johnson finished the season with 2,087 yards on 271 attempts, scoring 20 touchdowns.

October 9, 2004 — The first Penn State Student Whiteout made a strong and lasting impression on the Nittany Lions, the Beaver Stadium faithful and the opposition, as No. 9 Purdue escapes with a 20-13 win.

November 13, 2004 — The Nittany Lion defense stopped Indiana on four consecutive running plays from the Penn State one-yard line to preserve a dramatic 22-18 win in Bloomington. The victory began a streak that saw Penn State beat Michigan State at home the next week and post a 51-13 record through the end of the 2009 season.

September 24, 2005 — Penn State staged a critical come from behind 34-29 win at Northwestern in the Big Ten-opener. After falling behind, 23-7, and still trailing, 29-27, with less than 2:00 to play, the Nittany Lions converted a fourth-and-15 play from their own 15-yard line, gaining 20 yards on a pass from Michael Robinson to tight end Isaac Smolko.

Robinson then threw his third touchdown pass of the game, connecting on a 36-yard strike to freshman Derrick Williams with 51 seconds remaining for the dramatic win. All-America linebacker Paul Posluszny made 22 tackles (14 solo).

October 1, 2005 — Paul Posluszny's leaping tackle at the goal line highlighted the Nittany Lions' 44-14 thumping of No. 18 Minnesota, lifting Penn State to 5-0 and back into the national rankings.

Quarterback Michael Robinson (114) and tailback Tony Hunt (112) become the first Penn State tandem to gain 100 rushing yards in a Big Ten game.

October 8, 2005 — All-American Tamba Hali forces a fumble near midfield with 1:21 to play that Scott Paxson recovers to preserve the Nittany Lions' 14-10 win over No. 6 Ohio State in a primetime thriller. A crowd of 109,839 in Beaver Stadium helped will the Nittany Lions to the crucial win, which vaulted Penn State into the Top 10.

January 3, 2006 — Kevin Kelly's 29-yard field goal in the third overtime lifts Big Ten Champion Penn State to an exciting 26-23 victory over Florida State in the 2006 FedEx Orange Bowl. In a meeting of the two winningest major college coaches of all-time, the longest game in Penn State history ends at 12:57 a.m. The Nittany Lions (11-1) finish No. 3 in the final polls.

September 30, 2006 — Sophomore wide receiver Deon Butler makes 11 receptions for a school-record 216 yards, breaking O.J. McDuffie's mark of 212 (Boston College, 1992), to lead the Nittany Lions to a 33-7 win over Northwestern.

November 4, 2006 — Joe Paterno suffers serious leg and knee injuries in the third quarter at Wisconsin when two players tumble into him on the sideline. Paul Posluszny becomes Penn State's all-time leading tackler with 14 stops, passing Greg Buttle's mark of 343 that had stood since 1975. A two-time All-American and Bednarik Award winner, Posluszny finishes his career with 372 tackles.

November 11, 2006 — Joe Paterno misses just the third game in his Penn State coaching career, while recovering from surgery on his left leg six days earlier. The Nittany Lions limit Temple to two first downs and 74 yards in a 47-0 win in Beaver Stadium.

January 1, 2007 — Cornerback Tony Davis scoops up a fumble and returns it 88 yards to break a 10-10 fourth-quarter tie, lifting Penn State to a 20-10 win over No. 17 Tennessee in the Outback Bowl. Facing their fifth ranked opponent of the season, the Nittany Lions force three Volunteer turnovers and finish No. 24 in the final Associated Press poll.

September 1, 2007 — The Big Ten Conference launches its own network, the Big Ten Network, and Penn State makes its debut during the network's launch weekend, pounding Florida International, 59-0, in the season-opener in Beaver Stadium. The Big Ten Network would be available in more than 70 million homes by the end of its second year on the air.

September 8, 2007 — The first full stadium "Whitehouse" crowd of 110,078 sees Derrick Williams' punt return touchdown ignite the Nittany Lions to a 31-10 defeat of Notre Dame in front of an ESPN primetime audience.

November 3, 2007 — All-America linebacker Dan Connor records 11 tackles in the Nittany Lions' 26-19 Senior Day win over Purdue, moving him past Paul Posluszny to become Penn State's all-time leading tackler. A two-time All-American and winner of the 2007 Bednarik Award, Connor finishes his career with 419 tackles.

November 10, 2007 — Junior kicker Kevin Kelly becomes Penn State's all-time leading scorer in the Nittany Lions' 31-0 blanking of Temple in Philadelphia, kicking a 32-yard field goal and connecting on all four PAT attempts. Kelly surpasses Craig Fayak's total of 282 points from 1990-93.

December 4, 2007 — Joe Paterno becomes just the third active coach to be inducted into the National Football Foundation College Football Hall of Fame. Paterno is forced to delay his induction by one year due to leg injuries suffered in the 2006 game at Wisconsin. He had been scheduled to enter the Hall in 2006 with active coaches Bobby Bowden and John Gagliardi.

December 29, 2007 — Joe Paterno coaches his 500th game as head coach of the Nittany Lions. His team erases a 14-0 first-quarter deficit to defeat Texas A&M, 24-17, in the Valero Alamo Bowl. A diving 30-yard touchdown catch by Deon Butler and an 11-yard scoring run by Daryll Clark spark the win and a No. 25 ranking in the final USA Today Coaches poll.

September 27, 2008 — Kevin Kelly breaks the NCAA record for consecutive games with at least one field goal (25) when he connects on a 25-yarder in the third quarter of a 38-24 primetime victory over

Illinois in Beaver Stadium. Kelly's streak would reach 31 games, ending when he did not attempt a field goal in the season-finale with Michigan State.

October 11, 2008 — Senior Derrick Williams becomes the first player under Joe Paterno to return five kicks for a touchdown in his career (three punts, two kickoffs) when he brings back a punt 63 yards for a score in Penn State's 48-7 win at Wisconsin.

October 18, 2008 — Jared Odrick records a safety on a sack to break a 17-17 third-quarter tie and spark the Nittany Lions' 46-17 Homecoming win over Michigan. The 46 points are the Lions' highest total in the series. Kevin Kelly becomes the Big Ten career kick scoring leader when he connects on a 32-yard field goal, giving Penn State a 29-17 lead.

October 25, 2008 — Penn State scores 10 points in the final 6:25 to record a 13-6 win over No. 10 Ohio State in a primetime game in Columbus. Mark Rubin records a career-high 11 tackles and forces a fumble in the fourth quarter, which Navorro Bowman recovers in Ohio State territory to set up the go-ahead score. Ohio State is held to its fewest points at home since a 6-0 loss to Wisconsin in 1982.

November 8, 2008 — Kevin Kelly becomes the Big Ten leader in field goals when he boots the 73rd of his career, a 23-yard kick in the first quarter of a 24-23 loss at Iowa that ends the Nittany Lions' unbeaten season. November 15, 2008 — Deon Butler becomes Penn State's career receptions leader with 172, surpassing Bobby Engram, when he makes five catches in a 34-7 win over Indiana at Beaver Stadium.

November 22, 2008 — Daryll Clark throws for 341 yards and four touchdowns to propel No. 8 Penn State past No. 15 Michigan State, 49-18, to clinch the Nittany Lions' second Big Ten Championship in four years. Penn State passes for a school-record 419 yards, improving to 11-1 and earning a Rose Bowl berth against Southern California. Penn State becomes the sixth school in the nation to win 800 games.

December 11, 2008 — Senior A.Q. Shipley is announced as Penn State's first recipient of the Dave Rimington Trophy, honoring the nation's most outstanding center.

October 3, 2009 — Stephfon Green (120) and Evan Royster (105) gain more than 100 rushing yards to lead Penn State past Illinois, becoming the first tandem of Nittany Lion running backs to crack the century mark in Big Ten play.

Nov. 21, 2009 — Quarterback Daryll Clark delivers a record-breaking performance in his final Big Ten game, throwing for 310 yards and four TDs to lead a 42-14 win at Michigan State. Clark breaks the school records for season (22 by Todd Blackledge, 1982) and career (41) touchdown passes and finishes the season with 24 and 43, respectively.

January 1, 2010 — Penn State defeats No. 13 LSU, 19-17, in the Capital One Bowl on a Collin Wagner field goal with :57 to play. The Nittany Lions (11-2) secure their first consecutive 11-win seasons since 1985-86, and finish No. 9 in the final Associated Press poll. Daryll Clark becomes Penn State's season total offense leader with 3,214 yards and the first Nittany Lion quarterback to eclipse 3,000 passing yards in a season (3,003).

September 4, 2010 — Rob Bolden becomes the first Penn State true freshman quarterback to start a season-opener in 100 years (Shorty Miller, 1910) and leads Penn State to a 44-14 win over Youngstown State. Bolden goes 20-of-29 for 239 yards, with two touchdowns and one interception to deliver the best passing performance by a Penn State true freshman quarterback in program history.

September 18, 2010 — Penn State beats Kent State, 24-0, for its 500th victory since Joe Paterno joined the coaching staff in 1950. The shutout was the Nittany Lions' 41st since Paterno became head coach.

September 25, 2010 — Collin Wagner ties the school record with five field goals to lift the Nittany Lions past Temple, 22-13.

November 6, 2010 — Penn State rallies from a 21-0 deficit late in the first half to beat Northwestern, 35-21, giving Joe Paterno his 400th career victory on the field. Paterno becomes the first Football Bowl Subdivision coach with 400 wins and just the third in NCAA history. Matt McGloin throws a career-high four touchdown passes to lead the rally. The comeback is Penn State's largest at home under Paterno and matches the biggest comeback all-time under the Hall of Fame mentor (trailed 21-0 at Illinois in 1994; won, 35-31).

October 29, 2011 — Silas Redd rushes for 100 yards or more for the fifth consecutive game and scores the game-winning touchdown with 1:08 to play to lift Penn State to a 10-7 win over Illinois. The Nittany Lions improve to 8-1 overall and become the first team in Big Ten history to win five consecutive conference games by 10 points or less. The victory is the 409th of Joe Paterno's career on the field moving him past legendary Grambling coach Eddie Robinson for the most wins in NCAA Division I history and No. 2 all-time for all NCAA divisions. Paterno's career on the field record stands at 409-136-3 over 46 years as head coach in what would be the final game for the Hall of Fame coach and icon.

Chapter 4 The Rip Engle & Joe Paterno Era

Coach # 13

1950	Rip Engle	5-3-1
1951	Rip Engle	5-4
1952	Rip Engle	7-2-1
1953	Rip Engle	6-3
1954	Rip Engle	7-2-
1955	Rip Engle	5-4
1956	Rip Engle	6-2-1
1957	Rip Engle	6-3
1958	Rip Engle	6-3-1
1959	Rip Engle	9-2
1960	Rip Engle	7-3
1961	Rip Engle	8-3
1962	Rip Engle	9-2
1963	Rip Engle	7-3
1964	Rip Engle	6-4
1965	Rip Engle	5-5

Top row, left to right: Dan Radakovich, Joe McMullen, George Welsh, Joe Paterno, J.T. White Bottom row, left to right: Frank Patrick, Earl Bruce, Rip Engle, Jim O'Hora taken during the football Field Day in 1963

On April 22, 1950 Charles A. "Rip" Engle, who had been head coach at Brown University was named the new Penn State head football coach to replace Joe Bedenk.

Engle was the innovator of the famous Wing-T formation. His teams experienced tremendous success leading Engle to a career PSU record of 104-48-4.

In May of 1950 Engle named former Brown University quarterback Joseph V. Paterno to his Penn State staff. He promptly assigned Paterno to coach quarterbacks. Rip Engle coached his last game in 1965 with a win over Maryland, 19-7 ending a 16-year stint as Penn State head football coach.

During his tenure, Penn State did not endure a losing season. Engle officially retired February 18, 1966. A day later Joseph V. Paterno was hired head football coach of Pennsylvania State University. The rest, as they say, is history.

From 1950, when he was appointed head coach, through 1965, when he retired and was succeeded by Joe Paterno, Mr. Rip Engle's Penn State football teams won 104 games, lost 48 and tied 4. For his entire head-coaching career, which included six seasons at Brown University, his record was 132-68-8.

Charles Albert Engle became a great friend of Joe Paterno while at Brown University. He was born on March 26, 1906, in Salisbury, Pa. Like many Pennsylvanians in those days, he was a child mine worker. In fact, he was a mule driver in a coal mine at the age of 9,

He left Pennsylvania for Western Maryland College, where he was a skillful end on the football team and where he also was a great athlete in other sports such as basketball, baseball and tennis before he graduated in 1930.

Engle went right into high school football coaching, at Waynesboro (Pa.) High School, where he stayed for 11 years, before he was appointed assistant coach at Brown. In 1944, he was promoted to head coach in 1944. One of the greats on his Brown staff, besides Coach Paterno was Weeb Ewbank, who later earned fame as coach of the Baltimore Colts and the New York Jets. Of course, among his famous Brown players was Paterno, a quarterback and defensive back, as well as George Paterno, Joe Pa's brother who for years did a Penn State talk show.

With Paterno's help, Engle rebuilt the Penn State program at the time. When he took over the PSU football program was not considered among the nation's best. But by the time he retired, the Nittany Lions had become known for never having had a losing season in his sixteen

Besides a great record with Joe Paterno as assistant, Engle is credited with three major upsets over highly regarded Ohio State, in 1956, 1963, and 1964. Additionally, there were three times that Mr. Engle's and Mr. Paterno's teams—in 1961, 1962 and 1964, won the Lambert Trophy, which goes to the best college football team in the East.

Among the prominent players who helped the team in this period were Lenny Moore, Milt Plum, Jesse Arnelle and Roosevelt Grier.

Engle was a great mentor for Joe Paterno and was elected to the National Football Foundation's Hall of Fame in 1974. Mr. Paterno, by that time, had long since begun adding to the successful record created by his predecessor, including, by then Penn State's first National Championship as determined by news-agency polls in the university's history. Let's look briefly at the Rip Engle / Joe Paterno seasons.

1950 Penn State Football Season Coach Rip Engle

The 1950 Penn State Nittany Lions football team was coached by Rip Engle in his first year. Coach Engle compiled a 5-3-1 record in his first year with the Nittany Lions.

1951 Penn State Football Season Coach Rip Engle

The 1951 Penn State Nittany Lions football team was coached by Rip Engle. The team had a 5-4 record for 1951.

1952 Penn State Football Season Coach Rip Engle

The 1952 Penn State Nittany Lions football team was coached by Rip Engle and played a fine season with a record of 7-2-1. PSU was back to ten games per season.

1953 Penn State Football Season Coach Rip Engle

The 1953 Penn State Nittany Lions football team was coached by Rip Engle. They played home games in New Beaver Field in University Park, Pennsylvania. The Field had room for 30,000 fans at the time. This season's record was 6-3 and the team played nine games.

1954 Penn State Football Season Coach Rip Engle

The 1954 Penn State Nittany Lions football team was coached by Rip Engle in his fifth year. The team finished with a 7-2 record and achieved a #16 ranking in the coach's poll and a #20 in the AP.

1955 Penn State Football Season Coach Rip Engle

The 1955 Penn State Nittany Lions football team was coached by Rip Engle. The team talent pendulum swings and changes from year to year as one team is better than another and vice versa. This year's team made it above .500 with a 5-4 record but otherwise, it was not a stellar year. Rip Engle had better years as you will see. He coached the Lions until 1965.

Among great players on the team was Lenny Moore, who graduated in 1956.

Player Highlights Lenny Moore 1953-1955

Leonard Edward Moore was born November 25, 1933. He played halfback at PSU and he played pro for the NFL Baltimore Colts from 1956 to 1967.

Moore was simply great. He was NFL Rookie of the Year in 1956 and was a Pro-Bowler seven times. He was inducted into the Pro Football Hall of Fame in 1975.

Moore could to it all and Coaches Engle and Paterno had him do it all just as Moore always did in his great college and pro football career. He was both a great runner and receiver. He would line up both in the backfield as a halfback and split wide as a flanker, and the talented Moore was equally dangerous at both positions.

Moore was great at PSU and was named the NFL Rookie of the Year. Here is a pic from 2009 with JoePa at the Syracuse game. Joe Paterno was Assistant Coach when Lenny played in 1955. You can see just by looking at this picture that the two had great admiration for each other.

Pro football Hall of Famer and former Penn State running back Lenny Moore embraces coach Joe Paterno before the start of the Syracuse game at Beaver Statdium. Moore served as honorary captain for the Lions.

Joe Hermitt (jhermitt@pennlive.com) captured the essence of JoePa and Lanny Moore and their relationship in the above picture. This is from the Syracuse game September 15, 2009. Thank you to Pennlive for the use of the picture and the article to make this book and even more outstanding read for Penn Staters.

Here is Hermitt's article about Lenny Moore and their chance meeting:

"Ever have one of those moments when you just wish you could crawl under a rock and hide? You know, you do or say something so stupid that you would give your right arm to be able to take it back?

"Welcome to my world.

"It was about a half an hour before game time this past Saturday. Several recruits headed to their seats, both teams were leaving the field after pre-game warm-ups and Penn State coach Joe Paterno had just finished screaming at a cameraman who made the mistake of going onto the field to film him during stretches. In other words, it was business as usual at Beaver Stadium.

"I was following Paterno, shooting photos as he headed toward the tunnel. An older man approached the coach, reached out and grabbed him from behind. Paterno, at first surprised, immediately broke into a huge smile, as if seeing an old friend for the first time in a long while.

"The two embraced, not something you see Joe do very often, shared a few words and parted, as the coach needed to join his team in the locker room. Figuring the man must be someone special to Paterno, I headed over to find out who he was. I introduced myself, told him I had snapped his photo with Paterno and asked his name.

"The man smiled broadly and responded, "Sure, my name is Lenny Moore".

"After what seemed an eternity, I managed to coherently apologize. Profusely. To add to my trauma, his escort from Penn State burst out laughing, saying, "That was priceless, you should see your face."

"But a funny thing happened. Moore, wearing a perplexed look, asked why I was apologizing. In fact, he went on to say that he used to read the Patriot and would love to get a copy of the photo I had just taken. Would I possibly be able to send him one? I offered to email it to him but, much like Paterno, he doesn't have email. So, he pulled out a business card and handed it to me.

"Simple and to the point, the card read, Lenny Moore, his address and telephone number and in the top right corner, "Christ is Lord".

No mention of Pro Football Hall of Fame membership or of being one of the greatest players to ever play at Penn State.

"Moore played for the Nittany Lions from 1953-55 and as the Altoona Mirror's Neil Rudel writes, "In an era where the players went both ways, playing offense and defense, Moore averaged a ridiculous 8.0 yards per carry, a record that still stands among the season leaders - 55 years later. He also led the team in interceptions twice and punt return average three times, including a blurry 17.5 per in '54."

"Moore played for the Baltimore Colts from 1956-67, was selected to the Pro Bowl seven times, had his number, 24, retired and was elected to the Pro Football Hall of Fame.

"In his post-game news conference Joe Paterno said, "Lenny Moore was probably the best football player I've ever coached, all-around."

Baltimore Colts running back Lenny Moore in action.

"Wow.

"So as the legendary Moore stood on the sideline preparing to serve as honorary captain at the mid-field coin toss, he could not have been more gracious to a well-meaning, but foolish photographer who didn't even know his name.

"God, I still feel like climbing under a rock. Thanks Mr. Moore, your photo is on the way."

1956 Penn State Football Season Coach Rip Engle

The 1956 Penn State Nittany Lions football team was coached by Rip Engle in his seventh year as head coach. The team record was 6-2-1. Penn State had an independent football program at the time and were part of no football conference.

1957 Penn State Football Season Coach Rip Engle

The 1957 Penn State Nittany Lions football team was coached by Rip Engle in his eighth season. Engle directed the team to a nice 6-3 season.

1958 Penn State Football Season Coach Rip Engle

The 1958 Penn State Nittany Lions football team was coached by Rip Engle in his ninth year. Penn State played a tenth game in 1958 and without that game the season would have been 6-3, but with the tie at West Virginia on November 8 T (14-14) the record was 6-3-1.

1959 Penn State Football Season Coach Rip Engle

The 1959 Penn State Nittany Lions football team was coached by Rip Engle in his tenth season of sixteen with PSU. This was the first eight-win year for an Engle team and it brought them a shot at the Liberty Bowl which they won on December 31, 1959 v Alabama W (7-0). The Lions finished at 9-2.

Penn State was winning very game all year until it ran into some old rivals. By now, by reading this book's review of all the games by coach, you know who they are. PSU was 7-0 when it ran into an always stubborn Syracuse team at home. Syracuse was ranked #4 when they played at New Beaver Field. In a brawl, they barely beat Penn State L (18-20) to put the first blemish on Engle's 1959 team. Think about what would have happened if PSU won that game.

Syracuse went on to win their first and only National Championship with the help of future Heisman trophy winner Ernie Davis.

In the See-Saw end of season match, looking for every opportunity to have a one-loss season, Pittsburgh spoiled it for the Nittany Lions in a well-fought game L (7-22)

When PSU lost to Syracuse on November 7 L (18-20), the Lions were 8-0 and ranked # 7 in the nation. On November 14, the # 10 Nittany Lions got their breath with a home win against Holy Cross W (46-0)., Next was Pittsburgh at Pitt Stadium, an always-tough game to win. On November 21, Pittsburgh was energized and beat the Lions L (7-22)

After waiting a month for a chance for national exposure in the Independence Bowl, # 14 ranked Penn State knocked off # 11 Alabama in a real battle of the trenches W (7-0) PSU had a great season 9-2, finishing # 10 in the coach's poll and # 12 in the AP. 1959 was a fine year for Rip Engle and company.

1960 Penn State Football Season Coach Rip Engle

The 1960 Penn State Nittany Lions football team was coached by Rip Engle in his eleventh year. This year the Nittany Lions played their games in the newly opened Beaver Stadium in University Park, Pennsylvania. The team played ten games and finished their first season in their big, brand new stadium with a fine 7-3 record. PSU finished # 16 for the season and if the number of bowl games were as today, PSU would have assured itself of a bowl game match.

The 500-seat Beaver Field, then the 30,000 seat New Beaver Field, and in 1960, the new Beaver stadium were all named for James Beaver, President of the Board of Trustees. The Nittany Lions played at the original Beaver Field and New Beaver Field from when they moved off the lawn until 1959.

The university decided to disassemble the stadium and move it to its current location after the 1959 season. PSU played its first game in the rebuilt stadium on September 17, 1960 against Boston University. Beaver Stadium's horseshoe configuration enabled it to have a seating capacity of 46,284, but as we all know it fits well over 100,000 today after many expansions.

The stadium's inaugural season began in triumph against Boston University on September 17. There was a nice piece of history (30,000 original seats) packaged up as a starter kit for Beaver Stadium, and it sure helped for the first game at Beaver Stadium to be a triumph for the Nittany Lions W (20-10) over Boston University It had to be a great day.

The Nittany Lions had competed so well with its 6-3 record that it got a shot at Oregon in the Liberty Bowl on December 17 at JFK Stadium in Philadelphia, winning the game W (41-12).

1961 Penn State Football Season Coach Rip Engle

The 1961 Penn State Nittany Lions football team was coached by Rip Engle in his twelfth season. The lions pounded out a #19 finish and a #17 in the AP with an overall season ending 8-3 record including a Gator Bowl win v Georgia Tech.

1962 Penn State Football Season Coach Rip Engle

The 1962 Penn State Nittany Lions football team was coached by Rip Engle in his thirteenth of sixteen seasons. The team played its second set of home games in the brand-new Beaver Stadium in University Park, Pennsylvania.

At 9-1 with a fine year with just one blemish v Army L (6-9), the Nittany Lions were invited to play on December 29 vs. Florida at Gator Bowl Stadium in Jacksonville, FL. Florida won the close match L (7–17). PSU finished at 9-2 for a fine season.

1963 Penn State Football Season Coach Rip Engle

The 1963 Penn State Nittany Lions football team was coached by Rip Engle in his fourteenth of sixteen seasons. The team played its third set of home games in its brand-new Beaver Stadium in University Park, Pennsylvania. The regular season finale with Pittsburgh was postponed from Nov. 23 to Dec. 7 following the assassination of President John F. Kennedy on Nov. 22 in Dallas, Texas. Even football history cannot undue history, though we wish it could. PSU finished # 16 with a fine 7-3 record.

1964 Penn State Football Season Coach Rip Engle

The 1964 Penn State Nittany Lions football team was coached by Rip Engle in his fifteenth year. Even though the team was just 6-4, its strength of schedule prompted the coach's poll to rank PSU # 14 in 1964.

Pittsburgh, an old-time rivalry was doing poorly at 3-5-2 after a 9-1 season in 1962, marched into Penn State's Beaver Stadium on November 21. The Panthers marched back out after being shut down by PSU W 28-0)

There have been a lot of cold games in the history of Beaver Field, New beaver Field, and Beaver Stadium. In one of the two coldest games in the history of Beaver Stadium, Penn State dominated its bitterest rival before what was a record crowd of 50,144 before the big Stadium expansions.

They were forced to brave the wind, snow flurries, and wind chill temperatures of zero. It was just the eighth time since the Pitt series began in 1893 that the annual year-end game was played at Penn State and the first time since 1955. Penn State warmed the hearts and minds of their fans with this fine W (28-0) victory.

1965 Penn State Football Season Coach Rip Engle

The 1965 Penn State Nittany Lions football team was coached by Rip Engle's in his last season as head coach of Penn State. Penn State ironically had one of its worst records this year (5-5) as it proves the ups and downs of college football results. Rip Engle was a fine coach. With sixteen seasons of coaching PSU behind him Engle had had enough. He never had a losing season.

This 5-5 season was Rip Engle's last. Penn State appointed Joe Paterno as Head Coach of the Nittany Lions.

Chapter 5 Joe Paterno Era from 1966 to 1974

Coach # 14

1966	Joe Paterno	5-5
1967	Joe Paterno	8-2-1
1968	Joe Paterno	11-0
1969	Joe Paterno	11-0
1970	Joe Paterno	7-3
1971	Joe Paterno	11-1
1972	Joe Paterno	10-2
1973	Joe Paterno	12-0
1974	Joe Paterno	10-2

Coached 45 great seasons 1966 to 2010 and part of 2011.

With 409 victories, Joe Paterno is the winningest coach in NCAA FBS history.

Joe Paterno put together bowl victories, two consensus National Championships—1982, 1986, and five undefeated and untied seasons – 1968, 1969, 1973, 1986, and 1994. Four of Penn State's unbeaten teams (1968, 1969, 1973, and 1994) won major bowl games and yet were not awarded a national championship. You make the call on that one, please! At the end of the 2011 season, Joe Paterno was the winningest coach ever in Division IA with a 409-

136-3 record. Many of us who look at the number of years he coached and his fine record believe that He was the best coach ever!

1966 Penn State Football Season Coach Joe Paterno

The 1966 Penn State Nittany Lions football team was coached by Joe Paterno in his first season as head coach of Penn State. Paterno helped the team achieve a 5-5 record, which coincidentally was the record for PSU in Rip Engle's last season.

September 17 was the First Paterno-led game at home (Beaver Stadium). PSU beat Maryland in a lose match W (15-7).

It is always a good feeling and often a harbinger of good things to come when a new coach wins his first game, especially a home game. Paterno brought in the big one when he was still a kid at 40 years old. Tons of victories later, and Paterno teams would bring in over 400 victories for the good of Penn State University, a great school, and a great football program. September 17th was simply the first. The attendance was almost at max to see this game with 40,911 excited Penn State Fans ready to see the Nittany Lions play ball.

The first come-uppance for the team came soon after the first victory when PSU traveled to Army on October 1, and lost L (0-11). The next week on October 8, PSU was back at home and the Lions beat Boston College W (30-21) bringing the record to 2-1. The JoePa team went to the Los Angeles Memorial Coliseum on October 15 and were overwhelmed by UCLA L (11-49) Joe Paterno was getting a baptism of fire. But, this tough coach, a one-time quarterback would endure and succeed.

On October 22, The Nittany Lions played at West Virginia for a nice win W (38-6). The California University played PSU at Beaver Stadium on October 29, and PSU did quite good W (33–15_ before 33,332 fans. On November 5, at Beaver Stadium in what was termed an ABC Regional, PSU played Syracuse in a nail biter won by Syracuse L (10-12) before with 45, 126 in attendance—a veritable packed house at the new Beaver Stadium.

On November 12, PSU played at #5 ranked Georgia Tech and were shot-out L (0-21). Pittsburgh had been playing sporadic since its great years and in 1966, Joe Paterno's first team were ready in their annual venture, played this time at Pitt Stadium. Penn State was please to deliver a shellacking to Pitt W (48-24).

1967 Penn State Football Season Coach Joe Paterno

The 1967 Penn State Nittany Lions football team was coached by Joe Paterno and played its home games in the recently built Beaver Stadium in University Park, Pennsylvania. It did not take Joe Paterno long to break out of the regular pack of American coaches. Rip Engle and many PSU coaches were very good coaches.

Joe Paterno at 45 years was a remarkable, unquestionably great coach. In his getting to know you first year, he was 5-5 but those days for the most part were gone. In 1967 Paterno showed his mettle and delivered a great 8-2-1 season to PSU fans. Penn State had been a national power. Joe Paterno made Penn State a "you better notice us," national phenomenon.

Nobody likes to begin a season with a loss and when PSU traveled to Navy at Annapolis on September 23, the Nittany Lions planned to win. But a scrappy and tough US Navy team beat them by one point L (22-23). Miami Florida plays its home games at the orange Bowl, and in game 2 on September 29, PSU played Miami at this famous venue and beat the Hurricanes W (17-8).

UCLA, still very tough, and remembering their win the prior year came to Beaver Stadium on October 7, expecting an easy game like 1966 but it did not happen. UCLA beat the Nittany Lions but they worked for every point and the difference was just two points L (15-17). This PSU team hated to lose more than most teams. They would not suffer another loss for the rest of this season.

On October 14, PSU played Boston College at Alumni Stadium in Chestnut Hill, MA, and swamped the Eagles W (50–28). On October 21, West Virginia played the Lions at home W (21–14). On October 28, an always-tough Syracuse team coached by Ben Schwartzwalder played a tough game at Archbold Stadium but the Lions prevailed W (29–20) before 41,750. On November 4 at Maryland, Penn State took away a convincing win (38–3).

Back at home on November 11, the #3 ranked NC State team came into Beaver Stadium and the Nittany Lions won again W 13-8) in a very historical game. The Nittany Lions stopped a fourth-and-goal at their one-yard line with 44 seconds left to upset No. 3 North Carolina State and give Coach Joe Paterno his first signature victory. Paterno has called the tackle by Mike McBath, Dennis Onkotz, and Jim Kates: "one of the greatest plays in Penn State history." Joe ought to know.

Ohio was next on November 18 at Beaver Stadium in University Park, PA. PSU exploded for a win W (35–14). In the last regular game of the season, with a record of 7-2, PSU played its nemesis Pitt at Beaver Stadium on November 25, and beat their cross-state rivals in a blowout W (42-6). PSU finished the regular season in Joe Paterno's second season at 8-2, a great record with most wins on the back-end.

For this great record, the Nittany Lions were invited to the Gator Bowl which was on ABC TV played in Jacksonville Florida against

Florida State University on December 30, 1967. It was a really tough game and no team got the edge. This is one bowl game that ended in a tie (T 17-17) before 68,019—all of whom were disappointed.

1968 Penn State Football Season Coach Joe Paterno

The 1968 Penn State Nittany Lions football team was coached by Joe Paterno in his third season. The 1968 team was Paterno's first perfect season. He had gone from 5-5 to 8-2-1, to 11-0, and still could not get the pundits, the scribes or the coaches to give Penn State the championship it deserved. No matter what you think of the BCS, this is the scenario that it was created to avoid.

Was it fair that Penn State was denied the National Championship with a perfect record and eleven games played? How about going 11–0? Regardless of the fairness factor, the voters ruled. The Nittany Lions finished behind 9–0 Ohio State and 9–0–1 USC in both polls. Not fair for sure. PSU should claim a piece of this championship as many other schools have done when fairness was not achieved. Just a thought. Every game was a win in 1968. Every game, including the big Orange Bowl game on January 11, 1969

On September 21, a # 10 ranked Navy team lost at Beaver Stadium to Penn State in a convincing match W (31-6). After the game, PSU was ranked # 4. Kansas State then played at Beaver Stadium on September 28, and were beaten handily W (25-9). West Virginia then played a #3 ranked PSU at Mountaineer Field and lost the game to a powerful PSU team W (31-20).

PSU then played UCLA in California on October 12 and beat the Bruins for the fourth win of the season W (21-6). Somehow after this victory, Penn State had slipped down one notch to # 4 in the polls. Who knows why? After a week bye, PSU played at Boston College's Alumni Stadium in Chestnut Hill, MA, and won a shutout W (29-0) against the Eagles.

Army, always tough, were not tough enough in a really tough game to beat Penn State. The Lions won this close match W (28-24) before 49,653, a virtual sellout of the original Beaver Stadium. After these two wins, PSU was still in 4th place.

Regardless of the polls, Penn State could not have won this game against Army without a little intervention. Surely many were praying as it came down to an onside kick.

All-America tight end Ted Kwalick swooped up the football coming out of a pile of players on an onside kick attempt in this game with 2:29 left. Kwalick was not an All-American by acclamation. He had earned it. In this game, the tight end took the ball in addition to all hopes for an Army victory across the goal line 53-yards after he had snagged the kick in the air. This was a very important touchdown for the 1968 season as it avoided an upset that would have ruined Penn State's first undefeated season under Paterno.

Player Highlights Ted Kwalick

Ted Kwalick was inducted into the Polish American Hall of Fame on June 9, 2005. Having three children of Polish descent and living in a Polish / Irish family, I can say that I believe that Ted Kwalick enjoyed this honor as much as his College Hall of Fame induction.

Kwalick was born in Pittsburgh, on the other side of the state from where I live, but he came to mid Pennsylvania to play football. He became a star at Penn State University for his outstanding play. He put in a three year highly successful tenure with the Nittany Lions as a tight end, catching 86 passes for 1,343 yards and 10 touchdowns—all Penn State records.

Kwalick was the school's first two-time All-American (1968, 1969). He helped lead the Nittany Lions to a perfect 11-0 record and a victory in the Orange Bowl in 1969 (the season being reported).

He was selected seventh overall in the NFL draft by the San Francisco 49ers, and he quickly made an impact the way great players most often do. He made the NFC Pro Bowl three straight seasons (1971-73) playing in three NFL West Championship games.

Kwalick after the Maryland Game

In 1972, Kwalick scored nine touchdowns and averaged an amazing 18.8 yards per catch. After six seasons with the 49ers he played his last three years with the Oakland Raiders. In 1977 the Raiders beat the Vikings in Super Bowl XI giving Kwalick his Super Bowl ring. Kwalick was inducted into the College Football Hall of Fame in 1989.

Remaining 1999 Games

Always tough national power Miami played PSU at Beaver Stadium on November 9 and lost W (22-7). The crowd was more than capacity at 50,132. On November 16 at Maryland, a then-ranked #3 PSU won big W (57–13). Still not able to budge the pundits or the coaches who had something else on their mind, PSU smothered a tough Pitt Panther team on November 23 at Pittsburgh W (65-9). Even big scores against college powerhouses could not move the Lions up in the rankings.

The Nittany Lions were still ranked at # 3, though undefeated and untied when a tough Syracuse team came to Beaver Stadium on December 7. It was a respectable game W (30-12) but clearly PSU dominated against the national power Syracuse squad. Played before 41,393 at Beaver Stadium. Penn State, a team accustomed to cold Pennsylvania winters beat a cold-weather team that had yet to gain the comforts of the Carrier Dome. December 7 was a cold day and if I may after the game with the rankings, it appeared that it would have to be an even colder day in Hell for Penn State to get a break, and if not a break, some fairness.

Yes, the PSU Syracuse encounter was a tough cold game. Somebody, someplace, however was warm enough to be pleading the case for some other teams to advance in the standings while PSU was neutralized. PSU did not move up a nickel in the polls all season long. Everybody knew the PSU schedule when shortly after the season began PSU was ranked # 3.

Moreover, though the PSU record was about as good as it could get in football, at 10-0, PSU's opponent for the Orange Bowl was not either of the # 1 or # 2 ranked teams in America and neither had as good a record as the Nittany Lions.

As an independent, perhaps the conferences dominated the post-season voting for opportunities. Playing # 6 Kansas, a fine team in 1967, would in no way nudge the PSU record up a notch so PSU could play for the championship. Even if the battle between the # 1 and # 2 at the time found both teams losing, the obvious bias of the press and the coaches, I regret to say would still have denied PSU its due.

The university does not complain but perhaps it should. Nothing is over until it is over. The deck was stacked against PSU by a set of biased coaches and biased pundits. Who knows? Maybe they simply did not like Pennsylvania or perhaps it was third year coach Joe Paterno, who nobody knew because he was so new and thus did not deserve a championship. You tell me? Maybe somebody had an issue with Rip Engle or Bib Higgins or perhaps the Hollenback brothers that needed to be atoned. My only excuse is that it sure seems that some set of coaches and pundits with a relationship with a past Penn State coach or team believed they had experienced some animus that now had its chance to be righted. Again, who knows?

Nonetheless, Kansas and Penn State entered the Orange Bowl for this NBC televised game on January 1, 1969, both wanting to win this prestigious game and both hoping for the best. Both were great teams and nobody could deny that. Before 77,719 fans, Penn State played one of its best games ever against a very, very tough and respectable Kansas squad. PSU won the line battle and the scoring battle but just about won the game by one point W (15-14)

Quarterback Chuck Burkhart directed Penn State to its first two undefeated seasons under Joe Paterno in 1968 and '69. In the 1969 Orange Bowl against Kansas (above), Burkhart ran for a three-yard touchdown with eight seconds left and Bob Campbell's two-point run gave Penn State one of its most thrilling victories in program history, 15-14, to cap an 11-0 season and No. 2 finish in the Associated Press poll.

1969 Penn State Football Season Coach Joe Paterno

The 1969 Penn State Nittany Lions football team was coached by Joe Paterno in his fourth season. The 1968 team was Paterno's second perfect season in a row. He had gone from 5-5 to 8-2-1, to 11-0, and now again in 1969, 11-0, and yet the coaches and the pundits denied Penn State a National Championship for the second time in ten years. As I have said before, no matter what you may think of the BCS, this is the scenario for which it was created.

Despite posting its second consecutive undefeated, untied season, the Nittany Lions did not have a fair shot at the national championship. Somehow President Richard Nixon was polled about his thinking on the matter. He said that he would consider the winner of the December 6 matchup between the Texas Longhorns and the Arkansas Razorbacks, then ranked at the top of the polls.

The coaches and the pundits mysteriously agreed with the President and they set up a scenario from which Penn State could again not compete in a championship game on New Year's Day. Sometimes even though a university does not whine, it should. PSU should have received a share of two national titles that it had earned.

Though there are no real excuses for this travesty against fair play, national champions were selected before the bowl games were played in January. Joe Paterno, who was a great speaker and a great teller of great stories—at the 1973 PSU Commencement ceremonies four years later, was quoted: "I've wondered how President Nixon could know so little about Watergate in 1973 and so much about college football in 1969." This was a national shame.

When Nixon named Texas the national champion over Penn State

President Nixon's decision to name Texas the 1969 national champion over Penn State is explored in ESPN Film

Pennsylvania Governor Raymond Shafer got into the act and quickly got the White House's attention with Penn State's 2 season undefeated streak. Shafer quickly declared that Pennsylvania State University was the # 1 team in the nation.

A White House assistant called Paterno to invite him and the team to the White House to receive a trophy for their accomplishment. Paterno has stated many times that he responded with, "You can tell the president to take that trophy and shove it." Penn State and the entire state of Pennsylvania declined an invitation to play the Texas/Arkansas winner in the Cotton Bowl.

As we review the 1969 season, it helps to remember that now, many years later, there will be no drama reading the season's games as each and every game was won by Penn State. Not all games were blow-outs but there were many, but Penn State won all the games – the shutouts, the blow-outs, and the close-calls, one after another. Every game below that you read about was a victory for Penn State though these wins were not enough for the coach's and pundits who perhaps wanted a different team or coach to win the national prize. It sure was not right. Then again, that's why today we have the BCS

The first win came on September 20 at Navy at the Navy-Marine Corps Memorial Stadium • Annapolis, MD. PSU was rated # 3 to start. The Nittany Lions won the game handily W (45–22) before 28,796. On September 27, Colorado came to play a now # 2 ranked PSU at Beaver Stadium and lost the game W (7–3) with 51,402 in attendance. On October 4, Kansas State hosted PSU at KSU Stadium for a close Lions win W (17–14). By Beating Kansas somehow PSU went down 3 notches in the polls to # 5. On October 11, #17 West Virginia tried to move up in the polls by beating now #5 ranked PSU at Beaver Stadium but the Nittany Lions shut out the Mountaineers W (20-0).

On October 18, Ben Schwartzwalder's tough Syracuse team hosted #5 ranked, unbeaten and untied Penn State and gave the Lions quite a tussle but PSU prevailed W (15-14) After Syracuse, ranked # 8, yet still unbeaten and still untied, PSU played Ohio on October 25, at Beaver Stadium and beat the Buckeyes by a pile W (42-3), bringing back the reward of a return to #5 in the polls. At Boston College on week 7, November 1, PSU defeated the Eagles W (38-16) at Beaver Stadium before 46,652.

On November 15, after a bye week, PSU smothered Maryland at home W 4(8-0). Now #4 ranked PSU played Pitt and beat the Panthers at Pitt Stadium W (27-7). On November 29, Carter Stadium was the home for a match-up of North Carolina State v # 3 ranked PSU, still unbeaten and untied with a 9-0 record going into game 10 of the season. Penn State convincingly beat the Wolfpack W (33-8).

It looked like Ohio State would automatically be the National Championship as they were ranked # 1 and were precluded from a Bowl game so no matter what when the Bowl decision had to be made, PSU only had a chance if Ohio State lost its last game. The decision had to be made before the last game, however.

Joe Paterno admitted that he liked the way the team was treated the previous year in Miami for the Orange Bowl, but he always thought you should play the best team you could.

That means that at the time the highest ranked team in the Bowl game which when the game was played would have been either Texas or Arkansas in the Cotton Bowl. Yet, the players decided to go to Miami. When Ohio lost, it made the Cotton Bowl the battle for the National Championship or so it seemed to the coaches and pundits. Penn State and the people of Pennsylvania and Governor Schaeffer felt otherwise.

Ranked #6 Missouri put up a fight but were defeated by the #2 ranked Penn State Nittany Lions in the Cotton Bowl. Texas beat Arkansas and were crowned National Champions. Penn State finished the balloting at # 2.

1970 Penn State Football Season Coach Joe Paterno

The 1970 Penn State Nittany Lions football team was coached by Joe Paterno in his fifth season, and continued to play its home games in Beaver Stadium in University Park, Pennsylvania. After two undefeated and untied seasons, 1970 was a rebuilding season but well played nonetheless. Paterno's Lions finished with a 7-3 record, ranked #19 in the coach's polls and #18 in the AP pundits poll.

Jack Ham—a standout at Linebacker U.

Ham, Jack Raphael (nickname Dobre Shunka)
Born: December 23, 1948, in Johnstown, Pennsylvania
Vocations: Athlete, Radio Personality, Sports Analyst

Short Bio: Jack Raphael Ham, Jr. was born in Johnstown, Pennsylvania, on December 23, 1948. He attended The Pennsylvania State University where he became one of the school's all-time great football players. He then went on to a wildly successful career in the National Football League with the Pittsburgh Steelers. After retiring, he entered broadcasting and headed a drug-testing company. He currently resides in Pittsburgh with his wife, Joanne.

Here is the rest of the full "skinny" on Jack Ham. This biography was prepared by Wesley Kendle, fall 2007.

Jack Ham, a man who would leave his mark on the world of American Football, was born in Johnstown, Pennsylvania, on December 23, 1948. The undersized and underrated linebacker graduated Bishop McCort High School in 1967 and found that he had no place to go. Ham, worried that his football career might be finished, then went to Massanutten Military Academy in Woodstock, Virginia, with hopes of toughening up and honing his skills in order to work his way onto a college football team.

Just when Ham had thought his only option was to enroll as a student at The Pennsylvania State University and attempt to walk on to the football team, his high school friend Steve Smear convinced recruiter George Welsh to offer Ham a newly opened scholarship. The rest is history. Jack Ham would go on to an astounding career in football, both with The Pennsylvania State University and the NFL's Pittsburgh Steelers. He is now considered to be one of American football's greatest linebackers to ever play the position.

1970 games

On September 19, the season began well at home against Navy with an overwhelming victory W (55-7). It looked like the old stuff was back where it was. Colorado came to Beaver Stadium on September 26, and spoiled the party with a solid game v the Nittany Lions for the first loss of the season and the first loss in three years of play, L (13-41). It was back to back losses as PSU traveled to Camp Randall Stadium on October 3 to be beaten by Wisconsin in Madison L (16-29) PSU got a win back against Boston College at Alumni Stadium W (28-3.

At 2-2, with a win in the prior week, Ben Schwartzwalder's Syracuse Orangemen came to Beaver Stadium on October 17, and won the game handily L (7-24). On October 24, Army was next game at Michie Stadium in West Point W (38-14). Now, at 3-3, the win engine went into full gear as PSU defeated West Virginia at home W (42-8), followed on November 7 at Maryland W (34-0).

On November 14, Ohio was next at Beaver Stadium W (32-22). Penn State capped off its season against Pittsburgh at home W (35-15).

1971 Penn State Football Season Coach Joe Paterno

The 1971 Penn State Nittany Lions football team was coached by Joe Paterno in his sixth season. If the man, who would soon be known and loved as JoePa knew anything at all, he knew how to win. With just one loss in an 11-1 season, I was a justified whiner in 1971 when, for this stellar record, PSU was ranked at just #11 in the coach's poll and # 5 in the AP. A lot of coaches seemed to be unwilling to reward Penn State in the mid twentieth century for its valid accomplishments.

Joe Paterno's worst season so far was his first at 5-5. When any coach could follow this with 8-2-1; 11-0; 11-0; 7-3; and 11-1 records, that is one heck of a Division I coach. It is not coincidental that Joe Paterno is currently the winningest coach in the history of major league Division I football. Can you believe this fantastic start to a fantastic coaching career?

On September 18, PSU played at Navy and defeated the Middies in a blow-out 56-3. PSU then played Iowa in Iowa City and won big again W (44-14). Air Force, a very scrappy team that has a habit of beating big teams—a team which played in the Sugar Bowl in 1971, always played to win. On October 2, the Falcons were just about beaten by Penn State W (16-14). PSU played all three major service academies in 1971 with Army losing to the Nittany Lions at Beaver Stadium W 42-0) before a packed house.

With a 4-0 record, still ranked just # 9 in the nation, PSU traveled to Syracuse on October 16 and shut out a tough Orange team (31-0). PSU was hitting on all cylinders at Beaver Stadium on October 23 in scobbing TCU by a whopping W (66-14). On October 30, PSU at # 6 was off to Morgantown WV to defeat West Virginia W (35-7). Maryland was next on November 6 at Beaver Stadium in a shootout dominated by Penn State W (63-27) before an oversold attendance of 50,144.

NC State played at Beaver Stadium the next week on November 13, and were beaten by the Nittany Lions W 35-3). On November 20, Penn State pounded Pittsburgh at Pitt Stadium W (55-18). At 10-0, a #5 ranked PSU let its guard down on December 4 at Neyland Stadium in Knoxville v the Tennessee Volunteers and lost the game L (11-31).

With a 10-1 record, ranked # 10 in the nation, Penn State won a shot at Texas in the Cotton Bowl on January 1, 1972. The game was televised on CBS so that70,000 in attendance along with millions of fans on TV saw #10 PSU defeat #12 Texas W (30-6) in a well-played game for the Nittany Lions.

PSU Player Highlights: Franco Harris and Lydell Mitchell

What a blessing for any team to have Franco Harris and Lydell Mitchell playing in the same backfield. One might ask if linemen would be necessary at all. Let's briefly look teammates (FB) Franco Harris and (RB) Lydell Mitchell. They were responsible for a lot of PSU wins.

Running backs and fullbacks did well at Penn State. We'll look at both running superstars from 1971. Let's look at the guy called on to get the 1st downs first and then the guy called on to win the games—Franco Harris then Lydell Mitchell

Franco Harris

Franco Harris continues his loyalty to his college coach Joe Paterno. Surely, no matter how well you and a and several other million Penn State football fans think we knew Joe Paterno, the coach, nobody knew him like Penn State players and a lot of good guys like Franco Harris. Harris was a three-year starter and standout player for the Nittany Lions. Harris is a gentle yet very tough man. He still does not let anybody, including the press push his Alma Mater or his coach around. He hits back and stings and then continues to fight back

When you are talking about the all-time best players in the NFL from Penn State, you have to start with Franco Harris. Harris was named to nine Pro Bowls and seven all-pro teams, and won four Super Bowls with the Pittsburgh Steelers. Yet, his PSU years do not get him the same level of acclaim…but they should. He started for the Lions for three years and averaged over five yards per carry each year. I am convinced that because Franco's pro career was so stellar, that the write-ups of the day focused on who he was and not who he had once been.

Nonetheless, he was one heck of a PSU football player even though I cannot find him on anybody's top ten PSU player list. He is on mine for sure.

When you dig down into Harris's great career at Penn State there was a player on the team who cast a big shadow. Fellow running back Lydell Mitchell became an All-American. Despite Mitchell's great stats the Steelers scouts still saw enough in Harris's play to draft him with their 13th overall selection of the 1972 NFL draft.

Yet, he gained more yards as a pro in his first season than in any of his Penn State Seasons, in which of course, he averaged between 5 and 6 yards per carry. He rushed for 1,055 yards and scored 10 touchdowns in his first year in the NFL and he was named Offensive Rookie of the Year and chosen for his first of nine consecutive Pro Bowls. Franko Harris was one heck of a football player. Not taking anything from All-American Lydell Mitchell, it is ironic that he had to become a pro to gain his proper recognition.

Harris was named the MVP of Super Bowl IX, 1972 NFL Offensive Rookie of the Year and AFL-AFC Rookie of the Year by UPI, and was the 1976 Walter Payton Man of the Year.

Harris is most famous for The Immaculate Reception in the AFC playoffs against the Oakland Raiders and was voted to the NFL 1970s All-Decade Team. Harris finished his Hall of Fame career with 100 touchdowns and 12,120 rushing yards.

Rather than depend on the reader being omniscient about things like the Immaculate Reception, let's talk a bit about it since this is a book about the great moments in Penn State History. Undoubtedly this reception is one of the greatest moments and the most talked about moments in football history. Unfortunately for Franco Harris it did not affect his college stats as he achieved this career milestone as a pro.

It is the nickname given to what is what most living pundits today would agree is the most famous play in the history of American football. The Immaculate reception has a great ring to it. It was a divisional playoff game so it had much more than the normal coverage.

The game opponents were the Oakland Raiders vs the Pittsburgh Steelers with help from Franco Harris, and some say, help from the Lord himself. Even three Rivers Stadium could not prevent the miracle that was to occur on this Merry Christmas day December 23, 1972. Then, again if God is a Pittsburgh fan who had to worry?

Despite all of the spirits and the entire Franco Harris family and perhaps even a few Bradshaw's rooting for the right outcome, Pittsburgh was losing. So, with 30 seconds left in the game, Pittsburgh quarterback Terry Bradshaw, who still has lots of sputter during NFL game days, threw a pass attempt to John Fuqua. I cannot name one person today who knows who John Fuqua is but the ball did not reach him anyway.

It bounced off the hands of Raiders safety Jack Tatum; though it might have been Fuqua and with this more than likely the last play of the game, the world went into slow-mo. as everybody in the stadium and watching from TV sets across the land, saw the ball falling toward the ground like a rocket. Like a gift from the most-high, out of nowhere, Steelers fullback Franco Harris, who had purchased a discount halo helmet attachment the night before the game at K-Mart, was there to scoop it up, right into his arms before ground-touch, and then as a schooled running back, the young Harris had enough sense and wherewithal to tuck it in and he ran for the game-winning touchdown. And, that was that. Everybody accepted the outcome. Well, not exactly.

No play that starts off so needy goes so far south without a miracle intervention from above. Even the agnostics did not know what had hit them. This play remains a source of unresolved controversy and speculation ever since, as many people have contended that the ball touched either Fuqua or the ground before Harris caught it, either of which would have resulted in an incomplete pass by the rules at the time.

Kevin Cook's *The Last Headbangers* cites the play as the beginning of a bitter rivalry between Pittsburgh and Oakland that fueled a historically brutal Raiders team during the NFL's most controversially physical era. Either way, Pittsburgh won and Harris got another TD...one of many in his outstanding career.

Lydell Mitchell

Though he played football and graduated in 1972, Lydell Mitchell was elected into the SBC Cotton Bowl Hall of Fame on December 20, 2004 with the major tribute being his 146-yard running total in the 1972 Cotton Bowl win over Texas.

Former Penn State standout Lydell Mitchell earned on this day what some call his second hall of fame recognition of 2004. He was elected to the SBC Cotton Bowl Hall of Fame, less than two weeks after his induction into the College Football Hall of Fame. The All-America running back was be inducted with seven others on Wednesday, April 20, 2005 at Cotton Bowl Plaza in Dallas.

Lydell Mitchell was an outstanding PSU football player. He was a 1971 All-American. As a dangerous running back, he led the Nittany Lions to a resounding 30-6 victory over Southwest Conference champion Texas in the Cotton Bowl on January 1, 1972. He pulled it in for 146 yards on 27 carries and scored the go-ahead touchdown, as Penn State rallied from a 6-3 halftime deficit to score 27 unanswered points in the second half. It was nothing less than the Lydell Mitchell Show with fullback Franco Harris picking up the slack as needed.

Mitchell was the overwhelming choice as the game's Outstanding Offensive Player, as he led Penn State to its first Cotton Bowl victory. The Lions became 1-0-1 and as of 2015, are 2-0-1 all-time in the contest.

The win over the Longhorns was one of the landmark victories in the early years of the Joe Paterno era. Two years prior, an undefeated Penn State team had been overlooked, as President Richard Nixon spoke before he thought and declared Texas the 1969 national champions after a 15-14 win over unbeaten Arkansas, and the pollsters followed his lead. The 1969 undefeated, untied Nittany Lions finished No. 2 in the final AP rankings for the second consecutive year.

Lydell Mitchell was so good that the pundits did not fully notice Franco Harris but the Pittsburgh Steelers did. Mitchell led the nation in touchdowns (29) and points scored (174) in 1971. He also set three NCAA season records during his superlative 1971 campaign - most touchdowns (29), most rushing touchdowns (26) and points scored (174) - and finished fifth in the Heisman Trophy balloting. Franco Harris, one of the best football players in PSU history was kept in the shadows as the high-scoring Mitchell scored and scored and scored.

Mitchell still holds Penn State records for touchdowns in a season (29 in 1971), touchdowns in a career (41) and rushing touchdowns in a career (38) and his 246 career points scored rank fourth, the most among players other than kickers. His 1,567 yards rushing in 1971 stood as the Penn State season record for more than 30 years until Larry Johnson's 2,087-yard season in 2002.

During his phenomenal Penn State career, Mitchell won three varsity letters from 1969-71 and helped lead Penn State to a 29-4 record over that span. The Nittany Lions went 11-1 during his senior campaign to finish No. 5 in the final AP poll. In case you are not scoring at home folks, it helps to recall these fine teams were all coached by Joe Paterno, the master.

Mitchell is the first Penn Stater elected to the SBC Cotton Bowl Hall of Fame. He will join the following individuals in the SBC Cotton Bowl Hall of Fame: UCLA quarterback Troy Aikman, Arkansas halfback Lance Alworth, former CBAA executive director Jim "Hoss" Brock, Texas offensive guard Mike Dean, Tennessee fullback

Andy Kozar, Tennessee tailback Hank Lauricella, and former collegiate head coach Gene Stallings.

A 35-member judging committee comprised of media representatives and athletic administrators voted from a list of 52 original nominees that included players, coaches, bowl administrators and others who have made special contributions to the Cotton Bowl Classic.
On Dec. 7, Mitchell became the 19th Penn Stater to be inducted into the National Football Foundation's College Hall of Fame.

Think about how great Lydell Mitchell was and think about how great Franco Harris was. Consider that Joe Paterno was their coach and he got the most out of them and they loved him for it.

1972 Penn State Football Season Coach Joe Paterno

The 1972 Penn State Nittany Lions football team was coached by Joe Paterno in his seventh season. Penn State had another enviable regular season at 10-1 and with a #5 ranking in the national poll, they were invited to the Sugar Bowl in New Orleans against # 2 Oklahoma, and were defeated in a close match L (14-0), finishing the season at 10-2.

On September 16, though PSU played better than in 1971 against the Volunteers, #7 ranked Tennessee beat #6 PSU at Neyland Stadium in Knoxville L 21-28). It was the only loss of the regular season for Joe Paterno's squad. Navy played much better than the prior year at Beaver Stadium as the Lions prevailed W (21-10). On September 30, #13 PSU defeated IOWA at home in a close match W (14-10) After the win, PSU dropped to #16 in the polls and on October 7, at Illinois PSU triumphed W (35-17) over the Fighting Illini before 60,349.

On October 14, Penn State shut-out Army at West Point W (45-0). On October 21, Syracuse played the Nittany Lions but lost in a shutout W (17-0). PSU played at West Virginia the following week in a close call W (28-19). Maryland came to Beaver Stadium to defeat the #10 Nittany Lions but left with a big loss W (46-16).

On November 11, North Carolina State played # 10 PSU at Beaver Stadium. The Lions won W (37-22). On November 18, PSU was ranked # 6 and played Boston College at Alumni Stadium W (45-26). Still ranked #6, on November 25, PSU defeated the Pitt Panthers at home W (49-27).

The Sugar Bowl was played on December 31. PSU was ranked #5 with a 10-1 record when it met second ranked Oklahoma at Tulane Stadium in New Orleans before 80,123 and before million more on ABC TV. In one of its closest matches all season, Oklahoma defeated PSU L (14-0). This gave the Lions a nice 10-2 season, which for a number of reasons, could have been better.

Oklahoma had its second great year in a row under head coach Chuck Fairbanks. Offensive coordinator Barry Switzer had perfected the wishbone offense and Oklahoma could not be stopped. In 1971, the Sooners led the nation in both scoring (45 points average) and total yards (563 total yards' average).

Oklahoma set an NCAA record that year by averaging over 472.4 (5196 in 11 games) rushing yards in a season. The Sooners had another like year in 1972. They were phenomenal, and ran through every team they played.

There was a big discrepancy regarding the Sooners' record and the wins for which they got credit. It turns out that the NCAA never officially forced Oklahoma to forfeit games, but they were penalized on future scholarships. TV appearances, bowl appearances, etc. By rights, their team may not have been as good if their academic record keeping on their players was kept accurately.

The beef was that Oklahoma had used players (including Kerry Jackson, the team's first black quarterback) with falsified transcripts. It was such a big deal and such an embarrassment that at one point, Oklahoma University volunteered to forfeit all its games for the 1972 season.

Eventually, the Big Eight conference asked them to forfeit just three victories despite the fact that the NCAA still recognized them after time passed. Oklahoma in looking back, now recognizes all of its wins and it claims the 1972 conference title. Penn State was involved in the controversy as a team that had played an Oklahoma that had benefitted from using ineligible players.

At the time, as a result of using ineligible players, the Oklahoma Sooners were apparently ordered (though it was softened to a suggestion over time) to forfeit seven wins from their 1972 season, including their on-field win over the Nittany Lions in the Sugar Bowl. Joe Paterno's Nittany Lions were shut-out L (14-0) as noted but they had played a tough game against the Sooners.

Despite the prevailing thought on the legitimacy of the Sooners' season, Joe Paterno and the Penn State Administration refused to accept the forfeit, and the bowl game is officially recorded as a loss. There is some irony compared with how Coach Paterno was treated when it was his turn in the penalty box in 2011. Paterno, just about forty years earlier opted not to mess with Oklahoma's wins and losses.

Who knows if the QB and some other players made a difference? PSU had a shot at being 12-1 instead of 11-2. Who knows what that would have meant? Penn State was not interested in being handed any gifts that it had not earned on the field. As it turned out, officially PSU is listed as # 8 in the coach's poll and #10 in the AP poll.

1973 Penn State Football Season Coach Joe Paterno

The 1973 Penn State Nittany Lions football team was coached by Joe Paterno in his eight season. Penn State had another undefeated and untied season just four years after having two undefeated and untied seasons in a row. Despite having a perfect 12-0 season, PSU for the third time in six years was denied a proper ranking by the Coaches and by the AP. They slotted Penn State at # 5 after its third perfect season in six years. No wonder many felt that the system was rigged.

When like me, one walks slowly through the Paterno record—in my case because I am forming words and scribing it; in your case, as you are reading my words, you get the full sense of what an awesome achievement it was for the University, the players involved, and this awesome coach. Looking at the results season by season, nobody was as good as Joe Paterno in his eight seasons. You'd have to look outside of Penn State in 1973 to find a Rockne or a Leahy to match the outstanding record of Joe Paterno.

Penn State's third undefeated season under Joe Paterno was led by John Cappelletti who would become the first Penn State player to win the Heisman Trophy.

In an early season start on September 15, at Stanford #7 PSU defeated the Cardinal W (20-6). At Navy on September 22, PSU shut out the Middies W (39-0. At # 6 on September 29, the Nittany Lions played its home opener and scored a win against Iowa W (27-8). At Falcon Stadium on October 6, PSU beat the Falcons W (19-9).

Ironically after the win, PSU lost a point in the standings. The #7 Lions battered a game Army squad on October 13 at Beaver Stadium on October 20 W (54-3) Off to Archbold Stadium in Syracuse, #5 PSU beat the Orangemen W (49-6) After winning game after game, the 6-0 Nittany Lions would never get above # 5 in the polls for the rest of the season. It was as if other teams had a lock on the top 4 slots.

On October 27, West Virginia was roughed up by a tough Lions Team W 62-14 before an over-crowd of 59,138, an expansion built in in 1972 had brought capacity to 57,538. On November 3 #6 PSU defeated Maryland at Byrd Stadium W (42-22).

This was followed by a close win on November 10 at home against NC State W (35-9).

In this best of Beaver Stadium game, John Cappelletti, #22, solidified his credentials for the Heisman Trophy with his best running day ever in this wild shootout in freezing cold and snow. Cappelletti set a school record of 41 carries that is still unbroken in rushing for 231 yards and three touchdowns.

Ohio University was next at Beaver Stadium on November 17 W (49-10) At 10-0, ranked # 6, PSU played Pittsburgh at home and defeated the Panthers W (35-13).

The powers-that-be saw something that few at Penn State saw. These mysterious powers felt it appropriate to match the powerful 11-0, #5 ranked Nittany Lions against a twice beaten 9-2, #13 LSU in the Orange Bowl on January 1. PSU defeated LSU W (16-9). PSU ended its perfect season 12-0 and LSU finished with three defeats 9-3. It may not have been the Nittany Lions finest game but one thing is for sure. Joe Paterno knew how to win football game.

Orange Bowl Game Highlights

The Undefeated Penn State Nittany Lions moved its record to 12-0 on the season as it took advantage of consistently poor LSU field position to win 16-9.

LSU had a good game as it out-gained the Nittany Lions 274 yards to 185 and held Heisman Trophy winner John Cappelletti to 50 yards. Cappelletti nonetheless was the difference maker as he scored the Nittany Lions' final touchdown on a one-yard plunge in the second quarter. The game's big play was a spectacular 72-yard touchdown catch by Chuck Herd off a pass from Tom Shuman early in the second quarter.

LSU got a lot of yardage but not of lot scores. The Tigers scored first on a three-yard run by Steve Rogers, and Penn State retaliated with a 44-yard field goal by Chris Bahr to make it 7-3 at the end of the first quarter. Herd's catch and Cappelletti's plunge put PSU ahead 16-7 at the half. That was the game.

Although Penn State finished undefeated, the polls still had the Nittany Lions ranked at #5.

1974 Penn State Football Season Coach Joe Paterno

The 1974 Penn State Nittany Lions football team was coached by Joe Paterno and played its home games in Beaver Stadium in University Park, Pennsylvania. At # 7 in both polls and with a 10-2 record, and a fine Cotton Bowl win, Penn State had a remarkably great year after so many previous great years. It's like the flow of great athletes would never stop.

On September 14, #20 Stanford lost to #8 Penn State (24-20) at Beaver Stadium before a capacity overflow crowd of 58,200. On September 21, a tough and always crafty Navy team came to Beaver Stadium meaning business and they smacked PSU with a close loss L (6-7).

On September 28, PSU traveled to Iowa and shut out the Hawkeyes W (27-0). It was a tough year playing the service academies as PSU barely beat Army at West Point W (21-14). After a week bye, on October 12, Wake Forest suffered an overwhelming defeat, a shutout, at the hands of Penn State W (55-0). On October 19, PSU defeated Syracuse at home W (30-14). On October 26 in Morgantown, West Virginia, PSU defeated the Mountaineers W (21-12).

A #15 ranked Maryland made its way to Beaver Stadium to play #10 ranked Penn State on November 2. The Terrapins were defeated in a close match W (24-17). Then ranked # 7 PSU traveled to North Carolina State at Carter Stadium in Raleigh, NC on November 9, and were beaten in a lose match L (7-12). Ohio University next came to Beaver Stadium on November 16 and lost to #11PSU W (35-16).

On November 28, #10 PSU, at 9-2, challenged #18 Pittsburgh at Three Rivers Stadium in Pittsburgh, PA before 48,895 and the national ABC audience and succeeded in victory W (31–10).

The Cotton Bowl

With a 9-2 record, ranked # 7 ranked PSU won a berth to the Cotton Bowl and on New Year's Day, beat #12 Baylor in Dallas Texas before 67,500 onlookers as well as the entire CBS TV audience W (41–20).

Chapter 6 The Joe Paterno Era from 1975 to 1983

Coach # 14

1975	Joe Paterno	9-3
1976	Joe Paterno	7-5
1977	Joe Paterno	11-1
1978	Joe Paterno	11-1
1979	Joe Paterno	8-4
1980	Joe Paterno	10-2
1981	Joe Paterno	10-2
1982	Joe Paterno	11-1 National Champions
1983	Joe Paterno	8-4-1

Coached 45 great seasons 1966 to 2010 and part of 2011.

1975 Penn State Football Season Coach Joe Paterno

The 1975 Penn State Nittany Lions football team was coached by Joe Paterno in his tenth year. With a 9-2 regular season record and a berth in the Sugar Bowl at the New Orleans, Louisiana SuperDome on December 31, 1975, PSU, with Joe Paterno, an unbelievably successful coach at the helm, had a great season.

Seasons started to begin earlier and earlier form October twenty years earlier to September with games close to Labor Day weekend such as the September 6 nail-biter at Temple in Franklin Field, Philadelphia in which # 6 PSU won W (26-25). On September 13, Stanford played at Beaver Stadium and the #10 Nittany Lions winning the encounter W (34-14). #3 ranked Ohio State, coached by the master, Woody Hayes, hosted #7 Penn State on September 20 and defeated the Nittany Lions in Columbus L (9-17). Iowa played a #12 ranked PSU squad on September 27 at Kinnick Stadium and PSU triumphed W (30-0).

Next on the season agenda was Kentucky on October 4, playing at Beaver Stadium, the #12 Nittany Lions pulled of a close one W (10-3) bringing the season record to 4-1, A tough #10 ranked West Virginia team played # 9 ranked PSU on October 11 at Beaver Stadium and were shut out in a blow-out W (39-0). On October 18, the #9 ranked Lions played at unranked Syracuse and defeated the Orangemen W (19-7). The next week at Beaver Stadium (October 25), PSU shut-out Army W (31-0).

Ninth ranked PSU next played #14 ranked Maryland on November 1 and in a tough game beat the Terrapins W (15-13). In almost a reverse mirror image of the Maryland game a # 8 ranked PSU was beaten by NC State L (14-15) at home. The regular season ended after a one week bye with PSU barely beating Pitt at Three Rivers Stadium W (7-6).

PSU had a lot of close matches this year but as usual, in most of them at least Joe Paterno knew how to lead his team to victory. With a 9-2 record, an 8th ranked Penn State squad was invited to the Sugar Bowl to play a tough # 4 ranked Bear Bryant Alabama team on New Year's Eve, 1975. In a very close and tough match. Alabama defeated Penn State to win the Sugar Bowl L (6-13) before a nationwide TV audience in addition to 75,212 in the New Orleans Superdome. Penn State finished with a 9-3 record, ranked # 10 in both polls. It was another very good season for PSU and Joe Paterno.

1976 Penn State Football Season Coach Joe Paterno

The 1976 Penn State Nittany Lions football team was coached by Joe Paterno in his eleventh year and played its home games in a just expanded Beaver Stadium in University Park, Pennsylvania. In 1969, PSU found another 2000 seats for Beaver Stadium. In 1974, over 9000 seats, extended the capacity to 57,536. In 1976: South end zone bleachers expanded, adding 2,667, extending capacity to 60,203. Coming up in 1978, another big expansion of 16000 seats was coming and the growing still would not be done.

For any other program in any other year, Penn State's 7-5 record in 1976 would have been chalked up as well above .500 and very acceptable. Looking at the season, you will find an awful lot of close games that in other years went the Lions' way. Just one in the other direction and the team is 8-4, which sounds a lot better. Nonetheless, this was still a darn good year when you consider the problems that other teams with coaching instabilities have. Nice job again JoePa.

On September 11 Penn State ranked at # 10 played Stanford at home W (15-12). On September 18, Ohio State played the Nittany Lions in Beaver Stadium to a crowd of 62,503, and defeated Penn State in a tight slugfest L (7-12). Iowa came to Beaver Stadium on September 25, and for the second week in a row, PSU lost a nail biter L (6-7). Three makes a charm and Kentucky on October 2, defeated the Nittany Lions, then ranked at # 20, at Commonwealth Stadium L (6-22).

PSU defeated Army on October 9 at home W (38-16), followed by Syracuse at home on October 16 W (27-3). On October 23, it was off to Morgantown and a win against West Virginia W (33-0). No longer a ranked team, PSU pulled off a win in a very close game against Temple on October 30 at Veterans Stadium before 42,005 W (31-30).

Unranked North Carolina State, another tough team was ready when they came to Beaver Stadium on November 6 to play unranked PSU. The Nittany Lions won handily W (41-20). Then on November 13 came Miami, always tough, especially at home playing in the Orange Bowl stadium. PSU won W (21-7). Pittsburgh had become a player again after going to sleep for a few years. Ranked # 1 in the nation at the time, Pitt defeated #16 PSU at Three Reivers Stadium on November 26 L (7-24).

With 7 wins, ranked #20, PSU was eligible for a Bowl game. They played in the Gator Bowl in Jacksonville Florida on Monday, December 27, 1976 against the University of Notre Dame. Notre Dame won a tough battle v PSU L (9-20) before 67,827 and an ABC television audience.

1977 Penn State Football Season Coach Joe Paterno

The 1977 Penn State Nittany Lions football team was coached by Joe Paterno in his twelfth season. PSU recovered from a tough 7-5 season and experienced one loss to Kentucky at home on October 1, the fourth game of the season by just four points L (20-24).

Four points doth make a season as the Kentucky game is all that separated Paterno's tough Penn State squad from another perfect, undefeated and untied, season. The one loss made all the difference in the world as the Nittany Lions finished #4 in the Coach's poll and #5 in the AP poll. It was another great year for Penn State on the field.

In a rare Friday night game, on September 2, #13 ranked PSU began its season away at Giants stadium against Rutgers and won decisively W (45-7) before 64,790. It already looked like a great season. On September 17, after a bye week, Houston came to Beaver Stadium and were beaten by #10 PSU W (31-14). Maryland was the next home game on September 24 W (27-9). Operating at 3-0, and ranked #4 before the Kentucky game Penn State lost its only game of the season on October 1 L (20-24).

On October 8 Utah State were beaten by the #10 ranked Nittany Lions in a close match W (16-7). Then, on October 15 in the ongoing rivalry with Syracuse, #10 PSU beat the Orangemen in Archbold Stadium W (31-24). West Virginia was next on October 22 at Beaver Stadium W (49-28). An always tough Lou Saban coached the Miami squad, which rolled into Beaver Stadium on October 29 to play a # 9 ranked Nittany Lions team. Miami was not having a good year and won just three games in 1977. They were pounded by PSU W (49-7). PSU then traveled to Carter Finley Stadium to play North Carolina on November 5 W (21-17.

Penn State coach Joe Paterno and his quarterback Chuck Fusina discussed things late in the fourth quarter in Pittsburgh, Saturday, Nov. 26, 1977.

Ranked #9, PSU played Temple at Beaver Stadium on November 12 and defeated the OWLs W (44-7). The intrastate rivalry game between #10 Pitt and #9 Penn State was next on November 26, the Saturday after Thanksgiving. The Nittany Lions scored a victory in a nail biter W (15-13) in front of 53,000 at Pitt Stadium.

With a 10-1 record, ranked # 9, PSU played Arizona State on Christmas day in the Fiesta Bowl at Sun Devil Stadium, Tempe Arizona and won decidedly W (42-30).

1978 Penn State Football Season Coach Joe Paterno

The 1978 Penn State Nittany Lions football team was coached by Joe Paterno in his thirteenth year. This Chuck Fusina led-team was phenomenal. In 1977, four points to Kentucky in the fourth game separated PSU from a perfect season. This year, PSU did not lose a game until the Sugar Bowl when it was a seven-point difference against a Bear Bryant coached Alabama team that kept PSU from the National Championships.

PSU was 11-0 and ranked # 2 going into the game. Alabama was 11-0 and ranked #1. Alabama won the game and the National Championship. PSU finished 11-1 and were ranked # 4 in both polls. Joe Paterno was a phenomenon. SO was Bear Bryant. My buddy George Mohanco, a former Pennsylvanian has a saying, whether he invented it, I do not know but it applies to 1978. "Sometimes you eat the bear and sometimes the bear eats you." This time Bear Bryant had the better dinner.

Penn State started the season at # 3 with a game on September 3 at Veterans Stadium at Temple. Temple played extremely tough but the Lions got the W (10-7). This was a strange game. It was dominated by a typically unsung hero, punter Casey Murphy. Former Navy coach and relatively new Temple coach Wayne Hardin had Murphy punt "unexpectedly," on nearly every third down. Murphy averaged more than 48 yards on 11 punts. He backed up the surprised Penn State team inside its 6-yard line three times. PSU was fighting up-hill all day because of the Owls' punter

The Nittany Lions put together what it took to win W (10-7), but it was not easy. It was a late field goal. Joe Paterno honored Coach Hardin's cunning after the game: "That's the best coaching job anybody's done against us ever."

Rutgers was next at the newly enlarged (by 16,000 seats) Beaver Stadium on September 9 v #3 PSU. The Nittany Lions won W (26-10) in front of a newly enabled attendance of 77,154. Woody Hayes' # 6 ranked Ohio State Buckeyes expecting a win were turned back by # 5 ranked PSU at Ohio Stadium on September 16 W (19-0). SMU was defeated on September 23 at Beaver Stadium W (26-21).

TCU was blown away W (58-0) by #5 PSU on September 30. Kentucky, the team that spoiled the 1977 season with a four-point win were shown how it's done by # 4 PSU in an October 7 shutout in Lexington, KY W (30-0). After a bye week, Syracuse came into Beaver Stadium on October 21, and #2 PSU beat the Orangemen W (45-15). On October 28, the West Virginia Mountaineers were defeated by #2 PSU in a blowout at Morgantown, WV, W (49-21).

On November 4, 1978 in a home match at Beaver Stadium before 78,019, #2 ranked Penn State beat #5 ranked Maryland W (27-3). This was a nationally televised "Battle of the Unbeatens." It was the Nittany Lions' biggest--and most hyped--home game since the stadium was built in 1960. With 16,000 seats added since 1977, a record crowd of 78,019 watched No. 2 Lions overwhelm No. 5

Maryland, finally becoming a media darling in the race for the national championship.

Let's take a closer look at this game as it is one of the most memorable in PSU history. Maryland had a great team in 1978 and so did Penn State. Before they came to Beaver Stadium, the first Saturday in November, the Terrapins were rolling over their opposition.

They were ranked # 5 with eight straight wins behind them. They had already pummeled NC State 31-7. NC State would finish ranked # 18. Maryland had the ACC title in the bag if they beat Penn State.

PSU for its part was doing so well at #2. Maryland might be looking at a national title with a win. PSU however was on a 16-game winning streak and as expected, the welcome for Maryland would not be warm, and the Lions were prepared to play tough.

Maryland got the ball first, and then they got a feel for Penn State's defense on a 3rd and 8. Bruce Clark and Matt Millen pounded Terrapin QB Tim O'Hare for a 1-yard loss and a punt. The Nittany Lions began to drive down a short field immediately with nice runs by backs Booker Moore and Matt Suhey. This ended with a Matt Bahr 33-yard field goal.

Booker Moore then fumbled but it did not hurt Penn State as the "D" got the ball right back. From there, Mike Guman caught a 14-yarder and a nice 34-yard run set up a Chuck Fusina 1-yard TD drive as the second quarter began. Maryland seemed to get some adrenalin going and quickly converted a 39-yard field goal.

With PSU now ahead by 7, they held the Terrapins on a tough 3-and-out, and then after the punt when it was PSU's turn, Bob Bassett's snagged a 22-yard one-handed grab which put PSU again in field goal position. Matt Bahr was an automatic and he claimed the three points for PSU. Although the powerful defense held Maryland to just 12 rushing yards, the Nittany Lions still led by just 13-3 at the half.

In the 3rd quarter Pete Harris got an interception and the Terrapins benched their QB and put in reserve Mike Tice. It seemed like a good move as Maryland took the ball deep into PSU territory, but the drive was thwarted by Karl McCoy's interception. Fusina finished off this drive by pin-pointing a 63-yard pass to Tom Donovan making the score Penn State 20, Maryland 3.

McCoy grabbed another interception late in the third, and before long Booker Moore gobbled up 34-yards on a scamper to the Maryland 16. Four plays later, Moore scored on a 4-yard run for the touchdown.

As the game was closing, Maryland's kept in their starters and came to a fourth and goal from the 3 but were denied the score by Penn State's backup unit. The underclassmen got a standing ovation from the Nittany Lions fans.

Penn State's defense had been dominant all season long and this day would be no different as they brought forth their best performance in the 27-3 victory over #5 Maryland in Beaver Stadium. It was the Lions 17th straight victory.

For his role in the game, QB Chuck Fusina made the cover of Sports Illustrated. As noted in this 1978 season record, PSU just got by North Carolina State and #15 Pittsburgh to become # 1 in the polls. Even after undefeated seasons, this was the first #1 ranking in Joe Paterno's already legendary career. As an independent, PSU could go just about anywhere for their bowl, so they picked the SEC for a match-up with #2 Alabama in the Sugar Bowl – discussed at the end of 1978 highlights below.

A tough North Carolina team played #2 ranked PSU at Beaver Stadium on November 11 and were beaten by the Lions in a close call W (19-10).

This 1978 game was a typical nail biter. No. 2 Penn State was holding on to a 12-10 lead with 4:40 left and with the crowd of 59,424 growing restless, Penn State's Matt Suhey (shown on the left) returned a punt 43 yards for a touchdown to clinch the victory.

As soon as Suhey scored, it was announced that #1 Oklahoma had lost three days later, and so Penn State was ranked #1 for the first time ever.

<< Matt Suhey

Operating with a 10-0 record, ranked #1 in the nation, for the first time ever, playing nemesis cross-state rival Pittsburgh, anything could have happened on November 24.

PSU was steady and steadfast in its resolve to win and the Nittany Lions shut-out Pitt W (17-0) at Beaver Stadium and had just enough offense to keep Pittsburgh from thinking it had a chance. For its 11-0 season PSU was ranked #1 but there was another team with an 11-0 record, looking up at PSU from the # 2 slot.

The Sugar Bowl 1978

Alabama, coached by the inimitable great, Bear Bryant, a man with the great coaching stature of Joe Paterno, with a great team, was ranked #2. The Sugar Bowl eventually got the #1 and # 2 teams to play each other even though Coach Paterno would have preferred the Orange Bowl, the last game played on New Year's Day. That did not happen. Destiny was in the hands of both of these teams.

With its 11-1 1977 season behind them coming in with just four points separating PSU from a National Championship bid, PSU had high expectations for the 1978 season. Before game time. Nobody could say that the 1978 Penn State squad had disappointed anybody. PSU had a great season after barely escaping Temple in game 1.

While some games were relatively close, the Nittany Lions generally won each game with ease. Its defense was #1 in the nation. This was a Paterno hallmark at Linebacker U. It held teams to ten points or less. #1 ranked PSU had made it to the gates of the national championship. The great 1978 Penn State football team was ready for a win.

Alabama also had great expectations coming into the 1978 season. In 1977, they too were 11-1 11–1, losing only to Nebraska. They had devastated Ohio State in the 1978 Sugar Bowl much to Woody Hayes' chagrin. They were third in the country coming into their bowl game. The two top teams lost and Alabama naturally believed that it rightfully had earned the honor of being national champions. Notre Dame had rolled over #1 Texas in the 1978 Cotton Bowl Classic, and the Irish jumped from 5th to 1st to become national champions. The Crimson Tide felt robbed and it was their big motivation for 1978. There they were again with just PSU to get by. Alabama was also ready for a win.

And, so, this year's edition of the New Year's Day Sugar Bowl capped off the 1978 season and was the 45th edition of the Sugar Bowl, it was played in New Orleans, Louisiana on January 1, 1979 at the Louisiana Superdome. A close score of L (7-14) gave Alabama head coach Bear Bryant his fifth National Championship. After such a fine season, Joe Paterno was still looking for his first.

1979 Penn State Football Season Coach Joe Paterno

The 1979 Penn State Nittany Lions football team was coached by Joe Paterno. No team can have a championship every year. After back to back 11-1 seasons, PSU kept working hard. The University football program did not take the night off. Joe Paterno's squad compiled a 7-4 regular season record and won the Liberty Bowl, making the record 8-4. PSU was top-twenty ranked in both polls— #18 in the Coach's poll and #20 in the AP.

Ranked # 7, PSU defeated Rutgers W 45-10) on September 22 to begin the season at home September 15. On September 22, Texas A&M beat the Nittany Lions at Beaver Stadium L (14-27). #6 Nebraska played host to Penn State on September 29 and defeated the #18 Nittany Lions too easily L (17-42) Seems like a little bit of rebuilding was going on. Maryland was next on October 6 at Byrd Stadium. Penn State triumphed over the Terrapins W (27-7).

On October 13, Penn State beat Army at Beaver Stadium W 24-3 before an attendance of 77,157. Syracuse moved its October 20 game to Giants Stadium from Archbold Stadium and were shut-out by the Nittany Lions W (35-7). On October 27, the Mountaineers of West Virginia were beaten by PSU at Beaver Stadium W (31-6). PSU was coming back but there was another few tough ones on the schedule. The first loss was Miami on November 3. The Hurricanes played the #19 Nittany Lions at Beaver Stadium and prevailed L (10-26). The next loss was v #11 Pittsburgh at Beaver Stadium on December 1 L (14-29).

In between, PSU traveled to NC State and beat the Cougars in a defensive battle W (9-7). Temple was next to play #18 PSU at Beaver Stadium W (22-7). At 7-4, Penn State accepted an invitation to the Liberty Bowl

On December 22, the unranked Nittany Lions beat # 15 ranked Tulane in the Liberty Bowl W (9-6). The game was played in Memorial Stadium in Memphis Tennessee before a crowd of 50,021 and a nationwide TV audience on ABC. After the Liberty Bowl victory, PSU moved back into the top twenty—#18 in the Coach's poll and #20 in the AP.

1980 Penn State Football Season Coach Joe Paterno

The 1980 Penn State Nittany Lions football team was coached by Joe Paterno in his fifteenth season with Penn State. The team had a great season, winning two more games than in 1979, and finishing with a 10-2 record, ranked #8 in both polls. I am in awe about how consistent a winner, coach Paterno was with his PSU teams. Bravo!

Penn State began the season on September 6 ranked at #18 and playing Colgate at home. PSU had added about another 6500 seats to Beaver Stadium bringing its official 1980 capacity to 83,77. On September 10, after a bye week, PSU defeated Texas PSU walloped Colgate W (54-10). A & M at Kyle Field in College Station Texas W (25-9). #3 Nebraska, having another great year, beat the Nittany Lions at Beaver Stadium on September 27 L (7-21). Then it was Missouri on October 4 at Faurot Field in Columbia MO in a close match W 29-21).

On October 11, PSU traveled to Byrd Stadium in College Park MD to play Maryland and beat the Terrapins W (24-10). Syracuse played its annual game against Penn State, this year at Beaver Stadium before a capacity crowd of 84,000. The Lions came out on top W (24-7). On October 25, it was West Virginia at Mountaineer Field in a close win for PSU (20-15). Miami of Florida played at Beaver Stadium on November 1, and were beaten by the Nittany Lions W 27-12). North Carolina came to State College the following week on November 8 and were beaten by Penn State W 21-13).

Temple opted to play its November 8 home game v PSU at Veterans Stadium before 49, 313. The Nittany Lions thumped the Owls pretty good W (50-7). On November 28, Dan Marino led the # 4 ranked Pittsburgh Panthers in their win against #5 Penn State at Beaver Stadium L (9-14). Penn State was invited to the Fiesta Bowl with a 9-2 record.

Ohio State was coached by Woody Hayes who, like Joe Paterno knew how to coach young men to play football at its best. Paterno's Nittany Lions defeated the Hayes Buckeyes W (31-19) before 66,738 and an NBC national audience. The game was held won December 26 with Ohio State ranked #11 and Penn State ranked #10. It was a nice night at Sun Devil Stadium in the Tempe Arizona desert. Penn State was ranked # 8 in both polls after this victory. JoePa and a great team had brought another fine season to Penn State University.

Player Highlights Matt Millen

Matt Millen was an All-American Selection in 1978. The Hokendauqua, Pa. native played Defensive tackle of the Nittany Lions. He was also selected by Walter Camp and United Press International. Millen was a terror on Defense with 54 tackles, including nine quarterback sacks. He even blocked a punt and caused two fumbles as a junior.

He had an unfortunate senior year or he would have killed it in the stats and honors categories. He was a great football player. He missed most of his playing time during senior year with an injury. After graduation, he played with the Oakland/Los Angeles Raiders (1980-88), San Francisco (1989-90), and Washington (1991) of the National Football League.

Former player Matt Millen

In Millen's 12-year NFL playing career, he played on four teams that won the Super Bowl. Millen won a Super Bowl ring with each of the three teams for which he played; moreover, he won a Super Bowl ring in each of the four cities in which he played (the Raiders won championships in both Oakland and Los Angeles during his tenure). Millen was president and CEO of the NFL Detroit Lions until 2008.

1981 Penn State Football Season Coach Joe Paterno

The 1981 Penn State Nittany Lions football team was coached by Joe Paterno in his sixteenth season. Coach Joe Paterno did it again—a 9-2 excellent regular season and a victory over USC in the Fiesta Bowl giving a 10-2 combined record and a #3 position in both polls.

Cincinnati played #9 PSU on September 12 and were pummeled by the Nittany Lions in a home season opening shutout W (52-0). PSU went to Osborne. Ranked at #3, PSU traveled to Lincoln, Nebraska and beat Nebraska in a close match W (30-24). At home on October 3, PSU shut-out Temple W (30-0). PSU then took on Boston College at home and beat the Eagles W (38-7) on October 10.

On October 17, #2 ranked PSU traveled to the Carrier Dome to beat Syracuse W (41-26). West Virginia was next on October 24 to play #1 ranked PSU at Beaver Stadium W (30-7). #1 ranked Penn State traveled to unranked Miami to play the Hurricanes and were beaten in a heartbreaker L (14-17). The next week after the major disappointment in Miami, #6 ranked PSU took on North Carolina State in Raleigh NC and scored a victory W (22-15).

#5 Penn State got another shot at #6 Alabama, the team that had messed up its shot at a championship in 1978. Though it was an important game PSU was outplayed and lost to the Crimson Tide L (16-31). Unranked Notre Dame came to Beaver Stadium the following week on November 21, and were beaten by the Nittany Lions in a very close game W (24-21). After two losses, PSU was out of first place and down to # 11 in the polls.

The Nittany Lions delivered one of their most satisfying wins when quarterback Todd Blackledge (above) and the defense sparked a turnaround from a 14-0 deficit to a 48-14 win at No. 1 Pitt on November 28, 1981. Penn State beat Southern California in the 1982 Fiesta Bowl to finish 10-2 and ranked No. 3, setting the table for the Nittany Lions' 1982 National Championship.

On November 28, Penn State said enough is enough and shellacked #1 ranked Pittsburgh at Pitt Stadium W (48-14) in Dan Marino's last year. Incidentally, with Pitt's 11-1 record, PSU had put the only blemish on its season. The Pitt Team came back from the PSU loss, played and beat the # 2 team in the country Georgia 24-20 in the Sugar Bowl.

On this day in 1981, Penn State pulled off one of its finest come from behind victories, snapping back from a 14-0 second-quarter deficit to rout No. 1 Pitt, 48-14, and end the national title chances of the Sugar Bowl-bound Panthers before a national television audience and 60,260 at Pitt Stadium. The victory was sparked by interceptions of Dan Marino passes by Roger Jackson and Mark Robinson and the passing combination of Todd Blackledge to Kenny Jackson.

Player Highlights Todd Blackledge

Penn State Football, Todd Blackledge

When I first saw Todd Blackledge play at the Carrier Dome v Syracuse years ago, I was amazed at the passing after having seen so many games in which Penn State would run the ball almost all the time even if the situation clearly called for a pass. Before Blackledge, it seemed Paterno was always squeamish about passing.

On this day v Pittsburgh facing the consummate passer of all time, Dan Marino, JoePa had to let Blackledge throw—but would he? He sure did. Not only did Coach OK a vaunted passing attack, it was as if PSU had been a passing team forever. Blackledge could not do anything wrong. He played one heck of a game

He was so good that Todd Blackledge upstaged the best passer in football Dan Marino at quarterback. Penn State got its biggest upset since Joe Paterno became the head coach in 1966, a huge 48-14 victory over top-ranked Pittsburgh that ended the Panthers' 17-game winning streak, and ended their day in the championship sun.

Marino was a junior at the time, and as the QB, so far in the game he had put Pitt out ahead so quickly that it looked like the crying towels would be needed. Marino had already thrown for two touchdowns to put the Panthers ahead by 14-0 in the first 10 minutes.

Blackledge, Penn State's sophomore quarterback got some breaks and took advantage of them. There were a series of Panther mistakes that in a flash turned the game around. Before the Panthers knew it, the game was tied and then they were losing.

Blackledge threw two touchdown passes to Kenny Jackson, ran for one touchdown and wound up with 12 completions in 23 attempts for 262 yards before a crowd of 60,260 in Pitt Stadium.

Blackledge was elated. "This was the best game of my life," he said. Marino was not his usual pinpoint self with 22 completions in 45 attempts for 267 yards. His big problem was that he got only 80 yards in the second half. He was intercepted four times and his team lost three fumbles. The seven turnovers killed the Panthers.

"We can't cry," said Marino, who had taken Pitt to be the #1 team in the nation with 34 touchdown passes before this day in this season. "They did a good job and beat us outright today. We just made too many mistakes, and you can't win with so many fumbles, penalties and interceptions."

Paterno, an assistant coach at Penn State when the Lions beat Ohio State 17 years prior, said: "I didn't think this was an upset. Who says so?"

One of his former players, Irv Pankey, an offensive tackle on Penn State's 1978 team, added, "This without a doubt is the best victory ever." Pankey, then a member of the Los Angeles Rams, was at the game because the Rams were to meet the Steelers at Three Rivers Stadium Sunday.

Pitt began stumbling after its early two-touchdown lead. Marino gave Penn State its first chance just when it appeared Pitt was moving in for a possible third touchdown. When he passed from the Penn State 31 on the first play of the second period, the ball was intercepted by Roger Jackson deep in the end zone. This put the Lions on their 20 and Blackledge went to work immediately.

Helped by a face-mask penalty of 15 yards, Penn State got to the Pitt 31 in five plays. Blackledge then hit Mike McCloskey at the Pitt 2. Chuck Meade, the fullback, went over on the next play and the conversion made the score 14-7.

Penn State stopped Pitt with an interception and a fumble recovery the next two times the Panthers had the ball and the Lions took over on their 20 late in the second period. Blackledge completed three successive passes to get to the 7. The third of these was a 53-yard toss to Jackson.

Blackledge went in from there on a quarterback draw that caught Pitt with a huge defensive hole right in the middle.

Fumbles Plague Panthers

Pitt fumbled the ball away again on its final chance to score in the first half at the Penn State 22, then continued its series of mistakes when Bill Beach, a fullback, fumbled and lost the ball to Penn State at the Lions' 43 early in the third period. In the next three minutes, Blackledge won the game with his two touchdown passes to Jackson.

The first, for 42 yards, found Jackson at the 10, where he made a beautiful pirouette around Tim Lewis, the right cornerback, and left Lewis grasping out of bounds. The next, for 45 yards, was easier as Jackson get 15 yards behind the defenses and alone.

They were Jackson's fifth and sixth touchdown receptions of the season, tying a Penn State record. "Kenny Jackson really came through for me," Blackledge said. Jackie Sherrill, Pitt's coach, said, "Oh, the turnovers. Penn State did a fine job throwing the ball deep and Kenny Jackson is a great ballplayer."

After those two touchdowns by Jackson, Penn State scored again on two field goals by Brian Franco and two touchdowns. The first of these late touchdowns came when Curt Warner, the tailback, went 9 yards toward the end zone, fumbled and Sean Farrell, the Penn State strong side guard, fell on the ball in the end zone. Then Mark Robinson made the second of his two interceptions of Marino passes and ran the ball back 91 yards for a score.

When it was all over, PSU was # 3 in both post season polls whereas Pitt was # 2 in the Coach's poll and #4 in the AP poll. Texas, which had a loss and a tie played Clemson and lost but was given the #4 slot in the Coach's Poll and were ranked above Pitt at # 2 in the AP poll. The Clemson Tigers, who were unbeaten and untied, claimed the national championship with #1 ranking in both polls after their victory over Nebraska in the Orange Bowl. No wonder we have the BCS today.

As the standout quarterback at Penn State, Blackledge started for the Nittany Lions from 1981 to 1983, going 31-5 through three seasons. After leading Penn State to the national championship in 1982, Blackledge won the Davey O'Brien Award as the nation's most outstanding quarterback, and he finished sixth in the Heisman Trophy voting. His passer rating was 10th among the nation's quarterbacks that season.

In the 1983 NFL Draft, Kansas City selected Blackledge seventh overall. He played for the Chiefs for five seasons before joining the Pittsburgh Steelers in 1988. He retired in 1989.

Player Highlights—Mike Munchak

Mike Munchak was born about eighteen miles north of my home town. He was ready to play offensive lineman (Guard) for Penn State from 1978-1981 but he was injured in 1980 and he missed the season as his knee was recovering. Nobody has lots to say about offensive Tackles or Guards so just being honored is a big deal as everything is a team effort. Munchak came back and was fully healed in 1981. He was a talented starter in both 1979 and 1981. During his senior year, he was named a second team All-American and was subsequently drafted 8th overall by the Houston Oilers.

Mike Munchak

He had a great but short professional career. During the 1982 NFL Draft, Munchak was chosen as the Houston Oilers first round draft pick (8th overall), making him the first offensive lineman drafted that year. In his rookie season, he quickly earned a starting position at the left guard position. He remained in that position for 12 seasons. During that time he garnered nine Pro Bowl nominations, four All-Pro, nine Second Team All-Pro, seven All-AFC, and four second team All-Pro selections. He was a great player. In addition, he was selected for the 1980s All-Decade Team. Munchak's 12-year tenure tied for second most seasons played with the Houston Oilers.

Mike Munchak has been in the hunt for the PSU coaching job since 2011. As much was Munchak would be welcome, most PSU football fans want James Franklin to kill it again next year and break out of the 2011 funk for good.

1982 Penn State Football Season Coach Joe Paterno

The 1982 Penn State Nittany Lions football team was coached by Joe Paterno in his seventeenth season. After a disappointing loss at Birmingham to #4 Alabama in game 5 L (21-42), a resilient and very tough Penn State squad came back and brought home all the marbles. The Nittany Lions won every game for the rest of the regular season, and defeated the #1 Georgia Bulldogs 27–23 in the Sugar Bowl. Added to their 11-1 record Penn State's fine play gave Joe Paterno his first consensus national championship.

Watching the season records grow over the years, I still cannot get over how many games Paterno won and we are only in his seventeenth season. In 1982, JoePa was just in his mid-50. He surely knew how to get the most out of his players. That is the job of a great coach. Another great coach, Frank Leahy, at Notre Dame, a bit before Paterno's time, had a saying that I think was the same type of saying JoePa would use to get the most out of his lads. Leahy said: "Lads, you're not to miss practice unless your parents died or you died." That about says it all!

On September 11, # 7 ranked PSU defeated Maryland at Beaver Stadium in a very close game W (39-31). On September 18 Rutgers played a # 8 ranked Penn State and lost by a mile W (49-14).

2 Nebraska, coached by the Great Tom Osborne, with his own share of national championships, always a tough team played #8 PSU at Beaver Stadium on September 25. Osborne's team got its only loss (W (27-24) of the season in a very close game.

There are those that have this game characterized as the greatest game ever at Beaver Stadium. See write-up under picture.

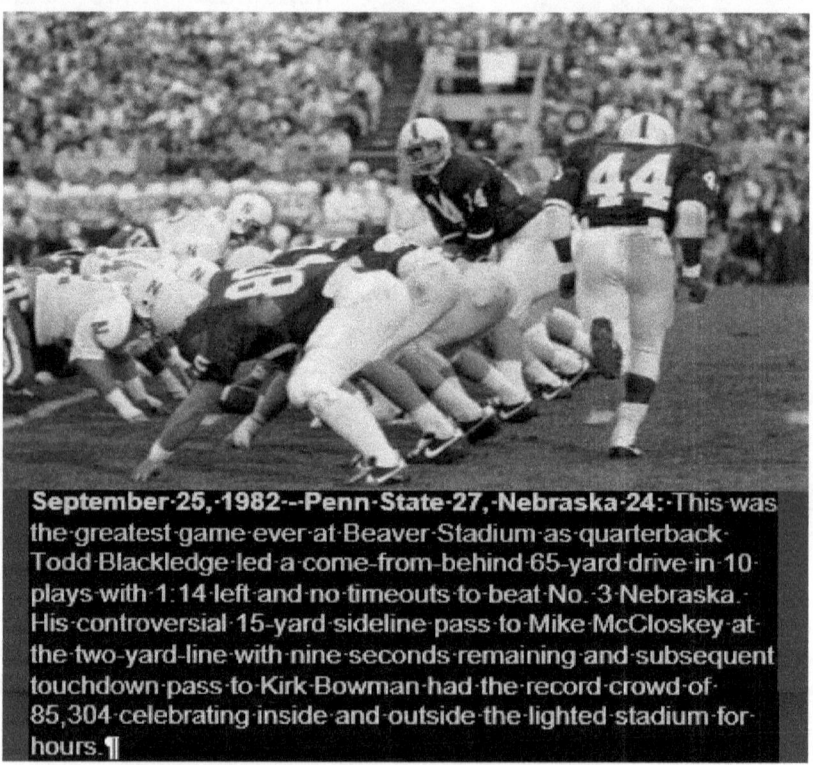

September 25, 1982 -- Penn State 27, Nebraska 24: This was the greatest game ever at Beaver Stadium as quarterback Todd Blackledge led a come-from-behind 65-yard drive in 10 plays with 1:14 left and no timeouts to beat No. 3 Nebraska. His controversial 15-yard sideline pass to Mike McCloskey at the two-yard-line with nine seconds remaining and subsequent touchdown pass to Kirk Bowman had the record crowd of 85,304 celebrating inside and outside the lighted stadium for hours. ¶

On October 9, came the loss at Alabama L (21-42). Alabama lost four of its next seven games which took them way out of the hunt for the championship.

Always ready to create havoc with a great PSU season, Syracuse played the #8 Nittany Lions at Beaver Stadium and lost W (28-7). West Virginia played #9 PSU in Mountaineer Stadium and gave up a loss W (24-0). Alumni Stadium in Chestnut Hill (Boston) was the scene for #8 PSU to shellack the unranked Eagles W (52-17). On November 7, #7 PSU then shut out and literally pounded NC State at Beaver Stadium W (54-0). #13 Notre Dame hosted # 5 PSU on November 13, as Penn State needed every win to have a shot at a championship. In a close match, #5 PSU (8-1) outplayed Notre Dame and got the W (24-14)

PSU v ND 1982

Yogi Berra may not have been a football player but his saying that it ain't over 'til it's over rand true in the 1982 matchup between Notre Dame and Penn State. In 1982, the Irish were coming off a 31-16 upset over then-No. 1 Pittsburgh when the No. 5 Lions came to South Bend.

Historical Nick Gancitano (Penn State) Field Goal against Notre Dame 1982

Notre Dame scored first, but a one-yard run by quarterback Todd Blackledge and two field goals by Nick Gancitano put the Lions up 13-7. Freshman sensation Pinkett, who would go on to have his best games of his career against the Lions, took a kickoff 93 yards for a touchdown and a 14-13 ND lead.

Blackledge, however, responded with a 48-yard-scoring strike to Curt Warner and Penn State went on to a 24-14 victory en route to its first national championship.

At 10-1, on November 26 # 2 Penn State played a tough #5 Pittsburgh at Beaver Stadium. The Nittany Lions controlled the game and won W (19-10). Penn State was the #2 team in the nation and they got a chance in the Sugar Bowl to play the #1 ranked team.

This year's Sugar Bowl was the type of game from which they make movies. The game would determine the 1982 national champions unless both teams played like pikers, which was highly unlikely for the recognized two best teams in the nation.

Georgia had a tough schedule and the Bulldogs had not lost a game. At 11-0, they thought they were pretty good. Penn State at 10-1, with a non-sequitur loss to Alabama felt pretty good about themselves. The game itself, for the first time in many trips to the great field for Penn State and Joe Paterno, would determine the national champion. Win, you're in; Lose, you're out and probably not even #2!

The game was played in the Louisiana Superdome in New Orleans, LA. It was called the Sugar Bowl but neither team had decided to sweeten anything for their opponent. Penn State at # 2, Georgia at #1—it was a game scheduled by the gods. And, so it happened on January 1, 1983 that the Pennsylvania State Nittany Lions defeated the great Georgia Bulldogs in a phenomenally tough football game W (19-10). 85,522 attendees plus a national ABC TV football audience enjoyed the game. Only half, my half, thankfully, enjoyed the score.

1983 Penn State Football Season Coach Joe Paterno

The 1983 Penn State Nittany Lions football team was coached by Joe Paterno in his eighteenth year. The team achieved an 8-4-1 record with an Aloha Bowl game victory over Washington. Even with four regular season losses, the Lions were ranked at #17 in the Coach's poll. Clearly after a national championship it is safe to call 1983 a rebuilding year for Penn State. New players equal a new team.

Nobody can win every game every season. Even Alabama, after doubling the score against PSU in their 1982 match could not sustain its good fortune and lost its last four games...of course this helped PSU in achieving the championship in 1982. So, unless students and coaches were all ironmen in football, the conclusion is that nobody can will all the games all the time. Yet great coaches such as Joe Paterno always try.

In its earliest season start since the inception of the program in the 1880's, on August 29, #4 Penn State lost to Tom Osborne's #1 ranked Nebraska team in the Kickoff Classic L (6-44). Teams do not forget the teams that have messed them up as PSU did the prior year to Nebraska. Cincinnati was next on September 10 at Beaver Stadium, and a Lions team that was not accustomed to losing lost again to the Bearcats. Iowa on September 17 kept throwing the bad sludge at Penn State. Not having won a game in this short season so far, PSU lost again to the Hawkeyes L (34-42)

Temple chose the Vet to play an unranked PSU on September 24 and came close to an upset over the Nittany Lions W (23-18) PSU had its first win of the season. On October 1, Rutgers asked PSU to play in Giants Stadium and the Nittany Lions defeated the Scarlet Knight. Not forgetting the Alabama loss, a year previous, Penn State took on Alabama's Crimson Tide on October 8 at Beaver Stadium and won a nice game W (34-8). On October 15, PSU then played Syracuse at the Carrier Dome and defeated the Orangemen W (17-6).

At the time, it was just as impossible to get a full bus trip to Beaver Stadium for a game but Syracuse was just two and a half hours from the IBM Scranton Branch Office. The tickets were affordable and available and so every other year, my IBM cohorts and I ran a bus trip to see PSU play Syracuse in the Carrier Dome.

I saw this game and many others until the series was canceled. I can remember how disappointed we all were when the games ended, but we kept going to Syracuse for a little while afterwards. One time an IBM football game flier read that *this year's Penn State Football game will be Syracuse v Army.*

I do recall one game in the balmy 69 degrees in which Todd Blackledge threw a pass on first down and before the clock had reached 14:50 in the first quarter, Penn State was up 7-0.

On October 22, #4 ranked PSU beat West Virginia at Beaver Stadium in University Park, PA W (41-23). On October 29, Boston College had its way with Penn State in a rare win at Foxborough MA. L (17-27). On November 5, at home, PSU beat Brown University W (38-21).

PSU was doing pretty well against Notre Dame at the time and in 1983, on November 12, things were no different. PSU beat the Fighting Irish in Beaver Stadium in a close match W (34-30) before 85,899.

The summarized scoop on this see-saw game between these rivals is that the two teams met on a frigid November afternoon at Beaver Stadium. Doug Strang had his best day as a Lion, completing 24 passes for 274 yards and three touchdowns. But his performance was overshadowed by ND's Pinkett, who would have his best game of his career (at least up until then) with 217 yards rushing and four touchdowns. In a see-saw battle, Notre Dame took a 30-27 lead late in the fourth quarter, but Strang's roll-out keeper with less than a minute to play enabled Penn State to win 34-30.

Cross-state rival #17 Pittsburgh hosted Penn State on November 19, and the teams tied T (24-24).

On December 26, PSU played Washington at Aloha Stadium in Honolulu, Hawaii in the Aloha Bowl. 37,212 watched the game on the field while millions of others watched it on ESPN. Penn State won the game W (13-10).

Chapter 7 Joe Paterno Era from 1984 to 1992

Coach # 14

1984	Joe Paterno	6-5	
1985	Joe Paterno	11-1	
1986	Joe Paterno	12-0	National Champions
1987	Joe Paterno	8-4	
1988	Joe Paterno	5-6	
1989	Joe Paterno	8-3-1	
1990	Joe Paterno	9-3	
1991	Joe Paterno	11-2	
1992	Joe Paterno	7-5	

Coached 45 great seasons 1966 to 2010 and part of 2011.

1984 Penn State Football Season Coach Joe Paterno

The 1984 Penn State Nittany Lions football team was coached by Joe Paterno in his nineteenth year at age 56. With a 6-5 record this can be called a rebuilding year to a rebuilding year. Lots of losses.

The pundits ranked PSU at #11 as this could have been the comeback year but it was not. On September 8, Rutgers was defeated just barely by the #11   Lions at Beaver Stadium W (15-12). Still winning some close games, #12 ranked PSU beat #5 Iowa

W (20-172) on September 15 at Kinnick Stadium • Iowa City, IA. On September 22, #7 PSU then beat William & Mary at Beaver Stadium W (56-18). Then #2 Texas came in to Giants Stadium to ruin the winning party. They played PSU before 76,833 and the Longhorns beat the Lions L (3–28.

Maryland played next on October 6 v a PSU team that had not yet begun to roll. In a very close game the Nittany Lions eventually prevailed at Beaver Stadium W 25–24. At Bryant-Denny Stadium, on October 13, Alabama squeaked out a victory against the Lions L (0–6). Syracuse then played at Beaver Stadium against #19 PSU but lost W (21-3). With a better team in 1984, on October 27, #18 West Virginia was ready for a win and they got it on their home field in a close game against a floundering #19 PSU team L (14-17)

PSU beat Boston College at home on November 3 W 37-30). Notre Dame had been beaten and roughed up a few times in the early 1980's and it wasn't forgetting the notion of payback. On November 17, in the old Notre Dame Stadium. PSU did not have what it takes and ND beat PSU with a big score L (7-44).

In a weak year, Pittsburgh was not about to get beaten by PSU so it played like the dickens and defeated the Nittany Lions L (11-31) at Beaver Stadium, with many PSU fans in attendance. It is much easier writing about Penn States big winning seasons than a slow-down season.

1985 Penn State Football Season Coach Joe Paterno

The 1985 Penn State Nittany Lions football team was coached by Joe Paterno for the twentieth year and played its home games in Beaver Stadium in University Park, Pennsylvania. You may recall in the 1983 summary, I suggested that the season was 8-4-1 because of rebuilding, and then with a 6-5 season in 1984 I admitted that the rebuilding needed rebuilding. Along the way, noticing that an Alabama team lost four games after beating Penn State, I realized that nothing is certain in college football. But, Joe Paterno knew how to win. That was certain and in 1985, he showed it again on his way to 1986.

On September 7, Maryland was ranked at #7 when #19 Penn State went to Robert Byrd Stadium to play the Terrapins. As season openers, often are as the sluggishness is removed from the routine, this game was very close and a fine Maryland team lost by just two points to Penn State W (20-18). Close was the order of the season as a tough Temple team came to Beaver Stadium ton September 14, to play ball, and play hard they did as PSU escaped with a two-point victory W (27-25).

East Carolina, not a frequent visitor to Beaver Stadium came to play the #10 Nittany Lions and they played a nice game but lost W (17-10). On September 28, Rutgers duplicated the East Carolina score W (17-10) in Giants Stadium before 54,560.

I am conditioned that when I see Alabama, I think tough and I think potential loss. I am sure Bear Bryant and subsequent coaches preach that message. Not in 1985. #8 ranked PSU beat #10 Alabama on October 12 W (19-17) in a nail-biter.

PSU was #6 when the Orangemen hosted the Nittany Lions at the Carrier Dome in 69-degree weather in Syracuse. PSU won another close game with a great defense W (24-20). PSU at #3 then played West Virginia on October 26 and triumphed with a shutout W (27-0). On November 2, BC came to Beaver stadium and were beaten in another close match by #3 ranked PSU W (16-12). On November 9, Penn State traveled to Riverfront Stadium in Cincinnati and won W (31-0).

On November 16, a new regular, Notre Dame, then an unranked opponent, played the #1 ranked Penn State at Beaver Stadium W (36-6).

In the Beaver Stadium, historical annals, no game ever had been played in such drenching, cold rain. The heavy rain started Friday night and did not let up until the game was long over. Despite regional TV able to take the fans out of the inclement weather, over 84,000 fans showed up. They expected to see a close game but watched as the top ranked Nittany Lions annihilated Notre Dame en route to an 11-0 regular season and berth in the national championship game vs. Oklahoma in the Orange Bowl.

On November 16, an undefeated PSU team beat Pitt at Pitt W (31-0). PSU was ranked #1 at 11-0 undefeated and were invited to play Oklahoma in the Orange Bowl.

Bowl Game Destroys Undefeated Season

The game was about five or six weeks after the team was in shape and had their last taste of a real football game. Miami had the same circumstances so there are no excuses but PSU had obviously lost its edge. On January 1, 1986, # 1 PSU played #3 Oklahoma in the Miami Orange Bowl and lost the game to a Miami team that played better than Penn State that day L (10–25). 74,148 saw the game on the field and NBC showed the game to the willing in the rest of the country. It was a great season, 11-1 with a #3 finish in both the Coach's and the AP polls.

1986 Penn State Football Season Coach Joe Paterno

The 1986 Penn State Nittany Lions football team was coached by Joe Paterno for the twenty-first year. Penn State defeated the Miami Hurricanes 14–10 in the 1987 Fiesta Bowl to win Paterno's second consensus national championship. Joe Paterno knew how to win football games.

On September 6, Penn State opened up this successful season at home against Temple. Temple had been having problems winning against PSU for some years and in fact it still does and this year was no different. #6 ranked Penn State won its home opener W (45-15). Boston College moved its September 20 game from Alumni Stadium to Foxborough to play a tough #5 ranked PSU team. The Eagles played a close game but lost to the Nittany Lions W (26-14). East Carolina lost at Beaver Stadium on September 27 against a #7 ranked PSU squad W (42-7). PSU had a knack of scheduling its easier games in the beginning to get the team accustomed to the routine before engaging tough game. PSU defeated Rutgers at Beaver Stadium next on October 4, W (31-6).

Cincinnati brought its football team to play #5 ranked PSU at Beaver Stadium on October 11. It was a close game but the Nittany Lions won W (23-17). On October 18, Syracuse played PSU at Beaver Stadium and were defeated easily by the #6 Nittany Lions W (42-3). A tough Alabama team waited for game seven when PSU was 100% ready for the Crimson Tide. The PSU squad made quick work of the vaunted Alabama team at Tuscaloosa W (23-3). At 7-0, with the Alabama game behind them PSU moved up in the rankings to #2 in the country. On November 1, PSU traveled to Mountaineer Stadium to play a fine West Virginia team and beat the Mountaineers W (19-0)

On November 8, #2 ranked Penn State played Maryland at Beaver Stadium and won a very, very close match W (17-15). A loss would have virtually ended PSU's championship dreams. Playing the unranked Fighting Irish at Notre Dame Stadium on November 15, it was expected to be close and it was but the #3 ranked 9-0 Nittany Lions prevailed W (24-19).

At 10-0, ranked # 2 on November 22, PSU needed just one more win v Pittsburgh at home to have a perfect regular season. The Nittany Lions got that win W (34-14) before 85,722, and also got a shot at winning the national title in the Fiesta Bowl v #1 ranked Miami.

PSU clinched a spot in the national championship game by beating arch rival Pitt. That it was Pitt made this an extremely gratifying moment. The bitterness of the long-time rivalry emerged with five fist fights, a number of late hits and four offsetting penalties for unsportsmanlike conduct. Many who watched every moment of the game, still enjoy the image of Joe Paterno running across the field late in the game to help break up a scuffle in front of the Pitt bench. They say that was a lifetime priceless moment.

A game marred by fighting!

Rob Biertempfel of the PSU Collegian Student Newspaper wrote about a "game marred by fighting. Here is how he saw the contest:

The Collegian Nov 24, 1986

> *Game marred by fighting*
>
> *A funny thing happened Saturday afternoon in Beaver Stadium. They started playing football and a hockey game broke out.*
>
> *The 86th gridiron clash between the Penn State Nittany Lions and Pitt Panthers was at times more like a boxing match than a football contest, as proved by five fights, three ejections, seven personal fouls and 77 yards in penalties. At one point, late in the fourth quarter, Lion Head Coach Joe Paterno sprinted across the field to help break up a scuffle near the Pitt bench.*
>
> *The image of Paterno running into a fight may have brought comparisons with Maryland Head Coach Bobby Ross' incident with a referee a few weeks ago, but this situation was different.*
>
> *The scoreboard showed 4:26 remaining and Penn State ahead 34-14 when Pitt's Teryl Austin returned a punt to the Panthers' 18-yard line. After he was run out of bounds, he flipped the ball into the facemask of Penn State's Brian Chizmar. Five Lions came to Chizmar's defense and the melee was on.*
>
> *"The next thing I knew I was surrounded," Austin explained afterwards. "Everyone got into it."*
>
> *The Pitt bench emptied, Penn State players rushed onto the grass and Paterno angrily ran into the fight. Television microphones picked up the coach calling the fighting players a disgrace to the game as he tried to separate them. When the mud had settled, the Lions were assessed a 15-yard personal foul penalty.*

Paterno was livid at the referees all day for doing what he thought was an inadequate job. After the game, he explained his anger.

"I thought the officials started wrong when they started with a personal foul here and a personal foul there," he said. "That means nothing and I think the game got a little out of hand. I'm going to sit down and tell my kids not to talk about it because I don't think it's good for football when you play in games like that.

"I've never been in a football game with Pitt when we had so much of that kind of stuff."

Pitt Head Coach Mike Gottfried, who got his first taste of the Penn State-Pitt rivalry Saturday, was much more direct in his comments.

"I'm not going to let an hour go by the rest of next year without remembering what they (Penn State) did," he grumbled after the game in a voice deadened by yelling. "I'm never going to forget what their coach did to me on that sideline, and how their fans embarrassed us."

The game's first confrontation came after Penn State's D.J. Dozier had sliced through the Panther defense for a 26-yard touchdown and a 17-7 Lion lead. As Dozier slowed down in the end zone, Panther cornerback Quinton Jones gave the senior tailback some assistance off the field with a slap and shove. Center Keith Radecic stood up to Jones and was joined by quarterback John Shaffer. The fight that ensued resulted in offsetting personal fouls which enraged the partisan crowd and Paterno, who responded by screaming at the officials.

Penn State cornerback Duffy Cobbs said that Paterno's vocal reaction surprised the team.

"Usually he's the one who tries to calm us down," he said. "When I saw him, I said, 'Anything goes now.'"

Radecic agreed, but noted that the afternoon saw more than its share of intensity.

"He did some things today that were a little uncharacteristic, but I think we all did," he said. "I think we all lost our poise a little bit. There were definitely too many personal fouls and unsportsmanlike contact calls. In the heat of the game you never know what will happen."

The rest of the game had its share of scuffles, taunts and shoves, and at least three players were ejected from the game. Pitt lost linebacker Jerry Wall and wide receiver Bill Osborn. Wall identified linebacker Don Graham as the Penn State player thrown out.

The players themselves seemed to take the fierce play in stride, saying that the nature of the rivalry caused spirited play to turn into violence.

Pitt's Steve Apke, who scuffled with former high school teammate Shaffer in the second quarter after Dozier's touchdown, said the game was out of the referees' hands.

"The refs tried to keep it under control, but things like that are going to happen," the senior linebacker said. "It's a big rivalry; that's just playing hard. When the score starts getting out of hand, people start getting frustrated."

Penn State's Bob White also tried to shrug off the scuffles.

"I think that in a lot of ways that's kind of expected," the senior defensive lineman said. "That's the nature of the game over the years. Things did get out of hand out there for a while. But when you've got a bunch of guys that are going at each other the way we were going at each other; those things are going to happen."

1986 Fiesta Bowl Game

Taking advantage of the long New Year's weekend, this January 2, 1987 encounter was scheduled for Friday. It was another game of the century with #1 Miami coached by Jimmy Johnson, the coach everybody loved to hate, and Joe Paterno, a great winning coach at the helm for the #2 ranked Penn State. The Fiesta Bowl game was played in Sun Devil Stadium in Tempe, AZ (Fiesta Bowl). It was televised by NBC and watched on the field by 74,098. PSU won the game W 14–10 and the national championship.

1987 Penn State Football Season Coach Joe Paterno

The 1987 Penn State Nittany Lions football team was coached by Joe Paterno in his 22nd year as head coach. The team's aggregate record including its Citrus Bowl major loss to Clemson L (10-35) Bowl was 8-4 and after a #1 finish in 1986, PSU finished out of the top 20 at #22. It was

Paying homage to the national championship team and recognizing the loss of senior athletes, PSU was ranked #11 to start the season on September 5 v Bowling Green at Beaver Stadium. PSU looked good v Bowling Green W (45-19). Alabama as a first test came early in Beaver Stadium and the Crimson Tide gave PSU their first loss since the Orange Bowl game after the 1985 season L (13-24). Overall, it was not a bad game. #20 PSU then shutout Cincinnati on September 19 at home (W (41-0). On September 26, the Nittany Lions played at Boston College W (27-17).

On October 3 v Temple at Beaver Stadium, the #14 Nittany Lions beat Temple W (27-13). The following week Rutgers came to town and PSU defeated the Scarlet Knight W (35-21). #13 Syracuse had picked itself up and dusted itself off while #10 PSU had been winning national championships. The Orangemen were waiting on October 17 at the Carrier Dome and they soundly defeated PSU L (21-48). On October 31, at home, PSU barely beat West Virginia played (25-21).

On November 7 at Maryland #16 PSU beat the Terrapins W (21-16) in another close battle. Pittsburgh had been getting shellacked in recent years by Penn State but this time, in a tough game on November 14, the Panthers beat the Nittany Lions at Pitt Stadium L (0-10). Notre Dame came to Beaver Stadium on November 21. In a nail-biter PSU beat the Fighting Irish by one point W (21-20).

This game may have been the coldest ever at Beaver Stadium with 30 miles an hour winds, snow flurries and wind chills of zero to 18 degrees the numbing 84,00 shivering fans. Notre Dame scored with 30 seconds remaining and went for the win but quarterback Tony Rice was tackled short of the goal by linebacker Pete Curkendall. "It was a moment that will always be frozen in the history of Penn State football," Paterno said.

PSU v ND

PSU was invited to the Citrus Bowl in which they played a tough Clemson Tigers team on January 1, 1988 in Orlando. Clemson won decisively L (10-35.

1988 Penn State Football Season Coach Joe Paterno

The 1988 Penn State Nittany Lions football team was coached by Joe Paterno in his 23rd season. With a 5-6 record, this is the first losing season in Joe Paterno's first 23 years. A double rebuilding process was underway. PSU was unranked and the team did not qualify for a bowl bid.

Penn State began its season fine with a nice win on September 10 at Virginia W (42-14). The wins continued the next week, September 17, at home v Boston College W (23-20). Rutgers came to Beaver

Stadium on September 24 and gave a signal that this would be a tough year by beating PSU L (16-21). Temple played PSU at the Vet and were defeated on October 1 by a wide margin W (45-9).

Cincinnati made the short trip to Beaver Stadium on October 8 and were rebuffed W (35-9). A Syracuse still feeling its oats from the prior year's major victory came to Beaver Stadium on October 15 and handed PSU another defeat L (10-14). By this time, PSU was ready for tough teams for sure. The Lions handled Alabama well on October 22 but not well enough to win L (3-8). West Virginia was ranked #7 when PSU played the Mountaineers in Morgantown. It was all about WV's offense L (30-51).

On November 5, PSU beat Maryland in a close home game W (17-10). Pittsburgh then came to PSU on November 12 and beat the Lions L (7-14). The next game was PSU's chance at a bowl win as Notre Dame was ranked #1 when it hosted the Nittany Lions on November 19. PSU could not match the Irish and lost L (3-21). Overall, this was PSU's worst season under Joe Paterno at 5-6 with no post season honors. Stay tune for our summary of 1989 to see how well the JoePa team recovered.

1989 Penn State Football Season Coach Joe Paterno

The 1989 Penn State Nittany Lions football team was coached by Joe Paterno in his 24th season. At 8-3-1, the team made a great comeback from the 5-6 record of 1988. Additionally, the Lions were #14 in the Coach's poll and #15 in the AP poll. Moreover, they played and beat BYU in the Holiday Bowl W (50-39).

PSU started the season ranked #12 on September 9 at home with a loss to the Virginia Wahoos L (6-14) before 85,956 at Beaver Stadium. Games at Beaver stadium attract even more fans than bowl games. Temple was next at Beaver Stadium on September 16 (W (42-3). On September 23, Boston College came to State College and were beaten by the Nittany Lions in a very close, low-scoring game, W (7-3). On September 30, Penn State traveled to Austin Texas and beat the Longhorns W (16-12).

On PSU shut out Rutgers at Giants Stadium in East Rutherford, NJ W (17-0). On October 14, PSU beat Syracuse at the Carrier Dome W (34-12). Then, in a nail-biter at Beaver Stadium, the #14 Nittany

Lions barely lost to #6 Alabama L (16-17). On November 4, at Beaver Stadium, #16 Penn State played #13 West Virginia W (19-9). On November 11, at Maryland PSU tied the Terrapins T (13-13).

On November 18, at Beaver Stadium, #1 Notre Dame defeated #17 Penn State W (23-34). A week later at Pittsburgh, PSU came back to beat the Panthers W (16-13).

Penn State was invited to the Holiday Bowl with a 7-3-1 record and the #18 Nittany Lions defeated the #19 Cougars at Jack Murphy Stadium in San Diego, California. The attendance was 61,113 plus a nationwide ESPN TV audience.

1990 Penn State Football Season Coach Joe Paterno

The 1990 Penn State Nittany Lions football team was coached by Joe Paterno in his twenty-fifth season. The team had a great 9-2 record.

Without the early almost-wins in the first two games of the season, Penn State would have been playing for another national championship. The first was a home opening loss on September 8 to Texas in a nail-biter to open the home season L (13-17) and the next was in game #2 in another nail-biter at # 6 USC in the Coliseum in Los Angeles California Southern California on September 15 (L (14-19).

Both were close but as the smoke shop manager would say, but "no cigar!" Until the Blockbuster Bowl loss to Florida State L (17-24), the Nittany Lions from game 3 on, had a perfect season. The final record was 9-3 and the team was ranked # 10 in the Coach's poll and # 11 in the AP poll.

On September 22, PSU beat Rutgers W (28-0) at Beaver Stadium to start a nine-game win streak. Temple was next in line at Beaver Stadium on October 6 W (48-10). Syracuse played very tough at Beaver Stadium on October 13 W (27-21). PSU then traveled to Boston College's Alumni Stadium W (40-21). Then came a great win in the Alabama rivalry game on October 27 in Tuscaloosa W (9-0)

#24 PSU played the next week, November 3 in Morgantown and beat the Mountaineers W (31-19). At #21 PSU played at home on

November 10 and beat Syracuse W (24-10). A tough #1 ranked Notre Dame squad hosted Penn State at Notre Dame Stadium on November 17 and JoePa's team, ranked #18 at the time pulled off its magic and destroyed the Fighting Irish's championship hopes W (24-10). #11 Penn State then played rival Pittsburgh at home on November 24 and beat the Panthers in a close game W (22-17).

PSU was then ranked #7 and they played Bobby Bowden's #11 Florida State team in the Blockbuster Bowl on December 28 at Joe Robbie Stadium in Miami Gardens, FL and were beaten in a heartbreaker of a game L (17-24.)

1991 Penn State Football Season Coach Joe Paterno

The 1991 Penn State Nittany Lions football team was coached by Joe Paterno in his 26th season. They won 11 games including the Fiesta Bowl W (42-17 v Tennessee.) Their two losses were at unranked USC on September 14, L (10-21) and against #2 ranked Miami in Florida L (20-26) on October 12.

#7 PSU was invited and accepted play in the Kickoff Classic on August 29 v #8 ranked Georgia Tech at Giants Stadium. PSU triumphed W (34-22). On September 7 at home, PSU shellacked Cincinnati in a humunga-scoring game W (81-0) before an attendance of 94,000. Beaver Stadium was enhanced this year. An upper deck was added to north end zone along with an additional 10000 seats added Then on September 14 came the loss to USC, followed the next week by a nice win against BYU in Beaver Stadium before 96,304 W (33-7). After the BYU game PSU was ranked # 10.

After a bye week, on September 28, Boston College were defeated by the #10 Nittany Lions at Beaver Stadium W (28–21). On October 5, PSU beat Temple at Veterans Stadium W (24-7). #9 ranked PSU then were beaten by #2 ranked Miami in Florida L (20-26). On October 19, Rutgers played the Nittany Lions at Beaver Stadium W (37-17).

On October 26, West Virginia played #8 Penn State at Beaver Stadium and lost big W (51-6). On November 9, PSU clobbered Maryland in Baltimore W (47-7). PSU was tough and they had one heck of an offense led by QB Tony Sacca. On November 16, PSU beat a Lou Holtz coached Notre Dame team at Beaver Stadium in University Park, PA) W 35–13 with 96,672 in attendance. On November 28 at Pittsburgh, #6 ranked Penn State beat the Panthers W (32-20)

#6 PSU played in the Fiesta Bowl on January 1 1002 v #10 Tennessee in Sun Devil Stadium before 71,133 onlookers and a National NBC TV audience. The Nittany Lions played a great game W (42-17). PSU finished 11-2 and were ranked # 3 in both polls.

1992 Penn State Football Season Coach Joe Paterno

The 1992 Penn State Nittany Lions football team was coached by Joe Paterno in his 27th season. After three great years, 8-3-1, 9-3, and 11-2, one could almost expect a rebuilding year. This year's 7-5 record was a winning season but it was not a contender season as the prior three.

The season opened at Nippert Stadium in Ohio against Cincinnati on September 5 as the #8 Nittany Lions beat a determined Bearcats team in a close match W (24-20). The home opener was on September 12 v Temple in a slugout. # 10 PSU prevailed W (49-8). Eastern Michigan played at Beaver Stadium before 94, 892 on September 19. #10 ranked PSU shellacked the Eagles W (52–7).

PSU played Maryland at home on September 26 and beat the Terrapins W 49-13). At 4-0, ranked # 8 PSU played Rutgers at Giants stadium and won a nice game W (38-24). PSU had five wins in a row. Having escaped anything bad so far in this season, the Penn State Nittany Lions unfortunately would soon notice that the losses were about ready to come home to roost.

October 10, it was another battle of the titans at Beaver Stadium in University Park, PA as #2 Miami (FL) had their sights on defeating PSU. The Hurricanes won the game but it was a nail-biter L (14-17). Boston College knew how to create nail-biting in the PSU stands also and just about beat the Nittany Lions on October 17, L (32-35).

On October 24, West Virginia hosted PSU in a tough contest and the #14 Lions beat the Mountaineers W (40-26). Two games that could have gone either way went the wrong way. First, a tough BYU invited the Nittany Lions to play at Cougar Stadium on October 29 and beat PSU L (17-30) in the biggest loss so far in the season.

Then, with PSU sporting a 6-2 record, the Nittany Lions traveled to Notre Dame on November 14. The #8 Fighting Irish squeaked out a thriller one point win v #22 PSU L (16-17). Pittsburgh then came to Beaver Stadium on November 21 and the Lions beat them handily W (57-13).

PSU accepted an invitation to the Blockbuster bowl with a 7-4 season. The game was played January 1, 1993 at Joe Robbie Stadium in Miami Gardens, Florida. #13 Stanford was hoping to make quick work of #21 Penn State. It was not quick and the game was tough but PSU was beat fairly that day by a Stanford team that had come ready to play ball L (3-24).

Chapter 8 Joe Paterno Era from 1993 to 2001

Coach # 14

1993	Joe Paterno	10-2	(6-2 Big 10)
1994	Joe Paterno	12-0	(8-0 Big 10)
1995	Joe Paterno	9-3	(5-3 Big 10)
1996	Joe Paterno	11-2	(6-2 Big 10)
1997	Joe Paterno	9-3	(6-2 Big 10)
1998	Joe Paterno	9-3	(5-3 Big 10)
1999	Joe Paterno	10-3	(5-3 Big 10)
2000	Joe Paterno	5-7	(4-4 Big 10)
2001	Joe Paterno	5-6	(4-4 Big 10)

Coached 45 great seasons 1966 to 2010 and part of 2011.

1993 Penn State Football Season Coach Joe Paterno

The 1993 Penn State Nittany Lions football team was coached by Joe Paterno in his twenty-eighth year. Joe Paterno figured it was time to stop his run as an independent and begin playing Big Ten teams more regularly. So, PSU joined the Big Ten Conference in 1990 and began play in 1993.

Penn State then won its first Big Ten championship in 1994, and the Nittany Lions won two more in 2005 and 2008. As a deep Penn State fan, all my life, after reviewing his life in his football record, I cannot believe what a great coach Joe Paterno was right from the start. The mold from which he was cut created the greatest football coaches of all time. And Penn State fielded the best teams.

At the end of the 1993 season, PSU was ranked #7 in the Coach's poll and # 8 in the AP with a 10–2 record (6–2 in Big Ten play). The complexion of the PSU schedule would change forever as a result of its playing in the Big Ten Conference. The same-ole same-oles were no longer on the schedule but the schedule was always exciting.

On September 4, Minnesota played #17 Penn State in a home game at Beaver Stadium. PSU won W (38-20) I think it was a nice gesture that PSU's first Big Ten encounter was at home. The Nittany Lions had gotten rid of that "rebuilding year," and were now moving on to their normal modus operandi of regular winning. On September 11, in a non-Big-Ten game, USC played #15 PSU before 95,992 and the Nittany Lions won the game by a sliver W (21-20). A win is a win. On September 18, #14 PSU traveled to Iowa and shot out the Hawkeyes W (31-0). Longtime foe Rutgers played on September 25 v the Nittany Lions and lost W (31-7).

On October 2 #9 PSU played at Maryland and ran roughshod over the Terrapins W (70-7). An always powerful Michigan team visited PSU on October 16 and beat the Nittany Lions in a close game W (13-21). Another tough opponent Ohio State, took command of the game at Columbus and defeated PSU L (6-24). Few teams ever beat Penn State by a large score. On November 6, Indiana played the Nittany Lions at Beaver Stadium and the Lions won W (38-31).

On November 13, #16 PSU defeated Illinois in Beaver Stadium W (28–14). The next week on November 20, at Northwestern, PSU gained another victory W (43-21). Still on the road a week later on November 27, #14 PSU beat #25 Michigan State at Spartan Stadium in East Lansing MI W (38-37). This was as close a game as it gets.

Let's talk about this game a bit more as from my perspective it is one of the best games and great moments in PSU football history. This game set the stage for the 1994 undefeated season and put out a fair warning that Penn State was for real. Some in the good ole boys crowd did not care as they seemed to like establishment football. We'll get to that after some great front work introducing this game, this one point victory, which demonstrates the mettle and the resilience of the Penn State football program. Go Lions!

The Season ends with a great game v Michigan State

As we have been touting in this book from way back when PSU won its first game in 1881, the Nittany Lions dominated college football as an independent for over 110 years before the university joined the Big Ten in 1993.

PSU won the National Championship again as everybody knows in 1994. But, because we are kind to our opponents, we just whisper about this triumph.

You see, the vaunted 1994 team was not awarded the big prize after a 12-0, undefeated, untied season. It was because the coach chose not to embarrass Indiana and the Hoosiers made the score closer than the game ever was. It was as if the football establishment was waiting to deny Penn State's possible best team ever, the national championship.

Paterno's teams had recorded great seasons before 1994 with a 37-12 record leading up to the great 1994 season in which nothing went wrong in games but the afterthoughts were mostly sour.

1993, the year in which we are now examining, was also a great effort and a great result though often overshadowed by the undefeated 1994 team. The pundits say that the final game of that season against Michigan State, set the tone for the run to the top in '94. Penn State showed its mettle and the future looked bright. Nobody could deny a great Penn State Team the Championship in 1994. All PSU had to do was win, win, and win again, and our great University did exactly that.

In 1993, Penn State was the new guy on the block in the Big Ten. The well talented but less experienced than talented Lions opened a great season with five back-to-back wins. Eventually, the team met Michigan and Ohio State consecutively and these opponents were a measurable cut above the five prior teams. Yet, Penn State was not intimidated at all.

The Lions competed with Michigan well for the first three quarters, but the Wolverines kept Ki-Jana Carter from the goal line in the opening play of the fourth quarter. It was hard to take, I regret to say that it sure seemed to take the oomph out of the PSU attack. Officially, the game ended when Kerry Collins threw a rare interception within the last minute of the game, but it seemed to end with Carter's almost TD.

Ohio State gave the Nittany Lions their second loss at Ohio Stadium just two weeks later. PSU had been 6-2 against Ohio State before this encounter but the last game was when they played the Buckeyes in the 1980 Fiesta Bowl. The Nittany Lions back then crushed OSU but the Buckeyes had improved for sure and they were ready for vindication against the Lions.

They got their day. The Buckeyes held Penn State to just two field goals and Kerry Collins was intercepted multiple times. The cylinders were not firing right on O or D. Ohio State finished the '93 season with just one loss.

Despite these two consecutive losses, in 1993 Penn State came back strongly and won-out the rest of their season. It was not a cake-walk. The season topping game was their close win in East Lansing, where they squeaked out the win against a stubborn Michigan State team to take home the legendary Land Grant Trophy.

The Big Ten was really on to something when they designated Penn State and Michigan State as rivals, meaning they would duel it out annually to prove which land-grant school was bigger and tougher and of course, badder than the other.

This great game is worth discussing. Michigan State was ranked #25, and Penn State was sitting at the number #14 spot. Neither team was a contender. However, as we know, the honor is everything in college football.

On game day, the field of play was a disaster, and the team play on both sides of the colors reflected that. Michigan State nonetheless broke out of the pack with a 13-0 lead early on. Soon, Joe Paterno would send Mike Archie right up the middle (in true Paterno form) to put some points on the board.

Michigan State wasted no time to respond with another seven points, and this is pretty much how this game went for the rest of the second quarter. By halftime Penn State had slimmed that difference to a one-score deficit, 23-17. The Nittany Lions were just down by 6, and they seemed confident in their stride.

The Spartans turned to their strong passing game in the third quarter, and they increased their lead to 37-17. Some were asking, "Is the Nittany Lions' recent winning streak over?"

All of a sudden, or so it seemed, the Lions were alive and roaring again: Collins completed a 40-yard pass to Bobby Engram, and Penn State was ready to control the game. They got even more when the reliable Linebacker U defense recovered a fumble on Michigan State's 38. Collins drove the Nittany Lions down the field again, and with a Brian O'Neal touchdown, he made it a one score game.

The defense took over and forced a three and out, and gave the ball back to the PSU offense on its own 48. Collins faked a handoff and lofted a beautiful 52-yard strike to Engram. That's three touchdowns in about four minutes, if like me, you are keeping track.

The Spartan offense was inert for the remaining ten minutes and the PSU D helped the team big time to take that Land-Grant Trophy back to Happy Valley. It was a good year for Happy Valley as The Nittany Lions finished their first Big Ten season at the number three spot in the conference.

After the win in East Lansing in 1993, Penn State didn't lose a game until late September, 1995. Yes, folks, that means there were no losses in 1994—not a one.

1994 Citrus Bowl

Penn State had a great 9-2 record going into the Bowl Season. The Lions were invited to the Citrus Bowl in Orlando Florida on January 1, 1994 at 1:00 PM (prime time New Year's Day) to play #6 Tennessee.

Penn State would not be denied the victory over this substantially higher ranked opponent W (31-13) before 72,456 plus the nationwide ABC TV audience. Nobody was more thrilled than I. Despite the outcome, it did not look good at first as the game began.

Tennessee got off to a great start at were ahead 10-0 after a quick 46-yard field goal and a 19-yard TD pass from Shuler to Cory Fleming. There were 72,000 singing Rocky Top and that was not the Nittany Lions favorite tune. At 10-0 but very early, it appeared the Vols might take it to the Lions with a big rout.

But with Kerry Collins calling the signals and Bobby <<< Engram catching the pigskin when thrown to him, the Nittany Lions were about to roar. On second down from their own 36-yard line, Collins hit Engram on a wide receiver screen over the middle. Engram picked up a block and outran the defenders down to the Tennessee 29-yard line.

After the game, Engram had no problem noting: "That play set the tone...They saw we had some speed after all, and you could just see it in their eyes they weren't sure they could stop us." It was not long before PSU scored on a 3-yard TD run by Carter, who had been sitting out with a knee injury since the Illinois game. Carter was ready.

Tennessee came right back with an impressive drive down to the PSU 28-yard line where linebacker Tyoka Jackson got a tip on the ball in the air, and safety Lee Rubin intercepted it for the Lions at the 13-yard line. This was as close as Tennessee would come to the goal line for the rest of the day. The rout was on but it was not as originally thought. Penn State got hot and The Volunteers were cold.

Before the break-away, Craig Fayak hit a field goal to tie the game and UT responded with a 50-yarder of their own to take a 13-10 lead. With 1:08 to go in the half, Collins moved the ball down the field with a 12-yard draw play to Mike Archi. He then tossed an eighteen yarder to Engram. With 10 seconds to go at the UT 14-yard line, Penn State called their final timeout. Everyone expected Joe Paterno to elect for the field goal, but to their amazement the offense went back out on the field.

Tennessee sat back in pass defense expecting the Lions to take a shot at the end zone, but Paterno called a draw play to Carter instead. Carter broke a tackle at the line and sprinted into the end zone to give the Nittany Lions a 17-13 lead at halftime. The pundits felt that PSU had sent this message to the Volunteers with this play: "We can do anything we want to do, and there is nothing you can do to stop it."

Joe Paterno let it out at half time in the locker room: "Who do they think they are, telling us they need a better opponent,"

Paterno yelled out to a fully-tuned in team of Nittany Lions: "I'm tired of this Orange team! I'm tired of this Orange Stadium! I'm tired of seeing Orange! Let's go out there and kick the Orange out of them!" Coaches inspire teams.

Penn State did exactly that. The Lions took the second half kickoff and marched 60 yards, with Collins hitting Brady wide open in the end zone to make it 24-13. Engram later added a 15-yard TD catch, and the defense shut out the Vols. The tough PSU D sacked Shuler four times. The final score was Penn State 31, Tennessee 13.

This was one game that even the players felt the negative hype and it had irritated them. Perhaps it had even inspired them. When it was all over, Kerry Collins let it be known that the Penn State team was irritated by the lack of respect for Penn State in the pregame media coverage.

"We heard all week about Heath Shuler and everybody was underestimating us, "Collins said. "We thought all along that we were the better team. All we had to do was come out and prove it." Paterno himself felt obliged to add: "We never thought Tennessee was better than us."

1994 Penn State Football Season Coach Joe Paterno

The 1994 Penn State Nittany Lions football team was coached by Joe Paterno in his 29th year. Hard as it is to believe Penn State had another perfect record at 12-0. But, again, they were not national champions. Instead, they were bequeathed a # 2 ranking, and thus were denied another national championship. Life sometimes is not fair. Some say the reason PSU did not win the championship is that the Big Ten was not a respectable conference.

I don't buy that. I think there are dominating love-fests by the coaches and the AP and they feel a successful program such as Penn State does not need the benefit of the doubt. They were right to a degree but how about fairness? This is not the first time being cheated for Paterno nor for Penn State.

During the season, just two days after beating Ohio State, 63-14, -- yes, 64-13, Penn State University received 28 first-place votes in the Associated Press media poll and 32 first-place votes in the CNN/USA Today coaches' poll. They should have and did and they played flawless perfect ball the rest of the way.

Yet, somehow, two months later, after winning its final five games, Penn State got just 10 1/2 first-place votes in the AP poll and just eight first-place votes from the coaches. Meanwhile Nebraska got 51 1/2 first-place votes from the writers and 54 firsts from the coaches.

What happened?

Nebraska was declared #1 and Penn State got the runner up spot at #2. Nobody could tell Joe Paterno his team wasn't the 1994 national champions.

"Who said we didn't win a championship?" Paterno mused. "(A portion of) the media (and the coaches' panel) said we didn't win a championship. We think we won a championship. We did everything we could and we're going to assume we're champions. And that's not to take anything away from Nebraska.

"But I think this team did everything it could, and it's certainly a national-championship-caliber football team. We're going to assume that, that's all. We're going to treat ourselves as champions. I'm going to treat them as champions. And I know Penn State will treat them as champions."

Whatever Penn State Fans or Nebraska fans or anybody who watches a lot of football thought about the ranking situation, it did not matter. What was clear, however, was that the coaches and media members were too lazy to analyze all of the top teams in depth to help them form a proper conclusion. This surely was a reason to get rid of such a system. It had become a popularity contest.

Reality often does not matter when perception is the deciding factor in any difficulty. The perception at this time in 1994 for those with a sentimental affinity for Nebraska was that Nebraska had beaten Miami by one touchdown in the January 1995 Orange Bowl and that made them automatic national champions. It was as if Richard Nixon had made the proclamation again against Penn State.

This time, rather than president Nixon's exuberance with his buddies at a football game, it was a media-driven perception that negated anything Penn State might have done in the Rose Bowl or anything the Nittany Lions accomplished in their record-setting season.

Find me another team that played the likes of Penn State in a year other than 1994 and I will show you a national champion. It did not matter that Miami, ranked # 3 when they played Nebraska had lost to Washington, a team that had four losses.

Miami in 1994 was not what Miami once was. They were ranked #3. Oregon, Penn State's Rose Bowl foe was not what it once was either. But Miami is perceived as a football giant, while Oregon is looked on as a joke. However, Oregon defeated Washington, a team that had defeated Miami 21-7 but none of the pundits cared that Miami was no longer Miami!

There was no way Penn State could overcome that dichotomy of impressions. Facts were not permitted on the table. To this day, I wish the University put 1994 on the table as a national championship. The players and the coaches earned it but the university went with the establishment.

Neither Penn State nor Nebraska played much of a non-conference schedule. Their conferences were supposed to be tough enough. Their best wins were over Southern California and UCLA, respectively. Who wants to make a bid on the better team USC or UCLA? Was the Big ten a tougher conference in which to excel or was the Big 8?

Other than Colorado, which got to pound a beleaguered Notre Dame team in the Fiesta Bowl, the Big Eight was comprised of six stiffs. There was no excellence there.

The Conference's only other bowl teams, Kansas State and Oklahoma, lost their postseason games to Boston College and Brigham Young, respectively, by the combined score of 43-13. So, how good was the Big 8 in 1994 and why were they given so much preference over the Big Ten? Why did the Big Ten conference not fight harder to claim a win for PSU, a new member of their prestigious organization?

Conversely, the other Big Ten bowl teams - Michigan, Illinois, Wisconsin and Ohio State - were 3-1 in their bowls. Ohio State lost to Alabama, 24-17, in the final minute. The other three won their games by the combined score of 88-34. So, how could PSU, the Big Ten Champion, be shut out in 1994 in their finest season by a bunch of blowhards that seemed to like a great coach such as Tom Osborne more than a clear championship team coached by Joe Paterno? Say it ain't so, Joe!

1994 Games of the Season

All-Americans Bobby Engram (left) and Kerry Collins celebrate Penn State's thrilling 31-24 win at Michigan on October 15, 1994 in Penn State's first game in Ann Arbor. Engram and Collins were among five first-team All-Americans that led the Nittany Lions to Big Ten and Rose Bowl titles, becoming the first Big Ten team to finish 12-0.

On September 3 to open the season, #9 PSU played Minnesota at 8:00 PM at the Hubert H. Humphrey Metrodome, Minneapolis. It was not scheduled to be a blowout but it was nonetheless W (56–3).

On September 10 at 3:30 PM, a #8 ranked PSU beat #14 USC, a tough team always, at Beaver Stadium in University Park, PA. USC was never in the game. On September 17, Iowa played #6 PSU at

Beaver Stadium W (61–21). Then on September 24, at home, #5 ranked PSU shellacked Rutgers W (55–27) before 95,379.

On October 1, #4 PSU traveled to Franklin Field v Temple W (48–21). On October 15, playing #5 Michigan, a #3 ranked Nittany Lions team had its way with the Wolverines in a tough battle against a powerful Big Ten opponent at Michigan Stadium, Ann Arbor, MI. W (31–24). The attendance was 106,382 in the Big House!

On October 29 at 3:30 PM. Penn State played a powerhouse of a team ranked at #21. Ohio State played the #1 ranked Nittany Lions at Beaver Stadium and in the biggest upset of an Ohio State team ever, Penn State could not hold back in its leathering the Buckeyes on National TV W (63–14). OSU was not a bad team at all but PSU was that good.

It is a sweet enough victory to repeat what happened. Penn State handed Ohio State its worst defeat in 48 years in what remains one of the most satisfying victories ever for Lion fans. The lopsided win by the No. 1 Nittany Lions over the No. 21 Buckeyes was impressive enough to write home about. However, it was not impressive enough to keep Penn State on top of the next AP poll. Penn State went on to win its first Big Ten Championship, becoming the conference's first 12-0 team, but as noted finished No. 2 in the final polls.

On November 5, somehow PSU was now # 2 in the game v Indiana at Memorial Stadium at Bloomington, IN. It was close but all Penn State W (35–29). Big Ten teams were tough to beat as PSU found out. On November 12 at Memorial Stadium in Champaign, IL, PSU beat the Fighting Illini W (35–31). On November 19, PSU defeated without a doubt the Northwestern Wildcats at home W (45–17)

On November 26, Michigan State came to win at Beaver Stadium v #2 PSU at Beaver Stadium in University Park, PA. The Nittany Lions won decidedly W (59–31) in a high scoring game.

With an 11-0 record, Penn State was ready to win the Rose Bowl on January 2, 1995 to assure itself of a National Championship. The Nittany Lions had beaten every team that it had played and it had one game left, the Rose Bowl

Having won the Big Ten Championship in just its second year and nationally ranked for some reason at # 2 instead of # 1, already declared the Big Ten champion, PSU accepted the Rose Bowl offer to play Pac 10 leader #12 Oregon. Oregon was no worse or no better than Miami at the time but Oregon had three tough losses heading into the Bowl game.

When the Rose Bowl was over in Pasadena California, shown on ABC and seen before 102,247 in attendance, Penn State had its way with Oregon W (38-20). Yet, the pundits were not swayed even a little.

This was such a great season, let's talk about it just a little bit more:

Penn State's Kerry Collins—:"Lots more than just a quarterback."

1995 Penn State Football Season Coach Joe Paterno

The 1995 Penn State Nittany Lions football team was coached by Joe Paterno in his thirtieth year as head coach. His PSU Nittany Lions had a great season at 9-3, and their record on the Big Ten was 5-3.

On September 9 v Texas Tech at Beaver Stadium, PSU beat the Red Raiders W 24–23. On September 16 at home PSU ranked # 7 at the time beat Temple in a mismatch W (66–14). Then, on September 23

@ 7:30 PM at Rutgers, played at Giants Stadium in East Rutherford, NJ # 6 PSU beat the Scarlet Knights W 59–34. Then, at the end of September (30), Wisconsin tried to beat # 6 PSU at Beaver Stadium and succeeded in a close match L (9–1).

On October 7, #5 Ohio State remembered how bad they were beaten in the prior year and the Buckeyes would have no more as they beat # 12 PSU at Beaver Stadium in a very close match L (25–28). On October 14, #20 PSU played Purdue in Ross–Ade Stadium • West Lafayette, IN, and squeaked out a win W (26-23). #18 Iowa was ready to take on # 19 PSU at Kinnick Stadium in Iowa City, IA but PSU won the game W (41–27) before 70,397. On October 28, Indiana played #16 PSU at Beaver Stadium and could not keep up, W (45–21)

On November 4, a good winning #6 Northwestern team took on #12 PSU at Ryan Field in Evanston, IL, and PSU lost to the Wildcats on ABC L (10–21).

On November 18 at 12:00 PM, #12 Michigan planned to beat #19 PSU at Beaver Stadium in University Park, PA on ABC TV, yet PSU prevailed before 96,677 W (27–17).

The Snow Bowl v Michigan Pre-Cleanup

To many football historians who love Beaver Stadium games, this match is simply remembered as "The Snow Bowl." Three days before the game, a surprise 18-inch snowfall made it necessary to use hundreds of paid volunteers to clear the field. But with snow piles all around them, 80,000 freezing fans watched holder Joe Nastasi score a two-yard touchdown off a fake field goal with 2:40 left to secure the Lions' second of three consecutive victories over the tough Michigan Wolverines.

Michigan State came so quickly afterwards at Spartan Stadium, after a long ride that the Lions were ready and PSU beat the Spartans W (24-20).

Having such a good year, 8-3, #15 PSU got to play in the Outback Bowl on January 1, 1996 at 11:00 AM v #16 Auburn in Tampa Stadium •at Tampa, FL. Penn State was up for the match and won handily W (43–14 (before 65,313. The Nittany Lions finished 9-3, #12 in the Coach's poll and #12 in the AP. Everybody was looking for 1996

1996 Penn State Football Season Coach Joe Paterno

The 1996 Penn State Nittany Lions football team was coached by Joe Paterno in his thirty-first year. Penn STtae had another great winning season with just a few disappointing games.

The 1996 season was also notable as it marked the end of ties in college football, as an overtime system was put into place across all of Division I-A. Penn State's first OT game came in 2000 v Iowa. The 1995 season had overtime rules, but only for postseason games.

The Bowl Alliance was formed to make post-season championships fairer but it did not really work well and over time the current BCS plan was adopted. For example, in 1996, there was a large controversy when #5 BYU was robbed of a spot in a Bowl Alliance game, as they were snubbed in favor of lower ranked teams from Bowl Alliance conferences. Believe it or not Congress got involved.

The Nittany Lions faced off against USC in the Kickoff Classic on August 25 before 77,716 at Giants Stadium in East Rutherford, NJ. PSU won the match W 24-7).

Player Highlights Curtis Enis

They called it Curtis Enis' coming-out party came when, in East Rutherford, NJ, the powerful sophomore tailback racked up 241 yards and three touchdowns on 27 carries in his first career start. The Trojans didn't score until pouncing on a fumble in the end zone in the final 30 seconds of the game. On November. 4: 1996, in his first try, Curtis Enis lifted #11 PSU over #7 Southern Cal by a score of 24-7. It was just the start of his college career.

As PSU's main running back while he played for the Lions from 1995 to 1997, Curtis Enis chalked up two 1,000+ yard seasons, including 1,369 yards and 19 TDs in 1997. He was 6th in Heisman Trophy voting in 1997. He was the 5th overall pick of the 1998 NFL Draft, though he played just 3 years in the NFL, retiring after the 2000 season because of knee problems. His best NFL season was 1999. He was a star. He rushed for 916 yards and 3 TDs.

Enis was not attentive to high school requirements. Coach Paterno made him attend The Kiski School in rural Pennsylvania for a year before enrolling at Penn State. At the Kiski School, Enis was able to work with Enis to get his grades and SAT score he needed to qualify.

Ironically, many Ohio State fans were upset that he chose to leave the state to attend college. There is some humor in how Ohio recruited Enis. The OSU recruiting computer had a few typos for example, and when they sent him a letter it was addressed to "Curtis Phenis." When they fixed the last name, they changed his first name to Chris. It has been reported that when Enis took a visit to Ohio State's campus, no one seemed to know who he was.

Enis was a standout player at Penn State for sure. With 3 seasons and two 1000 yarders, he was more than special. He was 6'0" and weighed a muscular 235 lbs. They say he was quite a load at running back. He earned All-American honors his junior year at Penn State and finished 6th in voting for the 1997 Heisman Trophy. He decided to leave school after that season and enter the 1998 NFL Draft, where he was selected 5th overall by the Bears. He was that impressive.

After the Kickoff Classic, it was back to every day games. On September 7, in the home opener, a # 7 ranked PSU defeated Louisville at Beaver Stadium W (24-7). In another home game on September 14, Northern Illinois came to Beaver Stadium for the first time and were shut out in a blowout by the Nittany Lions W (49-0). On September 21, PSU beat Temple at Giants Stadium W (41-0) in a shutout.

On September 28, #3 PSU defeated Wisconsin in a close Big Ten match at Camp Randall Stadium in Madison, WI W (23-20). On October 5, #4 PSU lost to a very tough #3 Ohio State Team coached by John Cooper at Ohio Stadium in Columbus, OH before 94,241 L (7-38). This was followed on October 12 with a win against Purdue at Beaver Stadium W (31-14). An unranked Iowa team beat Penn State the following week on October 19 in a nail-biter match at Beaver Stadium L (20-21)

On October 26, the #17 Nittany Lions traveled to Memorial Stadium in Bloomington IN, to beat Indiana W (48–26). The next week, November 2, at home, #15 PSU beat #11 Northwestern W34–9) before 96,596. On November 16, the #11 Nittany Lions traveled beat #16 Michigan at the Big House, Michigan Stadium in Ann Arbor, MI W (29-17). This victory followed the very next week at home by another against another Michigan team, Michigan State in a close call win W (32-29).

At 10-2, #7 ranked PSU had a great year and were invited to play on January 1, 1997 at 8:00 PM vs. #20 Texas in Sun Devil Stadium, Tempe, AZ, in the Fiesta Bowl. The attendance of 65,106 saw the Nittany Lions beat the Longhorns W (38–15).

1997 Penn State Football Season Coach Joe Paterno

The 1997 Penn State Nittany Lions football team was coached by Joe Paterno in his 32nd year. Penn State had a respectable season overall at 9-3 (6-2 in the Big Ten). The Nittany Lions were ranked #17 by the Coaches and #16 by the AP. Their season was capped off by being invited to the Citrus Bowl in Orlando but on January 1, 1998, the #11 Lions were beaten in this game by #6 ranked Florida L (6-21).

The home season began on September 6 as #1 ranked PSU defeated Pittsburgh W (34–17) before 97,115. On September 13, PSU beat Temple at home W (52-10). On September 20, still ranked at #1, the Nittany Lions beat Louisville at Cardinal Stadium in Louisville, KY W 57–21. After this convincing win, PSU fell to #2 in the rankings as they prepared to face Illinois in Champagne on October 4. The #2 Nittany Lions beat the Fighting Illini W (41-6) to hold second place.

The real big test of the season was next as a tough Ohio State team came to Beaver Stadium on October 11, and were beaten back by the Lions W (31-27). Now, back at #1, Penn State barely beat Minnesota on October 18 W (16-15). The closeness of this game put PSU in 2nd place as the Nittany Lions played at Northwestern and beat the Wildcats in a tug of war W (30-27).

Still ranked #2 with a 7-0 record, PSU faced #4 Michigan on November 8, and were beaten by the Wolverines L (8-34). Then at #6, on November 15, PSU played #19 Purdue at Ross-Ade Stadium and beat the Boilermakers W (42-7). The Nittany Lions followed this win with another on November 22 at home against #24 Wisconsin W (35-10). Then, it was off to East Lansing, Michigan on November 29 to lose to the unranked Spartans of Michigan State in a blow-out L (14-49).

Not having recovered from the two late-season crippling losses, #11 Penn State lost the Citrus Bowl to # 6 ranked Florida L (6-21).

1998 Penn State Football Season Coach Joe Paterno

The 1998 Penn State Nittany Lions football team was coached by Joe Paterno in his 33rd year. Penn State had another very respectable season overall at 9-3 (5-3 in the Big Ten). The Nittany Lions were ranked #15 by the Coaches and #17 by the AP. Their season was capped off by being invited to the Outback Bowl on January 1, 1999 in Raymond James Stadium in Tampa Florida where they beat #22 Kentucky W (26-14).

On September 5, #13 ranked Penn State played #21 Southern Miss at home and defeated the Golden Eagles W (34-6). On September 12 at home, the #9 Nittany Lions ran roughshod over Bowling Green W (48-3). On September 19, #8 PSU beat Pittsburgh next at Pitt

Stadium W (20-13). After Pittsburgh, the Big Ten Games began in force with #7 Ohio State first in waiting to play in Columbus. The Buckeyes played at their peak game and beat a 3-0 PSU L (9-28) before 93,479. Only Penn State and Ohio and Michigan had such huge stadiums.

On October 10, the # 13 ranked Lions flew out to the Hubert H. Humphrey Metrodome to beat a tough Minneapolis team W (27-17). Back at home the next week On October 17, PSU beat Purdie W (31-13).

On October 31, at Beaver Stadium, the Nittany Lions pitched a shutout against Illinois W (27-0). This game is known for LaVar's leap. If there is one single, memorable but isolated moment frozen in time it was LaVar Arrington's leap over the Illinois offensive line the instant the ball was snapped, tackling the runner in the backfield the millisecond the quarterback gave him the ball. That moment early in the third quarter when the score was already 21-0, had absolutely no impact on the game or the season but it will be forever known as "LaVar's Leap."

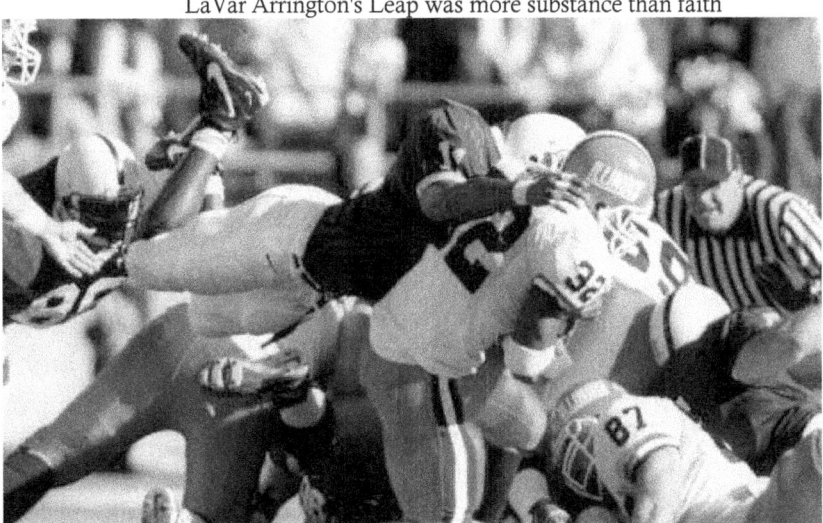

LaVar Arrington's Leap was more substance than faith

Always tough at home or away, Michigan was next on November 7 and they beat the Lions in a shutout L (0-27) at the Big House in Ann Arbor Michigan before a massive crowd of 111,019.

On November 14, an always scrappy Northwestern team were beaten by #19 Penn State at Beaver Stadium before an overflow crowd of 96,382. Then a week later on November 21 at #13 Wisconsin, the #15 Nittany Lions avoided a shutout but lost L (3-24). In a late season game v Michigan State at home, #23 ranked PSU dominated the shootout W (51-28). Overall, the #22 ranked PSU team was 8-3 and qualified to play unranked Kentucky in the Outback Bowl, winning the contest W (26-14)

1999 Penn State Football Season Coach Joe Paterno

The 1999 Penn State Nittany Lions football team was coached by Joe Paterno in his thirty-fourth year. This year the Nittany Lions had a nice 10-3 record (5-3 in the Big Ten), ranked # 11 in both polls. Their record was fine enough for a bowl game and they beat Texas A&M on December 28 in the Alamo Bowl in Texas W (24-0).

LaVar Arrington a Great PSU Linebacker

LaVar Arrington was one of The Lions best linebackers of all time. There is surely lots more that can be said as Arrington is one of the greatest Linebackers from PSU. Being a great linebacker was a big deal at Penn State but the University sure had its share.

LaVar Arrington was born in Pittsburgh, Pennsylvania. He played linebacker and running back at North Hills Senior High School in Pittsburgh. He was always a standout. After his senior year, he was awarded the 1996 Parade National Player of the Year, the Bobby Dodd National Offensive Player of the Year, the Gatorade Player of the Year and USA Today Pennsylvania Player of the Year.

He became the second player in Pennsylvania Class 4-A history to rush for more than 4,000 career yards. Yes, he was a running back. Before Arrington, PSU was breeding linebackers so it is not a phenomenon that the coaches picked Arrington out of the crowd to make him an outside linebacker. They bred another great player.

The 1999 Games of the Season

PSU was invited to the Pigskin Classic and so #3 ranked Penn State began its season on August 28 at Beaver Stadium against #4 ranked

Arizona. The Lions controlled the game and got the win W (41-7) before 97,168. On September 4, Akron took a try at the # 2 Lions at Beaver Stadium. PSU won in a high scoring game W (70-24).

Pittsburgh then played the #2 ranked Nittany Lions on September 11 at Beaver Stadium and Penn State won its third in a row W (20-17) to start the season. PSU then traveled to Miami before the summer was over to play the Hurricanes in the Orange Bowl. The Nittany Lions beat #8 Miami in a very close game W (27-23) and were now at 4 wins no losses for the season ranked at #2.

The Big Ten games began with Indiana on September 25 at home W 45-24). Next, on October 9 after a bye week was Iowa in Kinnick Stadium, Iowa City. Penn State triumphed again bring the season record to 6-0, and holding on to 2nd place. PSU played Purdue next on October 30 at Ross–Ade Stadium in West Lafayette, IN and won again W (31-25).

It was a very good year and the next week's game on October 30 at Illinois in Memorial Stadium • Champaign, IL, would add to #2 PSU's wins with a W (27-7) victory over the Fighting Illini. This was a special game, especially because of the hard play of Defensive End Courtney Brown which was simply outstanding.

For the third time in the last four weeks that season, a Nittany Lion—this time Courtney Brown was selected Big Ten Defensive Player of the Week, with defensive end. Courtney Brown earning the honor on October 30, 1999.

Brown was honored for his outstanding play in Penn State's 27-7 win at Illinois. The senior from Alvin, S.C. once again was sensational, surpassing his career-high with four sacks for minus-25 yards to become the school career leader with 32 sacks. Larry Kubin tallied 30 from 1977-80. A semifinalist for the Lombardi Award and a candidate for the Bronko Nagurski Trophy and Chuck Bednarik Award, Brown made eight tackles, second-highest of his career, forced a fumble and broke up a pass vs. the Illini.

The Nittany Lion defense had been ferocious the prior four weeks, including 24 sacks, with Brown one of the primary reasons for the unit's success. Against Illinois, Penn State allowed a touchdown, 113 yards and six first downs in the first quarter, but then virtually shut down the hosts, permitting only 135 yards, no points and six first downs over the final three quarters. The Illini gained 248 total yards and were 8 of 31 passing for 107 yards. In the second period, UI gained five yards on 12 plays and did not have a first down and in the third stanza, Illinois gained 29 yards on its first five possessions while the Lions were scoring 17 points to take a 24-7 lead.

Only one college player in the last 11 years -- former Buffalo star Khalil Mack -- has compiled more career tackles for loss. Penn State's had some dynamic defenders over the years but Brown took playmaking to another level.

Following the Purdue game, Brown received a ringing endorsement from Joe Paterno: "Courtney Brown is a great football player. I don't like to plug kids, but if he doesn't get the Lombardi Award there's something wrong with somebody."

The Rest of the 1999 Season

Penn State (9-0, 5-0) was ranked No. 2 and hosted Minnesota (5-3, 2-3) the following Saturday at 12:10 p.m. EST in an espn2 national telecast.

At eight and zero, Penn State was thinking championship but when Minnesota came to Penn State on November 6, the Gophers were thinking upset and they got it L (23-24). #16 Michigan added to #6 PSU's woes the following week at home in another close match L (27-31) Just five points separated PSU from an undefeated season at this point. Michigan State took the *special* out of this otherwise great season when it defeated the Lions at Spartan Stadium L (28-35) before 74,231.

#13 PSU was ready to play in the Alamo dome v #18 Texas A&M in the Alamo Bowl on December 28, and they won the game easily It sure was not a bad season. In fact, it was a very good season but with all the losses v Big Ten teams, PSU not only missed the National Championship but also the Big Ten Championship despite its fine (10-3) record (5-3 v Big Ten Conference teams).

2000 Penn State Football Season Coach Joe Paterno

The 2000 Penn State Nittany Lions football team's head coach was Joe Paterno. This was another one of those building years (5-7 with 4-4 in the Big Ten). It was just the second losing season for Coach Paterno in his 35-year stint so far at Penn State. Long time defensive coordinator Jerry Sandusky retired before the season began and he was replaced by Defensive coach Tom Bradley.

Penn State, ranked #15 to begin the season agreed to be in the annual Kickoff Classic held at Giants Stadium on August 2th. The Opponent was #22 USC. The Nittany Lions lost the game L (5-29). PSU would lose to Toledo the following Saturday, September 2 at home L (6-24). It took 'til the third win to get a win and it was at home against Louisiana Tech as PSU prevailed in a blow-out 67-7. After two weeks of losses the win felt pretty good. The good feeling would not last long as PSU traveled to Pittsburgh's Three River Stadium and were beaten by the Panthers on September 16 L (0-12).

Unranked and playing with a at 1-3 record, Penn State faced off with Ohio State on September 23 in Columbus. The Buckeyes dominated the Nittany Lions L (6-45). Purdue, a tough team in its own right came to Beaver Stadium on September 30, and lost to the Nittany Lions in a close match W (22-20). On October 7, PSU traveled to the Hubert H. Humphrey Metrodome in Minneapolis, MN and were beaten by the Gophers L (16-25). The Fighting Illini were next at home on October 21, and PSU collected a win against Illinois W (39-25).

On October 28 at 7:00 PM at Indiana, PSU played a close game and beat the Hoosiers W (27–24). A determined Iowa team came to Beaver Stadium to play some tough football on November 4 and beat the Nittany Lions L (23-26) in double overtimes. As of 1996, there would be no more ties.

On November 11, unranked PSU played at Michigan Stadium (The Big House) before 110,803. The #20 Wolverines beat Penn State L (11-33). The following week, November 18, Michigan State played the Lions at Beaver Stadium. Penn State triumphed in a nice season ending win. W (42-23).

2001 Penn State Football Season Coach Joe Paterno

The 2001 Penn State Nittany Lions football team was coached by Joe Paterno in his 36th season with the Lions. JoePa would coach for ten more seasons.

Penn State did not play Big Ten teams Minnesota and Purdue this particular year. Also, due to the events of 9/11, the Virginia game was rescheduled from September 13, 2001, to December 1, 2001.

Much to Nittany Lions Fans chagrin, this would be the second of two-rebuilding seasons. This team had one less loss than the 2000 team, finishing at 5-6 (4-4 in the Big Ten). If you'll look ahead, the agony ends in 2002 as PSU works its way back into the top twenty. But, not this year.

In a Baptism of Fire, The Nittany Lions began the 2001 season on September 1, against a #2 ranked Miami team at home before a home crowd of 109,313 in the newly renovated and expanded Beaver Stadium. Miami came in ready to go and beat the Lions L (7-33).

After the break for the country to heal from the 9/11 2001 terrorist disaster, PSU resumed play on September 22 at home and were beaten by Wisconsin L (6-18). On September 29 at Kinnick Stadium Iowa City, IA, PSU lost its third straight game against no wins yet for the season. L (18-24). On October 20 at Northwestern, the Nittany Lions finally came alive and beat the Wildcats W (38-35) in a close shootout W (38-35).

The Big Ten overall had a bad year in 2001. #12 Illinois (7-1) won the Conference. #20 Michigan came in second at 6-2. They were the only ranked Big Ten Teams. I 2001. Ohio State was 5-3 in third place, and PSU was 4-4, tied with Purdue and Iowa.

On October 27, Ohio State played the Nittany Lions at Beaver Stadium before 108,327. Penn State would not say no and beat the Buckeyes in a very close game W (29-27). This went down as one of the best games ever at Beaver Stadium.

PSU v Ohio State Oct 27, 2001 PSU Win 29-27 --- Johnson makes catch

The Beaver Stadium faithful honored their legendary coach when the Nittany Lions rallied from a 9-27 deficit to beat the Buckeyes. With this win, Joe Paterno passed Alabama's Bear Bryant as the winningest coach in major college football with 324 victories. Write-ups of the event after the game note that the genuine love and heartfelt emotion that flowed between the coach and the fans in the post-game ceremonies will always be remembered by those who were there.

Let's look at the specifics of the game. Penn State first received the kickoff. Paterno decided to start Matt Senneca instead of Zack Mills and of course a few Lions fans were upset. Senneca may have been a bit shaky from his concussion. He struggled on the first drive. Ohio State wasted no time when they gained possession. Their quarterback, Steve Bellisari quickly threw a 66-yard post to WR Michael Jenkins behind the secondary for the score.

Hoping to come back quickly, JoePa took Senneca from the game and put in Mills on the second possession. Things immediately went Penn State's way. Bryant Johnson made a leaping catch for 30-yards. But, then Mills got pasted on an option pitch which saw RB Larry Johnson gaining 31-yards.

There was no more offense left once PSU got inside the ten but Robbie Gould brought in three points from 23-yards out to make the score 7-3.

The Lions held strong on the next series, but OSU punted a huge one and pinned PSU inside the 10. Mills took off on a 5 for 5 passing trek reaching Eric McCoo on a nice 35-yard touch. Again, the drive stalled just outside the red zone, and Gould then hit his career-long field goal of 46 to bring PSU within one point.

DE Michael Haynes's got a sack on 3rd-down and this ended OSU's next effort. The Lions then went for broke. Mills threw a "to who?" pass under pressure and it was picked off by LB Cie Grant, who brought it back into PSU territory. Bellisari was effective running 18 yards, but the Buckeyes stalled.

Tressel opted for a field goal on 4th and 1, and Mike Nugent nailed a 28-yard field goal. OSU now had a 10-6 lead early in the second quarter.

PSU then put together a nice drive. It featured completions to TE John Gilmore and Bryant Johnson and the drive stalled again but Robbie Gould made a booming 46-yarder into the wind to bring the scoring difference to 1 point.

Ohio got one more possession in the first half, and they clicked. Bellisari hit Jenkins again on a post route for 68 yards and the Buckeyes were on the Penn State 2. The Nittany Lions defense again became a wall and Tressel's team from the end zone. The field goal was like an extra point and the Buckeyes lead 13-9 at the half.

The third quarter was dull with little action but that was after the second play for Ohio State when Jonathan Wells went like a dose of salt through the middle of the defense for a 65-yard touchdown. In just 57 seconds, the Buckeyes had a commanding 20-9 lead. Penn State continued its turnover problem just a few plays into their first drive. WR Eddie Drummond let a wide-open reception bounce off his helmet and into the hands of OSU's Derek Ross for a 45-yard touchdown return. The birds were booing as the 1-4 Lions fell behind by 27-9.

Senneca had watched Mills carry the team on his shoulders but there was always a show stopper. On the next PSU drive after the OSU touchdown, PSU executed an option run to the short side of the field, Mills saw a gap and leapt over his own downed lineman five yards down the field. The jump was unexpected by the safety and there was hesitation which permitted Mills to bounce off of tackle towards the sideline.

From there, the fleet-footed Mills trekked 69 yards with defenders almost catching up—but he got the score. The PSU attempt for two failed. Penn State and the boo-birds were now smiling and there appeared to be a change in momentum.

Lydell Ross fumbled in PSU territory and the Lions kept the momentum rolling. Mills rolled left and hit Bryant Johnson who dove for the 33-yard reception. One play later, Mills looked right and threw to the left, finding another Johnson—Tony, this time—just past the goal for a 26-yard score. The Lions were still down 27-22, but they could taste a difference in the game. Zack Mills had changed it all by taking the Nittany Lions 124 yards while chalking up 13 big points.

After the kickoff, Shawn Mayer and Anthony Adams sacked Bellisari to force a Buckeye punt. Penn State was on the move again. On the first play of the fourth quarter, Mills did the impossible. When the snap sailed over his head, he picked it up on the bounce and ran from the rush. He spotted a wide-open FB R.J. Luke, and the young QB Mills hit him with a perfect pass.

Luke did his part by running thirty yards down the sideline. On the next snap, Mills tossed a strike to Eric McCoo on a wheel route for a 15-yard touchdown. After having given up two touchdowns in the first five minutes of the second half, Penn State scored three of their own in the next ten—29-27. Penn State had the lead with the whole fourth quarter left to play.

Ohio State played back and forth ball with the Lions until late in the fourth quarter. Then, it got dangerous as OSU gained yardage each play down the field with impressive catches by WR Jenkins. All of Beaver Stadium including the boo-birds were holding their breath with just a two-point lead.

With OSU heading for a score on the PSU 32, an offsides call on PSU forced the Lions to give the ball back after a second Israel interception and it enabled the Buckeyes to keep moving. The PSU defense was on alert. Michael Haynes banged in and got a sack on Bellisari again, and the defense forced an Ohio State field goal attempt. The kicker, OSU's Nugent had trouble with the kick but got it off with a low trajectory. DB Bryan Scott jumped way up for the game-saving block. Penn State then had to hold the lead for just 2:55 more.

Larry Johnson rushed for one first down, and then on the next third down, Mills scrambled for 35 yards and stayed in bounds at the end of the play. Tressel's had no more timeouts. Three rushing plays later and Penn State had won a thriller and Joe Paterno got his Gatorade and win #324 of his career.

After an emotional embrace between Joe and wife Sue at midfield, players carried their leader from the field, and Penn State unveiled a 7-foot bronze statue of Paterno to commemorate the milestone. This bitter PSU season was sweetened by this one record-setting Saturday in Happy Valley.

For the rest of the season, with Zack Mills at the helm, PSU looked like a much better team. The Nittany Lions won three of their last five, which included another great comeback effort at Michigan State. The two losses were heartbreaking nail-biters against Rose-Bowl bound Illinois and Virginia.

In one of the write-ups on this game the one from the nittanylionsden.com was a wonderful postscript to Joe Paterno and the contrast between the coaches and their travails.

"Success may have been Tressel's after 2002, but the man on the other side of the field from Tressel in 2001 gave him a blueprint for success with honor; Paterno never fell under NCAA investigation for academic, financial, or recruiting illegalities in all his years of coaching. Yet even while he did things the right way, without any stigma as a cheater, Paterno found his name at the top of all the coaching record books."

JoePa had eclipsed the coaching record of the great Bear Bryant.

On November 3 at home, PSU beat Southern Miss W (38-20. On November 10, it was off to Illinois, the Conference Champions and a close defeat at the hands of the Fighting Illini L (28-33). The Hoosiers were next to play on the huge new Beaver Stadium field on November 17. Penn State prevailed in this game W (28-14).

On November 24 PSU played Michigan State in Spartan Stadium East Lansing, MI and won a close one (W 42–37) bringing the record to 5-5 on the season. On December 1, the make-up game from the 9/11 cancellation was played against Virginia in Scott Stadium, Charlottesville, VA. Penn State lost to the Wahoos in the last game of the 2001 season L (14–20).

Chapter 9 The Joe Paterno Era From 2002 to 2011

Coach # 14

2002	Joe Paterno	9-4	(5-3 Big 10)
2003	Joe Paterno	3-9	(1-7 Big 10)
2004	Joe Paterno	4-7	(2-6 Big 10)
2005	Joe Paterno	11-1	(7-1 Big 10)
2006	Joe Paterno	9-4	(5-3 Big 10)
2007	Joe Paterno	9-4	(4-4 Big 10)
2008	Joe Paterno	11-2	(7-1 Big 10)
2009	Joe Paterno	11-2	(6-2 Big 10)
2010	Joe Paterno	7-5	(4-3 Big 10)
2011	Joe Paterno	8-1	(5-0 Big 10)
2011	Tom Bradley	1-3	(1-2 Big 10)

JoePa Coached 46 great seasons 1966 to 2010 & part of 2011. This 15-year period, we find some of JoePa's worst but mostly his best. Nobody could make the team be a contender as well as Joe Paterno!

The overall record was 11-2, (6-2 in the Big Ten). Their record included a nice win against Texas in the Fiesta Bowl W (38-15). Penn State finished in the top ten in both polls at # 7.

2002 Penn State Football Season Coach Joe Paterno

The 2002 Penn State Nittany Lions football team was coached by Joe Paterno in his thirty-seventh year as head coach. The team improved substantially over 2000 and 2001, finishing the full season at 9-4 (5-3 Big Ten) and #15 in the Coach's Poll and #16 in the AP. Ranked #10 at game time, PSU was invited to the Citrus Bowl against #19 Auburn. In a game played on January 1 2003, in which neither team showed much offense, Penn State scored just four points less than the Tigers and lost the Bowl game in Orlando, FL, L (9-13).

On August 31, Penn State began its season at home defeating Central Florida W (27-24). #8 Nebraska played the Nittany Lions on before 110,753 on September 14, W (40-7). none of Beaver Stadium's treasure games the largest crowd of Penn Staters in Beaver Stadium history--110,753 were treated to a great football feast. The fans had to believe they were experiencing one of the greatest Nittany Lion games ever as No. 25 Penn State simply clobbered No. 8 Nebraska in a sizzling night time atmosphere weeks before the leaves would even begin to fall.

Like all routs, the game quickly lost its luster as the Nittany Lions pummeled a Nebraska team that went on to finish with its worst record (7-7) in 41 years. Regardless, all wins feel good.

On September 21, at home. Louisiana Tech was defeated by Penn State W (49-17). Before the game, the only tie-breaker game ever for PSU had been at Iowa and the Hawkeyes did it again on September 28 at Beaver Stadium—this time the tie was settled in just one controversial OT L (35-42). Let's look at this great PSU game though it ended in a loss, in some detail below:

PSU v IOWA, The Striped Shirts Won?
Iowa 42, Penn State 35, OT (2002)

At State College, this game was a heartbreaker for sure. Even though this game ended up in a PSU loss doesn't matter to the greatness of the game. It was full of fireworks, crazy drama, and an improbable comeback that almost was enough for the Nittany Lions.

The pundits agree that this outing against Penn State was the closest call a fine Iowa team had during what would be an undefeated Big Ten season. Yet, it looked like a rout early. Brad Banks and Dallas Clark led the Hawkeyes to a 35-13 lead more than halfway through the fourth quarter. There is no way to find much solace in that score.

It had been 23-0 at one point and probably should have been 30-0 with six minutes still left in the second quarter. However, the Big Ten officiating crew blew a call while blowing dead Antwan Allen's strip of Larry Johnson and the resultant fumble return for a TD. The officials had not ended their impact on the game.

Iowa could have punched PSU in the face for a knockout on two other occasions but Clark botched a would-be TD catch that was picked off in the end zone for a touchback and the Hawkeyes later fumbled at the Penn State 1 yard line. Tough winning when the players are nervous or they do not produce.

Iowa had been completely dominating this year against the Lions before PSU quarterback Zack Mills found a way to get Penn State back in it against all odds. Mills and PSU were nothing short of spectacular. The quarterback finished with a school-record 399 yards passing and four TDs.

The pundits replay of the game say that Mills had gotten frustrated with the cumbersome play-calling system that had been routinely delivered signals from the sideline too late. So, he decided to call his own plays at the line and the Lions got on a big roll.

Twenty-two straight points later, a spree that included a 36-yard Mills-to-Larry Johnson TD pass that ignited the rally and an 8-yard TD pass to Bryant Johnson with 1:20 in regulation that capped it, the Lions had incredibly forced overtime against the almost toughest team in the nation.

That's when the officials stepped back in to ruin a few students playing a game of football. Iowa scored 6 and 1 on its first OT possession thanks partly to an 11-yard bobbled catch by Maurice Brown ruled complete. Then the striped guys ruled a second-down catch by Tony Johnson at the 2 out of bounds. Mills ended up missing Bryant Johnson on fourth down to end it. The milk was sour and the stripes had made it sour but PSU most often does not complain when it losses—just we the faithful. This time was different.

Even when the game was over, the action wasn't. An incensed 75-year-old Joe Paterno, rightfully sprinted down the field to head referee Dick Honig. He grabbed the ref to speak to him as he entered the south tunnel just to vent in his ear. This game and another one full of gaffes at Michigan two weeks later are generally credited with creating college replay review.

We all could do better but the striped guys need to have their own version of replays!

On October 5, the #20 ranked Lions then traveled to Camp Randall Stadium in Madison, WI and beat the #19 ranked Badgers in a close match W (34-21). Always tough #13 Michigan then beat the Nittany Lions by just three points L (24-27) at the Big House before 111,502. Paterno's teams most often won and when they lost, they rarely were taken prisoners. There are so many one point to one touchdown losses that it makes one wonder how great a coach Joe Paterno really was. I know I am more impressed reading his record post facto and I was already impressed.

On October 19, unranked Northwestern scheduled a Big 10 opportunity to take down the Lions at Beaver Stadium but the Wildcats were not wild enough. Before 108,853, Penn State shut out and blew-out the fire in Wildcats W (49-0). Somehow no matter who was the coach Ohio State had a great team. The Buckeyes almost always gave Paterno's teams a game if not a loss.

The story was the same on October 26 at Ohio Stadium in Columbus, OH for this long-time rivalry game. Ohio State at #4 and

PSU at #18 squared off for the defensive battle. The Buckeyes persevered and got the win by six points L (7-13).

On November 2, at home, PSU recovered and beat the Fighting Illini of Illinois, W (18-7) Two weeks later, on November 16, Indiana played #16 Penn State on their home field in Bloomington and were beaten by the hard-charging defense and high scoring offense of the Nittany Lions W (58-25). In between on November 9 at home, Penn State beat Virginia W (35-14). Michigan State is nobody's pushover team but the determined #15 PSU Nittany Lions took on the Spartans at Beaver Stadium on November 23 and could not stop scoring W (61-7).

With a big win at Michigan State, and a five-and-a-half-week rest, some of the fire just was not there on January 1, 2003 at 1:00 PM when #10 PSU went against #19 Auburn in the Citrus Bowl at Orlando, FL. It was also called the Capital One Bowl. It was an exciting game for 66,334 fans and for a home ABC TV audience of millions. Everything was perfect but the outcome as Penn State's offense could not muster much L (9-13) in a 4-point loss.

Player Highlights Larry Johnson

Larry Johnson was an exciting Penn State football player at Tailback and he was accorded many honors for his great work. In 2002, he was selected by the Football Coaches, Associated Press, Football Writers, The Sporting News and Walter Camp. That is a lot of honors. He was also an All-American Selection for 2002.

Johnson also was the recipient of the Maxwell and Walter Camp Player-of-the-Year Awards and the Doak Walker Award, presented to the nation's top running back. He was third in balloting for the Heisman Trophy and was the Chevrolet National Offensive Player-of-the-Year.

Adding to the recognition for his great years was a unanimous first-team All-Big Ten selection.

Nebraska vs. Penn State 2002
Penn State's Larry Johnson pulls away from Nebraska defender

Johnson became just the ninth player in NCAA Division I-A history—and the first in the 107-year history of the Big Ten Conference -- to rush for more than 2,000 yards in the regular-season. He finished the season with 2,087 yards on 271 carries, for an outstanding 7.7 average, and 20 rushing touchdowns.

This effort put him on the top in the whole nation in rushing (160.5 ypg) and all-purpose yardage (204.2). He was fourth in scoring (10.8 ppg). He became the first Nittany Lion to lead the nation in rushing or all-purpose yardage and joined placekicker Matt Bahr (1978) as the only Penn Staters to lead the nation in two statistical categories in the same season.

Johnson shattered the Penn State game rushing record three times and blew by the 200-yard mark on four occasions, becoming the first Lion ever to post four 200-yard games in a season or career. His final record-breaking effort was a spectacular 327 yards at Indiana. He also tallied 279 yards against Illinois, 257 against Northwestern and 279 yards -- all in the first half -- in his home-finale with Michigan State.

Johnson posted eight 100-yard rushing games on the year and averaged an all-time Big Ten-best 8.8 yards per carry and 183.1 yards in eight conference games. His 2,655 all-purpose yards in 2002 shattered the Penn State record by more than 800 yards and were the fifth-highest total in NCAA history.

His 5,045 career all-purpose yards also were a school record. Chosen the Senior Bowl MVP, Johnson was selected by the Kansas City Chiefs in the first round of the 2003 National Football League Draft. He has played five seasons (2003-07) with the Chiefs and was selected All-Pro in 2005 and 2006. He set a National Football League record in 2006 for the most carries in a season. He had some issues with the Chiefs and did not play for a while.

From 2009, to 2011, Johnson met some good fortune and played with the Bengals, Redskins and the Dolphins at the end of his career, making at least twelve more $million and then he wrapped up his career in 2011.

2003 Penn State Football Season Coach Joe Paterno

The 2003 Penn State Nittany Lions football team's head coach was Joe Paterno in his thirty-eighth year. I bet JoePa in reflection would have still coached this year even though it was his worst ever. It was one of the worst seasons in PSU history. I guess if you bring home a lot of big ones, having a season in which there appears to be no harvest is expected. But, Penn State Fans get agitated when the W's are not there in the column.

Realistically all home teams feel the same. Our coach is supposed to win. Wins rarely happened in 2003. In a word, the year stunk with a 3-9 record and the second worst record in the Big Ten (1-7). Illinois at 0-8, had to live with its season for some time to come.

After some season background information, let me get right to the scores Rather than take this sequentially and drag it out, let me first share the wins with you and then we'll run quickly through the losses. I'll just give you the scores without a lot of supporting information. But, please be forewarned, even I can't make it better than it was.

The offense returned just five starters, including quarterback Zack Mills, who was on pace for a record-shattering season before he injured his left throwing arm. Clearly with a seasoned QB, the season would have been different. Penn State was expected to do much better. Starting the season ranked No. 25 in the Coaches college football preseason poll and unranked in the AP college football preseason poll. Though coaches really matter, when the fundamental players are missing, it is tough to make up for lack of players with great grooming.

On August 30, at home, PSU beat Temple W (23-10). On September 20, PSU beat Kent State at home W (32-10). Then, as the season went on one loss after another finally, a game Indiana team came into Beaver Stadium and gave the Lions a spiritual lift on November 15 W (52-7). That's all the wins she wrote in 2003.

The loss column was huge in 2003. Let me write the date, home/away and the score below on all the losses so you and I can get through them quickly.

September 6 at home v Boston College L (14–27)
September 13 at #18 Nebraska L (10–18)
September 27 at home v #24 Minnesota L (14–20)
October 4 at home v Wisconsin L (23–30)
October 11 at #18 Purdue L (14–28)
October 25 at #16 Iowa L (14–26)
November 1 at home, v #8 Ohio State L (20–21)
November 8 at Northwestern L (7–17)
November 22 at Michigan State L (10–41)

And, that was the games of the 2003 season.

It is always nice to find something good in a season so bad. The name of nice in this case is Michael Robinson, a special athlete. Let's take another look at the Temple Game and Michael Robinson's performance to get back on an upbeat path.

The Temple Game Michael Robinson

After the 2003 Temple game, Penn State's Michael Robinson looked like he had just walked the gauntlet about 12 times and though beaten, he was still standing. He had a bruised left eye which was swollen shut. It was a gauntlet of sorts against Temple and the young man kept moving, gaining, and enduring. It was a pack of Owls responsible for his swollen eye. Robinson felt that even with his helmet, the area around his eye was getting whacked every play.

This was the big change for Robinson, once thought to be just the future QB at PSU. Such a great athlete could play anywhere. It was just the second time in his career he started at tailback, lining up at wide receiver and quarterback within two series, and of course he also took time to return some punts on the side.

Who says Robinson could not do everything. Before the game was over, He even snagged a tackle statistic when he bought down Zamir Cobb, who had converted Temple's fake punt.

From early in his career to his moving on to the pros, Robinson created a major dilemma for his coaches. It is a great problem but a dilemma nonetheless. The problem of course is not "whether," but "where" to play him. Penn State football coach Joe Paterno, never really minded the problem of figuring out where to play him. He was always just happy to have him on the team.

"Robinson's such a good athlete. The problem with Robinson is that he's got to practice at quarterback," Paterno said. "He's going out on some tailback plays, he's running a lot of other things, he's running back punts and if he wasn't as strong of an athlete as he is, he probably couldn't do it all. He's an easy guy to coach."

Robinson finished the afternoon as Penn State's leading rusher with 84 yards on nine carries, most of which came when he broke free down the right sideline for 53 yards before being brought down from behind early in the fourth quarter.

"Joe [Paterno] came to me on the sideline, and he said, 'give it to him and let him go,' " Robinson said." The offensive line did a great job, and I bounced it outside."

The only pass that Zack Mills completed in the first quarter was to Robinson on a six-yard screen pass. Robinson returned two punts for 18 yards.

Robinson is listed as a quarterback. But, on this day against Temple, he took just five snaps before replacing Mills in the closing minutes and he didn't throw a pass. He would play less and less QB and more and more RB throughout his outstanding PSU career

2004 Penn State Football Season Coach Joe Paterno

The 2004 Penn State Nittany Lions football team's head coach was Joe Paterno in his thirty-ninth year. The wonderful coach JoePa and the same wonderful man over the prior two years had begun to have trouble winning games while in his later years of coaching. Some thought he had lost it. In 2004, he was 77 years old but still spry and he did have a number of player issues.

If this were a mystery novel you'd have to wait until next year's and the next to see how this comes out but it is not. It is real, it is fact based, and if you want to, you can look it up but soon, in the next few pages or so, you will have all your answers about the Penn State record under Joe Paterno. He stopped coaching in his forty-sixth year and in 2002, it was his thirty-ninth. He was one heck of a coach!

As we approach the end of Coach's career, we will provide some more information about what he faced at the beginning of the season and what the prospects were for success, etc. One thing is for sure, as long as JoePa was the coach, he had the energy to run the field with the best of them—well into his eighties.

In the spring of 2004, there were changes made to the coaching staff. As you will see by this year's less than sterling 4-7 overall record overall (2-6 Big Ten), coupled with last year's (2003) 3-9 record, something was wrong in the State of Denmark!

The changes affected long-time offensive coordinator Fran Ganter, who signed up as the new Associate Athletic Director for Football Administration, after 37 years as a player and coach for Penn State. Former Penn State quarterback Galen Hall joined the coaching staff as the new offensive coordinator and running backs coach. Mike McQueary, another former Penn State quarterback, joined the staff as the wide receiver's coach and also served as the recruiting coordinator.

In addition to the coaching changes, head coach Joe Paterno had his contract extended through the 2008 football season, despite having had three losing seasons out of the past four. Whenever a coach creates a bunch of potholes in his record, there are many who cry for his ouster. There was a major sentimentality for Coach Paterno but there was also a lot of rumbling under people's breaths.

Things that should improve only improve if there are ingredients of improvement. The 2003 second-leading receiver Maurice Humphrey, for example, was expelled from school and convicted of three counts of simple assault. He would not play another down for

Penn State. His absence created a major void of experience at the wide receiver position. Senior Gerald Smith was the most experienced receiver, and he had limited action and just 15 catches in 2003. Zack Mills was healed and he and Derek Wake were elected team co-captains by their teammates. Because of the dubious future for 2004, PSU was unranked at the beginning of the season by both the AP and the Coaches. The ranking was deserved.

Despite concerns for success, as the calendar ticked, the season began in September with Akron at Beaver Stadium W (48-10) On November 4, PSU made the trip to Alumni Stadium to play a determined, aggressive Eagles team. PSU never-quit though often over-manned by Boston College. The Eagles beat Penn State in a tough match L (7-14).

Central Florida, a team that has kept getting better and better, came to Beaver Stadium on September 18 and were handily beaten by the Nittany Lions W (37-13). Then, on September 25, it was off to Camp Randall Stadium •in Madison, WI for another PSU loss L (3-16).

On October 2, at the Hubert H. Humphrey Metrodome • in Minneapolis, MN at #19 Minnesota, PSU succumbed to the Badgers, L 7-16). Always tough and always surprising, #10 Purdue knocked off the Lions at Beaver Stadium, L 13-20). Iowa came to Penn State's homecoming and spoiled it in a close game L (4-6) before 108,062. Never to be taken lightly, PSU played OSU in Columbus and were beaten L (10-21)

On November 6, at Beaver Stadium, a confident Northwestern team beat Penn State L (7–14). Then, on November 13, at Indiana, PSU pulled out all stops and beat the Hoosiers in Bloomington W (22–18) before 24,092. On November 20, an often-great Michigan State team invaded Beaver Stadium in University Park, PA and were beaten by a full season experienced Nittany Lions Squad W (37–130 before 101,486 to end the season.

2005 Penn State Football Season Coach Joe Paterno

The 2005 Penn State Nittany Lions football team for the fortieth year in a row were coached by the one and only JoePa (Joe Paterno) in another of many great winning seasons. Just when you think there is a systemic reason for losses that may involve coaching, the same Paterno formula again brings in more wins than anybody could ever expect and guys like me and perhaps you too, regardless of where we were in the dark losing years would say, "Of course, that's JoePa. He's our coach."

This was Paterno's toughest mountain to climb. The Nittany Lions were coming off of back-to-back losing seasons, finishing 3–9 in 2003 and 4–7 in 2004, capping a stretch from late 1999 where Minnesota upset the #2 Nittany Lions with a late field goal until the goal line stand at Indiana. There were four of five seasons being losing seasons and the lone winning season in 2002 featuring many extremely frustrating close losses. You lived through these frustrations in this book, and this year is one of our chances to smile.

This stretch was called "The Dark Years", sometimes including 2002 as well. The team finished the sketchy 2004 season with wins over Indiana and Michigan State. As always, a strong finish helps springboard momentum into the next season (2005 in our case). So here we are with a great year which we are about to describe, having closed out 2004 with two nice wins. There was a ton of hope for continuance into the 2005 Nittany Lions season. It happened.

Instead of five starters in 2003, this year's team returned 18 starters from last year's squad. Eight starters returned on offense, led by starting quarterback Michael Robinson who also played at wide receiver, tailback, and punt returner during his first three years at Penn State. Robinson played exclusively under center after the graduation of Zack Mills.

PSU heralded the fact that it had nine defensive starters return from a unit that did not allow more than 21 points in a game in 2004. Also returning was safety Chris Harrell who suffered a neck injury in 2003 and missed the 2004 season. It was time to play.

Michael Robinson, Alan Zemaitis, and Paul Posluszny were elected tri-captains of the football team in 2005. Posluszny was the first junior captain since 1968.

Penn State had made the pundits wary in their last four out of five tough seasons. So, they started the season unranked in both the AP and the Coaches college football preseason polls. Who can argue with an excellent # 3 finish in both polls and an 11-1 overall record as well as a 7-1 record in and co-championship in the Big Ten, Penn State had recovered and the prognosis for the patient was good. Along with the team, JoePa had also recovered.

On September 3, PSU began the season and the home season by beating South Florida at Beaver Stadium W (23–13). On September 10, the next week, a tough Cincinnati team was taken down by the Lions at Beaver Stadium in University Park, PA W (42–24). Finally winning, PSU next engaged Central Michigan at home on September 17 W (40–3). Then, on September 24 at Ryan Field in Evanston, IL, PSU defeated a scrappy Northwestern squad W (34–29).

On October 1, the still down by the press but tough on the field degraded Nittany Lions, unranked after four straight wins, played at home against the #18 Minnesota Gophers and showed the stuff from which they were made before 106,604 at Beaver Stadium and ABC TV. PSU won big W (44-14). Somebody had to notice that Penn State was again playing Nittany Lions Football.

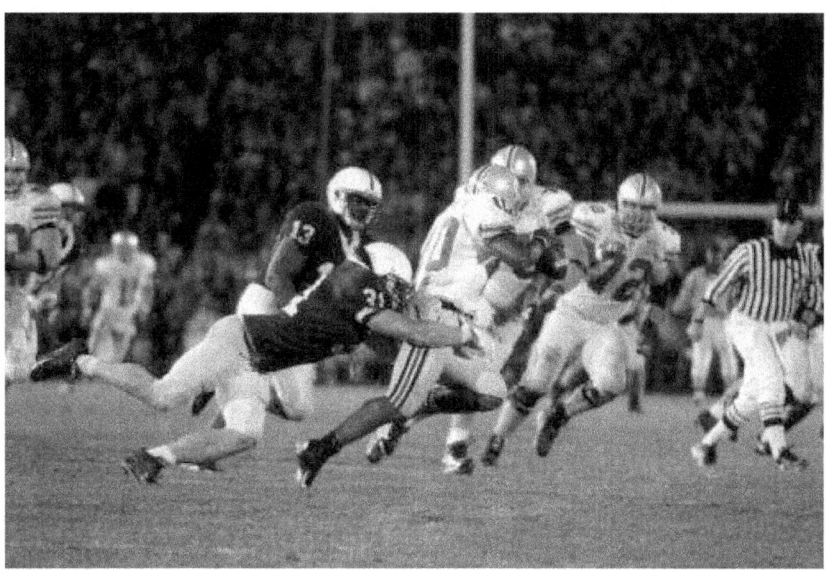

Never giving up in the tough games, on October 8, a finally ranked #16 PSU hosted the Ohio State Buckeyes before 109,839 at home and outlasted the Ohio Squad W (17-10).

The Nittany Lions' win over the No. 6 Buckeyes before another frenzied night time "whiteout" crowd of 109,839 was an epic milestone, marking the return of Penn State to the college football elite. The Lions took the lead in the Big Ten Conference and went on to finish No. 3 in the polls with a BCS Orange Bowl win and their best record (11-1) in 11 years.

Ready to play anybody and win, the 2005 Nittany Lions finally met a team that could beat them. Unranked Michigan was a different team at home than away. The Wolverines hosted the game at Michigan Stadium in Ann Arbor, MI (aka, the Big House) before a huge crowd of 111,249. They barely beat Penn State (two-points) L (25-27) but they won nonetheless. This tough Michigan team was the single reason why the Nittany Lions were not undefeated and untied in 2005. In his fortieth year Paterno was still outclassing all coaches as they came by. What a record! Michigan somehow survived Paterno in 2005.

On October 22 at Illinois the #12 PSU Nittany Lions won big…very big against the Fighting Illini W (63-10). On October 29, on Homecoming, PSU beat Purdue at home W (33-15). On November 5, another Big Ten Tough team, Wisconsin were beaten by #10 Penn State at home W (35-14) before 109,865 electrified PSU fans and maybe a few others. On November 19, PSU took out its Michigan frustration against a guiltless Michigan State at Spartan Stadium in East Lansing, MI with a convincing win W (31–22).

At 11-1, On January 3, 2006 at 8:00 PM, #3 ranked Penn State won a shot at the Orange Bowl against nemesis #22 Florida State at

Dolphin Stadium in Miami Gardens, FL (aka the Orange Bowl). After winning the opportunity to play during the season. PSU won the game in three overtime periods W (26-23).

2006 Penn State Football Season Coach Joe Paterno

The 2006 Penn State Nittany Lions football team's head coach was Joe Paterno in his forty-first year. As always, the Lions played home games at Beaver Stadium in University Park, Pennsylvania. Though not as clean as 2005, PSU was making everybody take notice again with a season record of 9-4 (5-3 in the Big Ten). PSU had a winning record in the Big Ten and against non-Big-Ten teams. Certainly, there were better years but this signaled an escape from the Dark Years back into the top 25 with a Coaches ranking of 25 and an AP rank of 24.

The 2006 season began with the Nittany Lions ranked #19 in the AP and Coaches preseason polls. With losses to Notre Dame and Ohio State, the team dropped out of the rankings, but snuck back into the top 25 at season end.

Everybody had been looking for an unprecedented 2006 after Penn State had some major unexpected success in 2005 after two consecutive losing seasons. The 2005 team was a big part of the 2006 team. As you recall from last year's synopsis in this book. The team began 2005 unranked in any poll, and yet finished 11–1 and ranked third.

With only one loss, the team achieved a Big Ten co-championship with Ohio State. Some great players achieved great milestones with linebacker Paul Posluszny winning both the Chuck Bednarik and Dick Butkus Awards. Also, consensus All-American. Quarterback Michael Robinson finished fifth in the Heisman Trophy voting. It was a fine year but this is 2006 and the old saying, what are you going to do for me now comes into play.

Paul Posluszny and Levi Brown were elected co-captains of the football team for 2006. Posluszny became the team's first two-time captain since 1969. No matter which PSU game you watched in 2005 or 2006, you would hear Posluzny's name accoladed for his fine play.

In 2006, Pozlusny kept at his excellence and was also named the 2006 Big Ten and consensus national pre-season Defensive Player of the Year. The Nittany Lions team was ranked No. 19 in both the AP and Coaches college football preseason polls. They made the top 25 and came close to an even better season.

Before we go on with the games of the season, let's profiled Paul Posluzny as this was his senior year. Posluzny was one of the greatest linebackers in the greatest Linebacker school in the country, Linebacker U, aka PSU.

Player Highlights: Paul Posluzny,

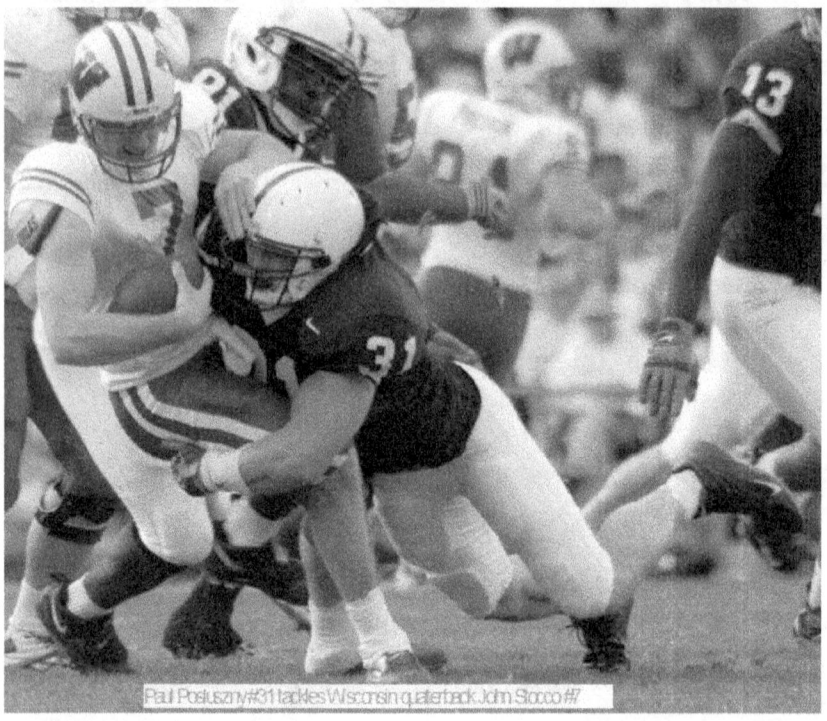

Paul Posluzny #31 tackles Wisconsin quaterback John Stocco #7

In 2005, Paul Posluszny was a junior outside linebacker at Linebacker U and captain for Penn State. He had a great year as a junior with 82 tackles, ranking third in the Big Ten and 11th in the nation with 11.7 tackles per game. In 2005 and 2006, Posluszny was named a semifinalist for the 36th Rotary Lombardi Award, presented to the nation's top lineman or linebacker. In both years, the 6-2, 234-pound linebacker was one of 12 semifinalists up for the prestigious award and in 2005, he was one of only three non-seniors chosen. On November, 15, 2005 Posluszny was selected a finalist.

Posluzny started playing when he was six, back home in the Pittsburgh area. He recalls his dad asking if he wanted to do something new and play football. So, he said sure and gave it a shot. He's been playing ever since. Paul Posluzny had a great high school career, was highly recruited, and he felt really comfortable coming to Penn State. He likes to say that one of his favorite notions about Penn State is that it is Linebacker U and he is a linebacker. He feels that anytime you play a position like linebacker at a school known for that, it's really an honor and a privilege. To Posluzny, it is something to try to uphold.

Posluzny has only good things to say about Joe Paterno: *"He teaches us about really just growing up and being a man,"* POZ once said. *"Besides the football, he's preparing us to be good men in life."*

Paul Posluzny was first Bills rookie to start the season-opener since 1987. He was the first player ever to record 100-plus tackles three times in a college career … Two-time winner of Bednarik Award for best defensive player in the nation. Paul Posluzny is the real deal and he is a Penn Stater.

Penn State began the season at home against Akron on September 2, W (34-16). Notre Dame then hosted PSU on September 9 after not playing for many years. ND took advantage of home-game spirit and pummeled the Nittany Lions L 34-16) in a game that was not as close as its score. PSU would even the score v Notre Dame the following year at home. On September 16, PSU beat Youngstown State W (37-3). Then, on September 23, the #24 ranked Nittany Lions traveled to Ohio Stadium in Columbus, OH and were beaten by #1 Ohio State W (L 6–28) before 105,266.

On September 30, PSU beat Northwestern at Beaver Stadium in University Park, PA W (33–7) before 108,837. On October 7 at Minnesota's Hubert H. Humphrey Metrodome in Minneapolis, PSU beat the Badgers in Overtime W (28–27).
On October 14 at home, PSU played #4 ranked Michigan and were defeated L (10–17) before a capacity crowd of 110,007.
Homecoming featured Illinois and PSU won the game W (26-12).

PSU then defeated Purdue at Ross–Ade Stadium • West Lafayette, IN W (12-0).

On November 4, PSU played at Camp Randall Stadium • Madison, WI, against Wisconsin and were defeated L (3-13). On November 11, Temple came to play PSU and the Lions won big W (47-0). Then, on November 18, Michigan State played a tough battle at Beaver Stadium but lost to Penn State W (17-13) before 108,607.

Penn State finished the regular season at 8-4, winning a berth to play on January 1 at 11:00 AM to play #17 Tennessee in the Outback Bowl in Raymond James Stadium, Tampa, FL. The unranked Nittany Lions triumphed in a nice game W (20-10) before 65,601. With its 9-4 record (5-3 in the Big Ten), PSU made its way into the top 25 with this win #25 and #24 in the Coach's poll and the AP respectively.

2007 Penn State Football Season Coach Joe Paterno

The 2007 Penn State Nittany Lions football team was coached by Joe Paterno in his 42nd year and played its home games in Beaver Stadium in University Park, Pennsylvania. Penn State was 9-4; 4-4 in the Big Ten. ranked #25the Coaches poll.

On April 27, 2007, State College police announced that six members of the squad were charged with a range of criminal charges related to an altercation that occurred in an apartment in downtown State College earlier that month. Most of the charges were eventually dismissed or were whittled away by pleas agreements.

For his part, not confining the issue to just six players,
Coach Paterno announced that, because of the incident, the entire football team will clean Beaver Stadium on Sundays after home games, a task usually handled by members of Penn State's club sports teams. The team began serving this punishment following their 59-0 victory over Florida International.

On September 1, #17 PSU defeated Florida International at Beaver Stadium W (59–0). Keeping their word, members of the squad cleaned the stadium on the Sunday after the game. On September 8, at Beaver Stadium, it was make-up time as Penn State thumped Notre Dame a good one before 110,078 W (31-10), one year after

The Irish had delivered a similar blow to the Lions at home. On September 15, Buffalo made a rare appearance playing Penn State in a rout by PSU W (45-24). On September 22, a stubborn Michigan State handed PSU its first loss of the season at Beaver Stadium in a close match L (9-4). The second loss came quickly the following week on September 29 at Illinois L (20-27)

PSU picked itself up after two losses in a row and hosted Iowa in Beaver Stadium. The Nittany Lions got back on track with a win against the Hawkeyes W (27-7). PSU beat Wisconsin at Wisconsin the following week in a nice win W (38-7). PSU then played at Indiana and beat the Hoosiers W (36-31) On October 27 Jim Tressel brought his #1 ranked Ohio State team to Beaver Stadium and overpowered the #24 Lions L (17-37). Back at it again against Purdue on November 3 at home. PSU won a close one W (26-19)

On November 10, PSU shut out Temple W (31-0 at Lincoln Field in Philadelphia. Then on November 17 in Spartan Stadium, PSU lost to Michigan State in another close battle L (31-35).

Ranked 8-4 after the regular seasons the Nittany Lions got a shot at Texas A & M in the Alamo Bowl in the Alamo Dome in San Antonio, TX. The game was played on December 29 at 8:00 PM before 66,166 plus a nationwide ESPN TV audience. In a close match, PSU prevailed W (24-17) and thus finished the season at 9-4 with rankings of #25 and # 24 in the Coaches and AP polls.

2008 Penn State Football Season Coach Joe Paterno

The 2008 Penn State Nittany Lions football team was coached by Joe Paterno in his forty-third year. Ranked #6, PSU had a great record of 11-1 going into the Rose Bowl v #5 USC L (24-38). The team finished with a great winning season of 11-2 and were ranked #8 in both polls.

In the good news and bad news category before the end of the previous-season, difference maker linebacker Sean Lee announced his plans to return for his senior season. Unfortunately, Lee, the mainstay on the defense, tore his anterior cruciate ligament in his right knee during practice and was sidelined for the entire season. Lee was permitted to use his redshirt and returned in 2009.

There was some bad news in Spring with five players being suspended prior to spring drills for their involvement in an October 7 fight at the HUB-Robeson Center during the previous season, including defensive tackle Chris Baker, linebacker Navarro Bowman, defensive back Knowledge Timmons, defensive tackle Phil Taylor, and receiver Chris Bell. Tight end Andrew Quarless was also suspended after a DUI incident in March. Later Bell was kicked off the team for brandishing a knife at a teammate.

Following spring workouts, Baker, Bowman, Quarless, Timmons and Taylor were allowed to rejoin and work out with the team. Baker was sentenced to two years' probation. When you are trying to be #1, it hurts when players off the field choose to not engage life as gentlemen. It hurts them, the university and the team. Good recruits are tough to find and experienced team members are even harder to find.

#22 ranked PSU started the season early on August 30 against Coastal California at home with a really big win W (66-10). On September 6, the next team to try their luck at the #19 Lions in Beaver Stadium was Oregon State. The Nittany Lions won by a large amount W (45-14)

Playing again at the Carrier Dome in Syracuse after eighteen years on September 13, #17 Penn State dominated long-time rival Syracuse, W (55-13). On September 20, Temple lined up at Beaver Stadium and were beaten by #16 Penn State, W (45-3). The #12 Nittany Lions were now 4-0 for the first time in years. #22 Illinois was next at Beaver Stadium and the Lions won W (38-24). On October 4, at Ross–Ade Stadium in West Lafayette, IN, #6 Penn State beat Purdue W (20–6).

The smell of a special season was again in the air as Joe Paterno had put together another great team. It was his forty-third season and after all that time to still be walloping great teams was a mark few coaches could ever achieve.

On October 11, at Wisconsin in Camp Randall Stadium, The Nittany Lions kept pouring it on W (48-7).

Michigan game – Say no more

On October 18, The Lions took on a very powerful Michigan team at Beaver Stadium, and were relentless in trouncing the always-tough Wolverines W (46-17).

The crowd went nuts after this long-sought victory. Huge carloads of exhilaration emanated from the first victory over Michigan after nine straight losses over 12 years. This bad record may fade from the mind in the future, but the 110,017 impassioned Homecoming fans thoroughly enjoyed the second half thrashing under the lights as Beaver Stadium rocked and rolled, and PSU picked up a fine W (46-17).

Like many other great PSU games at Beaver Stadium, there were thousands of white pompoms fluttering as 100,000 Penn State fans broke into a sing-along as the happy night fell on Beaver Stadium in the Happy Valley.

Joe Paterno had picked up many nemeses in this 60 years of coaching but they say his greatest nemesis was Michigan and its nasty, victory-seeking Wolverine football team. On this evening in October, these warriors from mid-America were about to be vanquished by a #3 ranked Nittany Lions and its 81-year-old coach. The post-game celebration would create the need for a bird's-eye view of party time in Happy Valley.

Though the season ended without a championship at the time, JoePa was getting a great look at some of the folks in his lineup that were about to make PSU a national championship contender.

Behind the running of Evan Royster and a few momentum-shifting plays by the defense and special teams, the PSU got the game going its way by withstanding the Wolverines' early moves and most importantly, the Nittany Lions worked as hard as they could to not only snap a nine-game losing streak to their Big Ten rivals, they whacked them a good one W (46-17) on this particular Saturday.

Paterno was limping and so he was not on the field to enjoy his record 380th victory. The outstanding master of the college coaching profession was relegated to working from the press box for a third consecutive week because of his sore hip and leg.

"My being upstairs -- it's funny, I'm not sure that's not the best place for a head coach," he said. "I mean you really get a view of things, I get a better view of football games from up there than I ever do on the sideline."

What Coach Paterno saw was a team that should be no worse than third in the BCS standings when it heads to Big Ten rival, and eternal powerhouse Ohio State next week.

"Am I starting to like it up there? I'll never like it, it doesn't mean that the team might be better off with me up there," Paterno said.

No team had ever won as many in a row against Penn State during Paterno's 43 seasons at the helm than Michigan. But if ever there was an opportunity for the Nittany Lions (8-0, 4-0) to break the streak it was 2008. The Wolverines at (2-5, 1-2) were struggling in their first season under coach Rich Rodriguez, but like many teams with new coaches, they expected things to get better as time went by. Nonetheless, they were a powerful team.

"It's a fact, you take it year by year, game by game, we lost to them last year, and coach has made a great point this week, that this Penn State team has not lost to this Michigan team," center A.Q. Shipley said.

Michigan came in the game as a 23 1/2-point underdog because they were not at prime under their new coach Rodriguez, for sure. The Wolverines were unaccustomed to being low in the odds maker's opinions.

Michigan looked like a good bet early with their spread offense clicking as they sped to a 17-7 lead early over Penn State in the second quarter. But the Lions (8-0, 4-0) soon deciphered the spread, and got its own high-powered version of Rodriguez's offense rolling. The lions delivered the knockout punch with a safety, a partially blocked punt and a forced fumble on consecutive second-half Michigan possessions. Michigan did not look good.

"Oh, we executed for a while and then we didn't," said Rodriguez, whose team needs to win four more games to avoid Michigan's first losing season since 1967. "That's what happened. We executed, we moved the ball a little, and when we didn't, we didn't."

Jared Odrick gave Penn State its first lead of the game at 19-17 when he dragged down backup quarterback Nick Sheridan in the end zone with 4:39 left in third quarter.

The free kick set the Nittany Lions up at midfield, Royster's 21-yard run put them at the 1 and Daryll Clark sneaked in at 3:04 to make it 26-17.

Royster, one heck of an athlete, ran for 174 yards on 18 carries, with a 44-yard TD run in the first quarter.

A minute later, Nathan Stupar blocked Zoltan Mesko's punt deep in Michigan territory and Penn State turned the short kick into a Kevin Kelly 32-yard field goal on the first play of the fourth.

60 seconds or so after that, Aaron Maybin sacked Steven Threet, who fumbled, and the Lions took over at the Michigan 19. A sore elbow forced Threet to miss a few series.

Clark's second 1-yard sneak turned the final 12 minutes into a Beaver Stadium celebration bash, with Penn State fans singing along to "Sweet Caroline" and enjoying their team's first victory against Michigan since 1996. It was as Lawrence Welk would say, "Wunnerful!"

The Wolverines had surely tormented Paterno and his Nittany Lions over the prior 12 seasons, with too many lopsided losses and heartbreaking defeats. In 2005, the last time Penn State was in the hunt for a national title, it was Michigan that scored a touchdown on the final play to hand Paterno's team its only loss of the season.

This one couldn't have started better for Michigan but things that start well do not always end well. After a three-and-out for Penn State, Michigan put together its longest drive of the season. The 14-play, 86-yard march featured all the best of Rodriguez's spread offense. The option cleared running lanes for Threet and Randon Minor, who surpassed his season high on the drive with 42 yards rushing.

The second half would have its rewards for the Nittany Lions as they soundly beat the Wolverines W (46-17). And ain't that sweet!

After Michigan, it seemed nothing could beat the Lions. But, Ohio State was the next on October 25, week and #10 Ohio State always played its best at home and rarely lost to Penn State. Would this game, played at Ohio Stadium, with so much on the line be different? ..... Answer = Yes! This was a different Penn State team.

One point and you're out!

PSU won this important game W (13-6. Sometimes when a team triumphs over its biggest threat in a season, they relax a bit and the next tough team claims a victory. On November 8 at Iowa, Penn State lost its first game of the season in what would have been an undefeated championship season, to a really tough Iowa Team by just one point L (23-24).

#7 PSU came back on November 15 v Indiana and defeated the Hoosiers at Beaver Stadium W (34-7). On November 22, #17 Michigan State played the Lions at Beaver Stadium. Penn State had fully recovered from the Iowa loss and beat the Spartans in a blowout-shootout W (49-18.

On January 1, 2009, #6 Penn State had another shot at greatness as it took on #5 USC in the Rose Bowl. USC was always tough and this was a special year for the Nittany Lions. The setting was Pasadena California in the Rose Bowl Stadium. The game was televised by ABC and the attendance was 93,293. It was a great game. PSU lost by 12 points in a really determined battle L (24-38) PSU finished the season 11-2. It was a fine # 43 season for Coach Joe Paterno.

2009 Penn State Football Season Coach Joe Paterno

The 2009 Penn State Nittany Lions football team was coached by Joe Paterno in his forty-fourth year. The Nittany Lions continued to play home games in the newly massive Beaver Stadium in University Park, Pennsylvania. As an aside, for those concerned about academics and athletics, in 2009, Penn State University had the highest graduation rate among all of the teams on the Associated Press Top 25 poll with 89% of its 2002 enrollees graduating. Miami and Alabama tied for second place with a graduation rate of 75%.

2009 was also another great year for football, though the two losses were heartbreaking, coaches are paid gazillion dollars a year to achieve records such as PSU's 11-2 record this particular year. Though 82 years of age in the 2009 season, Paterno never weakened.

He was strong and the squad was strong. How can you argue with an 11-2 record? The Nittany Lions also won the Lambert-Meadowlands Trophy award to the best team in the ECAC for the 28th time and the second consecutive year. Penn State is an impressive team and Joe Paterno, even in his few losing seasons, was an impressive coach.

There are always a few personnel setbacks in preparing for a season. In December, 2008, for example, QB Pat Devlin decided to transfer from Penn State and did not play in the Rose Bowl. Devlin appeared in ten games for the Nittany Lions, passing for 459 yards, four touchdowns and no interceptions.

In January, redshirt sophomore defensive end Aaron Maybin announced that he was skipping his final two seasons of eligibility and declared for the 2009 NFL Draft. Junior defensive end Maurice Evans, also declared for the draft. On top of these three losses of key players, the defense lost its entire starting secondary to graduation. The good news was that all-everything linebacker Sean Lee had healed and returned to the line-up for his senior season. The offensive unit had its own woes losing three-fifths of the line to graduation. Despite the losses, the team still looked strong and performed very well.

Ranked #8 pre-season, on September 5, in the home opener, PSU defeated Akron W (31–7) for a fine start to the season. On September 12, Syracuse returned the favor and came to Beaver Stadium to be beaten by an on-cue # 5 ranked PSU Nittany Lions Team W (28-7). Next, on September 19, at home, PSU beat the Temple Owls W (31-6). Ranked #4 with a 3-0 record PSU was off to the races until IOWA stopped by on September 26. The Lions lost to Iowa L (10-21). Back on the Big ten schedule at Illinois, PSU defeated the Fighting Illini in Champaign on October 3 W (35-17).

On October 10, Eastern Illinois made a rare trip to Beaver Stadium and were beaten big by the Nittany Lions W (52-3). Minnesota came to Beaver Stadium on October 17 and the Gophers were shut-out by the Nittany Lions W (20-0) PSU then traveled to the Big House in Ann Arbor Michigan and beat the Wolverines W (35-10). Staying on the road on October 13, PSU beat Northwestern W (34-13).

Always a nemesis and always tough, #10 ranked PSU played #12 ranked Ohio State at home on November 7, before 110,033 and lost this year's match, L (7-24). At home, again on November 14, The Nittany Lions beat Indiana W (31-20). Moving on to the Michigan State game, the Lions traveled to East Lansing and defeated the Spartans in a well-played game W (42-14).

Ranked #11 with a 10-2 record, Penn State got to play on New Year's Day in the Citrus Bowl—aka the Capital One Bowl—in Orlando at 1:00 PM, the best time for a January 1 football game IMHO. I saw the game on ABC TV and 63,025 saw the game live in

Florida. The opponent was a tough #15 ranked LSU team who like PSU, were planning to win the game. I

It was a real close match but the Nittany Lions held tough and beat Louisiana State W (19-17). With an 11-2 record with the bowl win and a #8 rank in the Coach's Poll and #9 in the AP, it was a fine year indeed for PSU football and for Coach Joe Paterno. It was a fine game to kick off the Master Coach's next to last full season.

Player Highlights Sean Lee

Sean Lee was in the on-deck circle at Linebacker U to be the Linebacker Apparent. He had been a three star recruit out of Pittsburgh but he broke into the Paterno lineup early. He made his Penn State debut as a true freshman in the 2005 classic whiteout win over Ohio State. He started every game as a true sophomore, ending the year third on the squad in tackles. He maybe had become a PSU Linebacker as in his junior season in 2007, he finished the year second in the whole Big Ten in tackles, and he was named second team All-Big Ten.

He would have had an even bigger 2008 when an ACL tear in spring practice crippled him while it was repairing after surgery. He sat on the sidelines wearing a head set during the games watching for things to report. Penn Staters were hoping that after such a nurturing Lee would be back at Beaver Stadium in 2009. It was not what it was expected to be.

During 2009, he simply was not the same player as in 2007. He just was not as strong physically as in 2007. He was forced to sit three games due to lingering injuries, but despite all that he did end the year with 86 tackles (39 solo) in the middle, right alongside NaVorro Bowman. He used his innate football sense and intensity and then he was drafted by Dallas in the second round, 55th overall.

Player Highlights NaVarro Bowman

PSU star Linebacker NaVarro Roderick Bowman was born on May 28, 1988 in District Heights Maryland. From day one, he worked every day of his life to become a great football player. He was so good, nobody wanted to see him leave PSU but the pressure to change life status for players is very difficult to refuse. On January 4, 2010, after a great PSU career, Bowman's mother announced his decision to forgo his final year of NCAA eligibility and enter the 2010 NFL Draft.

On the second day of the Draft, Bowman's ticket was punched in the third round as the 91st overall pick. The San Francisco 49ers gained a powerful player for their roster. Bowman wears number # 53 for the 49ers.

After the redshirting season Navarro played every game in which he was physically capable. He missed 2 games in 2007 due to a sprained ankle suffered at Illinois. He had 16 tackles, with one sack, a forced fumble, a fumble recovery, a blocked kick, and a pass breakup that season.

He played a lot more in 2008, mostly because All-American Dan Connor moved to the NFL but also because of an injury to presumptive starter Sean Lee. Despite the attrition, however, Bowman kept the Nittany Lions ranked in the top ten among three primary defensive categories. Individually, Bowman led the Nittany Lions in total tackles (106), solos (61), and assisted tackles (45), was second in tackles for loss (16.5) and tied for third in sacks (4.0). He also forced two fumbles, recovered a fumble, grabbed an interception and had five pass breakups.

When his last season was over Bowman had gained a lot of great recognition:

- First-team All-Big Ten selection.
- Maryland Defensive PoYr (2005)
- Maryland All-State (2005)
- Washington Post All-Met (2005)
- Big Ten Defensive PoYr (9/20/2008), (11/14/2009)
- All-Big Ten (2008)

2010 Penn State Football Season Coach Joe Paterno

The Penn State Nittany Lions football team was coached by Joe Paterno in his forty-fifth and last full season with Penn State University. Team captains for the 2010 season were wide receiver Brett Brackett and defensive tackle Ollie Ogbu. After a number of great seasons in a row, especially the outstanding 2009 season, it was again time for some rebuilding. The Nittany Lions finished the season 7-6, with a 4-4 record in the Big Ten play. They qualified and they played in the Outback Bowl where they were defeated by Florida L (37-24). The bottom line is that it was another winning season.

As an aside, it was Ohio State that had big troubles with the NCAA this season. On July 8, 2011, long after the 2010 season had ended, in the wake of NCAA violations for improper benefits to student athletes and the subsequent cover, Ohio State vacated all of its victories, as well as the conference and Sugar Bowl championships, from the 2010 season as self-imposed sanctions. Since Penn State lost to Ohio State, the official record for the Lions is 7-5; not 7-6 for 2009.

On September 4, at Beaver Stadium in the season home opener, #14 PSU beat Youngstown State W (44–14). On the road, again—this time at Bryant–Denny Stadium in Tuscaloosa, AL, on September 11, #14 ranked PSU lost to the #1 ranked Alabama Crimson Tide L (3–24). On September 18 Kent State came to Beaver Stadium to play the #20 Nittany Lions and the Lions Prevailed W (24–0). Temple played the Nittany Lions on September 25 and were beaten in a nice, close game W (22-13).

Penn State has had bad luck with Iowa since joining the Big Ten. October 2 was no different.as the Lions lost at Iowa City L to the Hawkeyes L (3-24). On October9, PSU lost to Illinois at home L (13-33). Then, on October 23, at Minneapolis Penn State won a nice match against the Gophers W (33-21). By the time Michigan came to Beaver Stadium, the Lions were hungry for the old winning days. PSU took care of business with Michigan W (41-31) before 108,539.

On November 6, PSU beat Northwestern at home W (35-21) and followed that up with a loss away at Columbus to the Ohio State Buckeyes L (14-38). This loss was vacated about a year later because of some issues with special favors for certain Ohio athletes. On November 20, PSU played Indiana at FedEx Field in Landover, MD and beat the Hoosiers W (41-24) On November 27, PSU wrapped up its season losing to #10 ranked Michigan State at home L (22-28).

Having had a winning Season (7-5), PSU played Florida in the Outback Bowl on January 1 at Raymond James Stadium in Tampa, FL and lost a tough battle L (24-37) in Joe Paterno's last bowl game as head coach.

Player Highlights Stefan Wisniewski

In 2008, Stefen Wisniewski was the first Nittany Lion true freshman offensive lineman to start a game since center Joe Iorio in 1999, Wisniewski was a starter in 12 games at guard in 2008, and a starter in 25 of the last 26 games.

Selected a 2010 first-team preseason All-American by Athlon, Lindy's, Sporting News and Phil Steele's College Football Previews, Wisniewski was a 2009 third-team All-America honoree by Collegefootballnews.com. Wisniewski became Penn State's first three-time Academic All-American

In 2009, his Junior Season, Wisniewski was shifted from guard to center prior to spring practice and emerged as one of the nation's top offensive linemen. Starting every game, he was selected first-team All-Big Ten by the coaches and media and was named a third-team All-American by Collegefootballnews.com.

At the beginning of the 2011 season, coach Hue Jackson named Wisniewski the Raiders' starting left guard, placed between Samson Satele at center and Jared Veldheer at left tackle. On opening day of the 2011 NFL season, the offensive line cleared the way for 190 rushing yards and a victory over the Denver Broncos.

Stefen Wisniewski was made to play football. He was immediately named the Pepsi NFL Rookie of the Week for Week 3 of the 2011

2011 Penn State Football Season Coach Joe Paterno

The 2011 Penn State Nittany Lions football team was coached by Joe Paterno in his forty-sixth and final year. Coach Paterno was the head coach for the first nine games of the year in what looked like it might be another championship season after the rebuilding year. As everybody knows there was a major scandal at Penn State and the

Coach was asked to resign in the wake of the devastating allegations involved.

Defensive coordinator Tom Bradley took over the team for Joe Paterno. Without discussing the merits of the case as this was well covered in many other books and articles during the period, many PSU fans are still not pleased with how it all happened, especially the undeserved and immediate fall from grace, with which Coach Paterno was subjected.

Under Bradley, the Nittany Lion players continued to work hard and they were clearly innocent victims of the situation and they continued to play but with heavy hearts.

Penn State finished the season 9–4, 6–2 in the Leaders Division of the Big Ten to be co–division champions with Wisconsin. Due to the head-to-head loss to Wisconsin, they did not represent the division in the inaugural Big Ten Championship Game. They were invited to the Ticket City Bowl where under Tom Bradley's best efforts as interim coach, they lost to Houston 14–30.

You may remember that Penn State began the season with an unsettled quarterback situation. There was a battle between sophomore Rob Bolden and one-time walk-on junior Matt McGloin split starting duties in the 2010 season. Rob Bolden was named the starter for the season opener against Indiana State, but things changed.

Matt McGloin was the first walk-on quarterback to start at Penn State since scholarships were reinstated in 1949. Prior to his college career, McGloin was a Pennsylvania all-state quarterback while attending West Scranton High School, a few miles from where I live. He became the starting quarterback for Penn State Nittany Lions football team and led the Lions from 2010 to 2012

The season began like any other on September 3 at Beaver Stadium v Indiana State. #25 ranked PSU defeated the Sycamores W (41-7). On September 10, the #20 ranked Paterno forces got their first setback of the season against #3 Alabama L (11-27). This would be the very last loss in Joe Paterno's excellent career. Penn State would win their last seven games coached by Paterno. When PSU played

Nebraska in game 10, Tom Bradley would be the new interim head coach.

On September 17 PSU beat a tough Temple team at Lincoln Financial Field in Philadelphia, PAW (14-10). On September 24, the Paterno forces beat Eastern Michigan at Beaver Stadium W (34-6). PSU then traveled to Bloomington Indiana before 42,621 on October 1, and the Lions beat the Hoosiers W (16-10). When Iowa came to Beaver Stadium on October 8, Penn State finished them off in a close match W (13-3).

Purdue was the next win for the Lions at Beaver Stadium in October 15, W (23-18). These were all typical Paterno close matches where the defense does a yeoman job. On October 22, #21 ranked PSU then beat Northwestern at Ryan Field in Evanston, IL W (34-24). PSU then finished off Illinois in another close game at Beaver Stadium on October 29. The #19 Nittany Lions beat the Fighting Illini W (10-7).

The Illinois game at Beaver Stadium was the end of Joe Paterno's season and the end of Joe Paterno's 45+ year head coaching career with Penn State. He finished his part of the season with another great record at 8-1, losing only to #3 ranked Alabama. When he gave up the team to Tom Bradley, to play Nebraska, Paterno's nine-game season Penn State team was ranked # 12.

Tom Bradley's shot at being coach came shortly after the November 4 grand jury report was released on Friday, November 4. There was no game Saturday. On November 9, Joe Paterno offered to retire at the end of the season, which was going pretty good for the players at the time. PSU officials appointed Bradley interim coach just three days before one of the toughest games of the season—#19 ranked Nebraska

On November 12, Tom Bradley's team, clearly upset by the week's happenings lost at home to the Nebraska Cornhuskers in a close game L (14-17). Having regained some composure by November 19 at Columbus Ohio, the #21 PSU squad beat Ohio State in a close game W (20-14). The #19 Nittany Lions finished off the season with a big loss at #12 Wisconsin L (7-45).

Tom Bradley led the disenchanted PSU Nittany Lions to the Cotton Bowl and PSU lost L (14-30). From the Nebraska game on, nothing seemed real as the whole football program was in disarray.

Player Highlights Michael Mauti

Michael Mauti had no clue his 2011 season would be abbreviated by injury. He was a Linebacker U Linebacker all over the field making the big plays for the first three games of 2011 season. He was earning recognition and would have surely gotten the plaudits with a completed senior season. But it was not to be.

He suffered a torn anterior cruciate ligament in his left knee. Before his injury, Mauti had recorded 21 tackles, with 3.0 tackles for loss, one interception and three pass breakups in three-plus games. In the meeting with an ever-tough No. 2 Alabama, Mauti led the team with a career-high 13 tackles and had two pass breakups. If there were more Mauti's on the team, the outcome would have been different.

In his junior season, he played in 11 games, with seven starts. He garnered 5.5 tackles for loss (minus-18), with two sacks and a pass breakup. Mauti rewrote his career-high in tackles in three consecutive games during the season.

He was selected Big Ten Co-Defensive Player-of-the-Week against Northwestern, after making a career-high 11 tackles and a career-best 3.0 TFL in the historic comeback win. In his first game since the 2009 Rose Bowl due to a serious knee injury, Mauti made five tackles against Youngstown State.

Mauti's pro career began when he was drafted by the Minnesota Vikings in the seventh round, 213th overall of the 2013 Draft.

Mauti, as many other PSU players enjoyed Penn State; enjoyed PSU Football, and enjoyed playing for the most decorated coach who has ever lived—Joe Paterno!

Chapter 10 Joe Paterno: The Fine Man, The Great Coach, & The Legend!

Only one Joe Paterno was ever built by God!

Before 2004 game: Penn State football coach Joe Paterno leads his team onto the field

We all know Joe Paterno as the inimitable and accomplished head football coach at Pennsylvania State University. He was without a doubt one of the most successful coaches, if not simply the most successful coach in the history of collegiate football. Paterno is well known for his quotes to help others succeed such as the following:

"Believe deep down in your heart that you're destined to do great things."

"The will to win is important, but the will to prepare is vital."

"Success without honor is an unseasoned dish; it will satisfy your hunger, but it won't taste good."

Joe Paterno had substantial success and many great successes and he had his success with honor. He was always a great man. He never changed to fit the times. His greatness and his legacy of respect for humankind will only increase as time goes by. Joe Paterno was not superhuman, god-like, or all-seeing, and he spent his time coaching football.

Contrary to popular belief, Joe Paterno was not born a coach in a manger. As a new born, little baby Joe knew that few colleges would hire him to coach their great football teams if he needed his mom and dad to take him to the practice field and to the games. But, this would soon change.

Like all of us, Paterno was born of regular parents who happened to be Italian. They pressed upon him early the importance of education and Joe, a quick learner, never forgot his parent's lesson. His date and place of birth is December 21, 1926, in Brooklyn, New York. Brooklyn was in his accent and he never lost that special voice.

Before he turned to college, Paterno was already turning heads. As a high school senior, Joe Paterno and his younger brother George, then a junior, gained notoriety throughout the New York metropolitan area for their exploits on the football field and basketball court. Hard as it to believe, neither were close to six foot tall.

The "Gold Dust Twins," as they were known, had led Brooklyn Prep to an 8-1 season in 1943, with the only loss against St. Cecilia's School in Englewood, N.J. At the time, St. Cecilia School was coached by none other than Vince Lombardi, who would go on to become a Hall of Fame coach with the Green Bay Packers.

After his HS graduation, Paterno attended and graduated from Brown University in 1950, where he played football both ways as the quarterback and a cornerback. It was not easy getting to Brown as dad wanted both boys, Joe, and George, to attend the same college together. The boys were small but star athletes nonetheless.

Finally, a wealthy alumnus from Brown University offered to pay for both Joe and George to attend the Providence, R.I., school in 1944, it was legal for donors to pay for player scholarships. Like Ed Kelly, my dad would have said if an alumnus from King's College had offered me such a deal, "Stop thinking…take the deal!"

JoePa had a great career at Brown. He was inducted into Brown's Athletic Hall of Fame in 1977. His former Brown coach, Charles ("Rip") Engle, became head coach at Pennsylvania State University (Penn State) and hired the 23-year old Paterno as an assistant coach.

That just about ended dad's hope for his son Joe to become an attorney. After 16 years as his assistant, Paterno succeeded Rip Engle as Penn State's head coach in 1966. JoePa as he was called often talked about how he wanted one day to be a lawyer.

The Paterno brothers George 1950 and Joe 1950

Joseph Vincent Paterno was nothing less than phenomenal as a head coach in his very late thirties right from the start. Paterno led Penn State to consecutive undefeated seasons in 1968 and 1969 and another undefeated season in 1973. He had to wake up the pundits and the other coaches to ever gain in the rankings. He did.

Like many of his time period, Joe Paterno served in the U.S. Army during

World War II. After the war, Paterno went to Brown, where as noted, he dominated the gridiron as the school's quarterback and led his team to an 8-1 season in his senior year. He graduated from Brown in 1950, and after settling down at Penn State, he married Suzanne Pohland in 1962. The couple had five children together, all of whom later became graduates of Penn State.

None of these fine people, who know their dad and husband like no other people know him, will let his legacy, or the legacy of the football program at Penn State University remain tarnished because of the rash judgment of a board of directors that had read a book about how to get monkeys off backs.

PSU Head Coach Paterno

In 1966, as noted, Coach Paterno became the head football coach of Penn State University. His first season was a draw, with 5 wins and 5 losses, but he worked especially hard to build up the school's football program.

Before long, Paterno racked up impressive scores, including coaching the team to two undefeated regular seasons in 1968 and 1969. Over his 61 years as assistant and as head coach, Joe Paterno became not just a revered coach but he also became a beloved figure at the university. Of course, he became known for his trademark thick, square-shaped glasses and for his leadership skills.

He was always in shape and ran with the team onto the field for football games. He had a revered nickname "Joe Pa," which stuck with him from the first time it was used. He dedicated himself to his team, the Nittany Lions. Joe Paterno could have made a lot more money and could have coached anywhere he wanted. He even turned down a chance to coach professional football with Pittsburgh and with the New England Patriots in 1973.

Though PSU was not awarded National Championship status for the many perfect records (undefeated and untied) that Paterno accumulated with Penn State, he did lead the Lions to two National Championships—in 1982 and again in 1986. Both of these are consensus and unquestioned. In recognition of his contributions to his winning team, he earned the Sportsman of the Year honor from Sports Illustrated in 1986.

Overall, Paterno had an impressive record as the Nittany Lions' coach. In 46 seasons, he led his team to 37 bowl appearances with 24 Bowl wins. The list goes on. In October 2011, Paterno set a major record of his own when Penn State defeated Illinois. This victory marked his 409th career win, making him the leader in career wins for Division I coaches. Think of all the greats that coached in Division I.

Al Browning, from the Tuscaloosa news wrote this piece about Joe Paterno from when the Coach first came to Penn State. Not everybody in life starts out with a silver soon but good people and good friends let them use their spoons until they can use their own.

By AL BROWNING
News Sports Editor

NEW ORLEANS — At age 24, Joe Paterno was lonely, practically broke and en route to farm-dotted woods from a concrete jungle.

The streets of Brooklyn had made him wise, but State College, Pa., offered strange surroundings. There were no Dodgers to watch on Saturday afternoons, no sidewalk bums to dodge and very little night life.

Paterno admits he was scared the night he arrived at Penn State University to begin his career as a college football coach. His salary was $3,200 a year — just enough money for spaghetti and Spanish Rice, as it turned out — and he was in bad need of a place to hang his coat.

Then the door opened at the house owned by Steve and Virginia Suhey, who were to produce three sons who would play for Paterno after he became head coach at Penn State.

The two surviving principals of that story — Paterno and Virginia Suhey — were caught rehashing those trying first days at Penn State here Thursday afternoon.

Two of the sons watched in the background, before joining their Penn State teammates at practice in preparation for a Monday afternoon Sugar Bowl game against Alabama. The gleams in the eyes of running back Matt Suhey and linebacker Paul Suhey indicated they were proud of the hospitality their family had shown a stranger who would later become one of the coaching elite of college football.

"Joe shared our two-bedroom apartment," said Virginia (Ginger) Suhey. "It was a difficult time for him, a young man in new surroundings. He enjoyed meeting our young friends and we enjoyed having a thoughtful, intelligent person in the house. We played bridge by the hours, which is what you did when you did not have a lot of money to socialize, and we ate Spanish Rice.

"He ate so much of that rice back then, I doubt he can look at it today."

The year was 1950,

Joe Paterno in 1950 arriving at Penn State Looking Sharp!

Chapter 11 Words about Joe Paterno from Penn Live

No man can do everything 100% perfect.

At his very essence, Joe Paterno was human as all of us. My deepest convictions from having studied the man is that he was and still is the real deal. I would have been proud to know him better. In another book that I wrote about Penn State, I included most of an article written by Penn Live that was very well done. This book is about Joe Paterno the coach and the man and so, it does not contain information about the dark days of 2011 and 2012, etc. There is what I would call an epitaph of Coach Paterno by Bob Flounders. It ran on Penn Live on Jan. 24, 2012 at 3:53 PM. In my version, I applied some poetic license as I did not agree with everything that was written. Nonetheless, you can come to your own conclusions if you choose to read what is mostly a well-done article about the life of Joe Paterno.

You can find Flounders piece titled, Joe Paterno: A Life. He was Penn State at this web address:

http://www.pennlive.com/specialprojects/index.ssf/2012/01/joe_paterno_a_life_-_he_was_pe.html.

Chapter 12 Please Tell Me More about Coach Joseph V. Paterno.

Joe Paterno, A great coach and a fine man.

Much of the biography information in this piece memorializing Joe Paterno was contributed by the PSU Sports Department and made available to the general public. I have used poetic license as information in the form in which it was provided was about six years old. I would hope Penn State chooses to add the one year necessary to its biographical information on Coach Paterno as I am sure many, like me, are searching for an official repository.

Joseph Vincent Paterno, often referred by fans as "JoePa", was a fine American college football player, but he was mostly known as an athletic director and an immortal coach. He served as the head coach of the Penn State Nittany Lions from 1966 to 2011 and for sixteen years before then he served as assistant coach of the football program at the University under Coach Rip Engle. To say the least, Joseph Vincent Paterno, "JoePa" made his mark on Penn State University and American Football.

Coach Joseph V Paterno's storied career was marked with distinction, glorious accomplishments and immeasurable contributions to The Pennsylvania State University. In his second to last season, 2010, the year of which many facts were written and hosted in what is his official PSU Sports Biography, Mr. Paterno added yet another compelling and thrilling chapter to his great legacy. Of course, we also know that in 2011, in his last game as an active coach, he passed Eddie Robinson of Grambling as the winningest Division I Coach with victory # 409.

In the 2010 season, having been head coach of any Division I program longer than any other, since 1966, Joe Paterno saw his resurgent and determined squad wipe out a 21-0 deficit to score touchdowns on five consecutive possessions to beat Northwestern,

35-21 on Nov. 6, 2010. This victory was big. It was the # 400 win in Paterno's career. He became the first Football Bowl Subdivision coach to reach that milestone.

The 100,000-plus fans in State College's huge Beaver Stadium on that day, reveled as the Hall of Fame coach was well-honored in a post-game on-field ceremony. Not only had they witnessed win No. 400, but also the greatest Nittany Lion comeback at home in Coach Paterno's 278th game coaching in Beaver Stadium.

It was a great game. The rally from 21 points down also tied the greatest comeback under the legendary mentor, matching the memorable win at Illinois in 1994, when the Nittany Lions trailed 21-0 in the first quarter and won, 35-31 en route to the Big Ten and Rose Bowl titles.

Just as was the case with the 1994 Nittany Lions and 25 times overall, Paterno's 2010 edition earned the opportunity to play in a New Year's Day Bowl Game.

By the way, this is another Paterno record. He is the all-time leader in post-season wins (24-12-1 record) and appearances (37). This particular year, 2010, Joe Paterno guided Penn State to a berth in the Outback Bowl, the squad's sixth New Year's Bowl in the past seven years. Penn State is 17-8 in New Year's bowl games under Paterno. Penn State is proud of Joe Paterno's great record.

Since the start of the 2005 season, Mr. Paterno and his highly competent staff have led Penn State to a 58-19 (75.3) record, a figure that ranks among the top 10 percent nationally.

The success of what some call Paterno's "Grand Experiment" of combined academics and athletics paid off and continued unabated in 2010. Senior guard Stefen Wisniewski led three Nittany Lions who were selected first team CoSIDA Academic All-Americans.

Academics were always very important to Joe Paterno and he drilled that into the players on each of his teams over the years. This is a record. It is the most Academic All Americans in the nation for the third consecutive year. Senior linebacker Chris Colasanti and sophomore defensive end Pete Massaro joined Wisniewski, giving

Penn State a nation's-best 15 Academic All-Americans since 2006. Joe Paterno was as proud of that record as his many victories.

Penn State acknowledges all the time how Joseph V. Paterno has passionately served the Penn State football program and the university with principle, distinction and success with honor since matriculating to State College in 1950. After 16 years as an assistant coach, he was rewarded for his fine work in 1966 with the head coaching responsibilities surrendered by the retiring Rip Engle. Engle had been Paterno's college coach at Brown. He liked what he saw and he appointed JoePa before he was JoePa to the Penn State staff in 1950 as a brash young 23-year old.

In 2010, Joe Paterno was a lot older (83), and wiser than in 1950 at 23, but he was no less enthusiastic and no less dynamic. He was, simply put, the most successful coach in the history of college football -- a fact that was validated during the 2001 season when Coach JoePa moved past Paul "Bear" Bryant to become the leader in career wins by a major college coach.

Joe Paterno is one of the most admired figures in college athletics, an acknowledged icon whose influence extends well beyond the white chalk lines of the football field. Ask his players and peers.

In 2010 when the facts for this article were collected, Coach Paterno was entering his 46th year of pacing the sidelines as head coach of the Nittany Lions. 2011 would be his last year but it too was a banner year of victories on the football field for the immortal coach.

Joe Paterno had faced every situation imaginable on the gridiron and had used his preparation, experience and understanding of the game that he loved, plus a bit of self-taught psychology, to respond to keep the Penn State program among the nation's elite for over six decades. He did exactly that in 2010 in this great comeback victory, chronicled on the PSU Web Site.

Paterno had posted a 401-135-3 mark as head coach as of his second-last season. He finished his career on the winning side at 409-136-3. This gave Joe Paterno the distinction of being the leader in career wins among all major college coaches (second all-time in all divisions). Joe Paterno passed his long-time friend and colleague, Bobby Bowden, on Sept. 20, 2008, for the lead among FBS coaches.

He then passed Coach Eddie Robinson on October 29, 2011 to become the winningest coach in Division I college football.

In 2010, Paterno's winning percentage was 74.7 and it gave him a ranking of # 4 among active Football Bowl Subdivision coaches (10 or more years). He was second all-time in games coached at the time (539) among major college coaches. With a final record of 409 wins out of 545 games as of 2011, Coach Paterno's winning percentage increased to 75.04. So we can now say that better than ¾ of JoePa's wins and losses were wins.

On October 29, 2011, at Beaver Stadium in State College, Joe Paterno orchestrated his most important personal victory on the field –# 409. Though he was in the press-box coaching, healing from a summer hip injury after being knocked down in a late pre-season practice, he was still in control of his team as its head coach.

On Oct 29 in this historical game, Joseph Vincent Paterno broke Eddie Robinson's record for victories by a Division I coach with his No. 409 in Penn State's 10-7 win against Illinois. It was Joe Paterno's last game as an active coach and a great game it was, as great as the game which was discussed in the first paragraph of this essay.

The # 19 Nittany Lions (8-1, 5-0 Big Ten) at the time in the 2011 season, overcame six fumbles with Silas Redd's 3-yard touchdown run with 1:08 to go in the game. It could not have been sweeter for the team, the fans, the institution, or for Coach Paterno.

Illinois (6-3, 2-3 Big Ten) drove from its 17 to the Penn State 25, but Derek Dimke's 42-yard field-goal attempt bounced off the right upright as time expired. God was with Joe Paterno on his big day. I am convinced of that. The immortal coach would not have ever gotten another game to break his record or to make it 410.

Redd, one of Penn State's great backs, had a career-high 30 carries for 137 yards for Penn State. None of his runs that day were bigger than his late run set up after Illinois corner Justin Green was whistled for pass interference after breaking up a fourth-down pass for Derek Moye in the end zone. Redd won the game for JoePa and the Penn State University and all its fans.

Among all NCAA coaches, Paterno now trails only John Gagliardi, who in 2010 was still active at Division III St. John's, Minn.. At the time Gagliardi had 481 victories.

I surely respect Coach Gagliardi but in many ways, comparing Joe Paterno's 409 with Coach Gagliardi's 481 and probably more now, is much like comparing a high school coach to Coach Gagliardi. His record is very respectable but the two are in a different league.

Joe Paterno injected some of his famous Italian humor when he took the mike to thank all those who had come out to root for the team on Oct. 29. He knew they were also rooting for JoePa:

"This is something I'm very proud of... Something like this means a lot to me, an awful lot." He ended his message by saying: "For all the fans out there, thanks for sitting through that today... You've got to be nuts!"

We've still got more to say about Joe Paterno

As of 2010, when most of these indisputable facts were collected by the PSU Sports Department, Paterno's overall postseason record was 24-12-1. This gave him a winning percentage of 66.2, which is #3 all-time among coaches with at least 15 bowl appearances. The Nittany Lions are 12-5 in contests that comprise the Bowl Championship Series. Including his time as an assistant coach. Coach JoePa's wins represent well over 60% of all PSU wins.

Penn State is one of just eight teams with 800 wins all-time and Paterno at the time, had been a member of the Nittany Lion staff for 505 of them -- 62 percent of the 818-all-time win total. Penn State owns a record of 505-183-7 (73.3) since Paterno joined the staff in 1950, the nation's third-highest winning percentage. He has missed just three games of a possible 695 Penn State contests over 61 seasons. I'm not going to check, but I'll take a bet most of those three games were losses. That is my confidence factor.

Since Joe Paterno began leading the program in 1966, Penn State has had 78 first-team All-Americans, with guard Stefen Wisniewski earning the distinction in 2010. Wisniewski was selected first team All-Big Ten for the second consecutive year and a National Football

Foundation Scholar-Athlete. He was joined by senior tailback Evan Royster as a three-time all-conference honoree.

During Paterno's remarkable tenure, the Nittany Lions have counted 16 National Football Foundation Scholar-Athletes, 37 first-team Capital One/CoSIDA All-Americans® (47 overall) and 18 NCAA Postgraduate Scholarship winners. Penn State has had at least one Academic All-American in each of the past nine years, with 13 first team honorees since 2006.

Winner of the 2005 Butkus and Bednarik awards, All-America linebacker Paul Posluszny was selected the 2006 CoSIDA Academic All-American of-the-Year in Division I football and was a two-time first team Academic All-American.

Penn State's 89 percent graduation rate and 85 percent Graduation Success Rate were tops among all teams in the Associated Press' final 2009 Top 25 poll, according to NCAA data. The Nittany Lions' GSR and four-year federal graduation rate were second only to Northwestern among Big Ten Conference teams, according to the NCAA's 2010 graduation report.

Paterno's coaching portfolio includes two National Championships (1982, 1986); five undefeated, untied teams; 23 finishes in the Top 10 of the national rankings; an unprecedented five AFCA Coach-of-the-Year plaques, and more than 350 former players who have signed National Football League contracts, 32 of them first-round draft choices. All-America defensive tackle Jared Odrick was a 2010 NFL first round draft choice by the Miami Dolphins and defensive end Aaron Maybin was the No. 11 overall choice in 2009.

His teams have registered seven undefeated regular-seasons and he has had 35 teams finish in the Top 25. Penn State has won the Lambert-Meadowlands Trophy, emblematic of Eastern football supremacy, 24 times in Paterno's coaching run, including in 2008 and `09.

Since Paterno's first day as a head coach in 1966 to 2010, there had been 883 head coaching changes among Football Bowl Subdivision programs, an average of more than six changes per I-A institution! (Includes 22 changes after 2010 season). Meanwhile Coach JoePa was loyal to Penn State and never wavered, and donated more to PSU than any coach ever in College Football.

Joseph V. Paterno is the only coach to win the four traditional New Year's Day Bowl games -- the Rose, Sugar, Cotton and Orange bowls -- and he owns a 6-0 record in the Fiesta Bowl. He loves to win and he has been successful in teaching his players how to win and how to want to win.

He was selected by the National Football Foundation and College Football Hall of Fame as the first active coach to receive its Distinguished American Award. Paterno also was the 1986 Sports Illustrated Sportsman-of-the-Year. This book would have a lot less pages if we chose to not include Coach Paterno's awards and accolades.

A member of the Nittany Lions' coaching staff spanning the administrations of 13 U.S. presidents (starting with Harry Truman), Paterno passed Bear Bryant on October 27, 2001 when the Lions secured his 324th victory. The Nittany Lions rallied from a 27-9 deficit to defeat Ohio State, 29-27, in the greatest Beaver Stadium comeback under the legendary coach—except the others.

Obviously, Joe Paterno was never a person of misplaced priorities regarding the game of football. He saw his football role as primo as it helped all aspects of his life, including his family who educated five children because of his hard work. Doctors and Psychiatrists are not equipped to coach Division I Football and Joe Paterno had no interest in separating conjoined twins or solving the psychological issues of the day. His concentration was always football, PSU, family, and players. Even JoePa could not do everything.

Yet, Coach Paterno always has concentrated on seeing that his student-athletes attend class, devote the proper time to studies and graduate with a meaningful degree. He often has said he measures team success not by athletic prowess but by the number of productive citizens who make a contribution to society.

The 2009 NCAA Graduation Rates Report for Division I institutions revealed that the Penn State football program earned an 89 percent graduation rate among freshmen entering in 2002-03, which was No. 1 among teams ranked in the 2009 final Associated

Press poll. Penn State's figure was an astounding 34 points above the 55 percent FBS average.

The NCAA data also showed that Penn State posted a program record 85 percent Graduation Success Rate, also the highest among 2009 AP Top 25 teams. The national average among FBS teams was 67 percent.

Paterno was never too fond of looking back, but it was certainly a memorable period for the legendary mentor, who had been a member of the Penn State staff for 695 games as of 2010. Most of the games were fun for all PSU fans and alums, and the administration to watch.

In January 2011, NCAA President Mark Emmert presented the Gerald R. Ford Award to Paterno at the NCAA Convention. The award honors an individual who has provided significant leadership as an advocate for intercollegiate athletics on a continuous basis throughout his or her career. "For me, Coach Paterno is the definitive role model of what it means to be a college coach," said Emmert. There are some who today regret they did not come immediately to the coach's defense. There is no time limit on granting forgiveness. Ask the Lord.

In December 2010, the Big Ten Conference announced the winning team in the Big Ten Football Championship game will earn the Stagg-Paterno Championship Trophy. The trophy pays homage to Paterno and Amos Alonzo Stagg, who won 199 games at University of Chicago when the Maroons were Big Ten members. Paterno ranks fifth among Big Ten coaches all-time with 154 wins since the Nittany Lions began conference play in 1993. Stagg's win total is second-highest total in Big Ten history.

PSU did not qualify in 2011, but has twice since 2010.

"It's an honor for our family and Penn State to have my name associated with the Big Ten Championship Trophy," stated Paterno, who is the Big Ten's all-time post-season victories leader (10-4 mark since 1993). Think of all JoePa did and know that this good man only wished to do more good.

The Maxwell Football Club announced in March, 2010 it was renaming its top college coaching honor the Joseph V. Paterno College Coach of the Year Award. "The Maxwell Football Club is privileged to honor the legacy of Coach Paterno, his values and his successes on and off the field," said Executive Director Mark Wolpert. I say, Amen to that! Keep the accolades coming as it all helps the legacy of a great coach.

In 2009, Paterno banded together a squad of highly-motivated and dedicated student-athletes and coaches into a squad possessing outstanding work-ethic, commitment and senior leadership delivered the Nittany Lions' fourth bowl victory in the past five seasons with a hard-fought, thrilling last-minute win over LSU in the Capital One Bowl.

The 2008 and '09 Nittany Lions earned consecutive 11-win seasons for the first time since 1985 and '86, when Penn State played in back-to-back National Championship games. Paterno's 21st season with double figure victories and 23rd team to finish in the Top 10 added to the litany of coaching records he owns. The Nittany Lions won at least 11 games for the 15th time under the Hall of Fame coach.

The 2008 Nittany Lions and their head coach displayed resiliency and toughness to capture the Big Ten Championship and the program's second Bowl Championship Series berth in four years. Nothing in life worth having is ever easy.

Trailing rival Ohio State in the fourth quarter in a late October night game, the visiting Nittany Lions made a momentum-swinging play and went on to score the game's final 10 points to post a hard-fought victory en route to their third Big Ten crown.

Paterno also was resilient, as he fought through a hip injury that occurred two days before the 2008 season-opener, displaying toughness and fortitude to his squad when in obvious pain. The day after the Big Ten-clinching win over Michigan State, Paterno had successful hip replacement surgery and led the Nittany Lions during their preparations for the Rose Bowl clash with Southern California.

Paterno was selected the 2008 Big Ten Dave McClain Coach-of-the-Year, winning the honor for the third time, second only to Bo

Schembechler's four selections in the award's history. He also was a finalist for three national Coach-of-the-Year honors: the Eddie Robinson Award (FWAA), Liberty Mutual and George Munger (Maxwell Football Club).

When many had written Coach Paterno off their pundit charts because they felt he was too old, especially after the "dark period," with Paterno at the helm, the University Football Team earned an 11-2 mark in 2008, finishing No. 8 in the Associated Press and USA Today Coaches polls. A school-record 10 Nittany Lions were selected first-team All-Big Ten, more than double the second-highest total, and a record 14 players earned first or second-team all-conference accolades.

Four Nittany Lions received All-America honors and A.Q. Shipley became Penn State's first recipient of the Rimington Trophy, presented the nation's outstanding center. Yes, Joe Paterno was the coach that year.

It was a record-breaking year for academic accomplishments as well. A program-record five players were selected to the 2008 ESPN/CoSIDA Academic All-America® team, with four on the first team. Penn State's four first-team selections and five overall selections led the nation, becoming the first school to have five Academic All-America® football players since Nebraska in 1997.

A program record 55 Nittany Lions earned at least a 3.0 grade-point average during the Fall 2008 semester. Among the 55 football student-athletes, a record 19 garnered Dean's List recognition by posting a 3.5 GPA or higher. Joe Paterno did not want dummies playing on the PSU varsity so he helped make them smarter.

In December 2008, Coach Paterno agreed to a contract extension through the 2011 season. He loved his job. He may not have seen all of the other entanglements of his job but in the coaching, nobody has ever done it better.

In 2007, Paterno was inducted into the National Football Foundation and College Football Hall of Fame. They do not nominate or select bad people—just the best such as Joseph Vincent Paterno.

The five-time National Coach-of-the-Year was selected for induction in 2006, and was set to join two more legendary coaches -- Bobby Bowden and John Gagliardi -- as the first active coaches or players to be inducted into the Hall of Fame. Paterno loved being among the greats. He understood them. They understood him. They loved being among a pile of greats in which Joe Paterno had a speaking role.

Coach Paterno's induction into the Hall of Fame had to be deferred until 2007, as the injuries he sustained during a sideline collision in a November game at Wisconsin prevented him from traveling to the 2006 event.

"I have mixed feelings because there were so many people that are not with me anymore who made it possible for me," stated Paterno during the December 4, 2007 induction ceremony. "How good has it been? What we share in football; there's never been a greater game. We've been involved in the greatest game, the greatest experience anybody could hope for. Great teammates. Guys you could trust. Guys you loved. Guys you would go to war with tomorrow. We're so lucky...we're so lucky. If we lose what we have in football, we'll lose an awful lot in this country and we've got to remember that."

Paterno and Bobby Bowden, who rank No. 1-2 in victories among major college coaches, received the prestigious Gold Medal, the National Football Foundation's highest honor, at the 2006 Hall of Fame Dinner via a video presentation.

The 2007 season saw Paterno reach two more significant milestones and one tremendous honor. He eclipsed another college football legend, Amos Alonzo Stagg, for longevity at one institution among major college coaches. Stagg was a head coach for 57 years, including 41 at the University of Chicago. Paterno was head coach for 46 years at Penn State thus beating Stagg and if we can include his assistant years with Rip Engle, Joe Paterno put in 62 good years of coaching for the Nittany Lions. Ask Lenny Moore, a great PSU athlete who hugged JoePa hard each time he would see him/

In December 2007, Patrick and Candace Malloy honored Paterno's contributions to the University by committing $5 million to create the Malloy Paterno Head Football Coach Endowment at Penn

State. The Paterno's are not selfish. Sue and Joe have given lots to PSU and its adjunct efforts such as the Malloy Endowment.

"All of Penn State has benefited from Joe's commitment to success with honor," said Patrick Malloy, a 1965 alumnus of the University. "He is so much more than a coach -- he's an educator. He teaches his players how to win in life as well as in football, and he teaches every Penn State fan how to make the world a better place through integrity, honesty, and excellence. We are also fortunate enough to know Sue Paterno, and we have the deepest admiration for her volunteer and philanthropic leadership at Penn State and beyond."

The Nittany Lions' capped 2007 by defeating Texas A&M in the Valero Alamo Bowl in Paterno's 500th game as head coach. Can you imagine how wonderful it would be and how tough it would be to come into life a regular guy and then finding out you had to live Joe Paterno's life or Sue Paterno's life. I think they did pretty darned good.

As day's end the writing on the wall stays the same. Penn State always hoped to be in a January Bowl game, a wish shared by many of the greatest coaches.

Penn State made another January Bowl appearance under Paterno in 2006 and the Nittany Lions defeated Tennessee, 20-10, in the Outback Bowl. It came as no surprise that less than two weeks after undergoing surgery on his left leg in November 2006, Paterno was back in Beaver Stadium, observing his team from the coaches' booth for the regular-season finale against Michigan State. Joe Paterno was no slouch and he was not a famous brain surgeon. He was simply the greatest football coach who has ever lived. Let's let it go at that!

The 2005 Nittany Lions are a squad the legendary coach also would remember fondly. The players and coaches passionately toiled every day to return Penn State to the national championship picture. In this year, the Nittany Lions compiled an 11-1 record. With the guidance of their coach, JoePa, they captured the Big Ten Championship and produced a thrilling triple-overtime decision over Bowden's Florida State squad in the FedEx Orange Bowl. Who could ask for anything more.

The 11-win season represented another milestone, as Penn State recorded at least 10 victories under Paterno in a fifth decade and for the 19th time overall. The Nittany Lions were listed as # 3 in the polls. They had earned their 13th Top 5 finish under the veteran coach, who could still out jog three quarters of the members of the PSU faculty, regardless of their age.

For his leadership in restoring the Nittany Lions to the nation's elite teams, Joseph V. Paterno was recognized with numerous National Coach-of-the-Year honors in 2005, capped by an unprecedented fifth selection by the American Football Coaches Association (AFCA).

Mr. Paterno also received national honors from the Associated Press, Bobby Dodd, Home Depot/ESPN, Maxwell Football Club (George Munger), Pigskin Club of Washington, D.C., The Sporting News and the Walter Camp Football Foundation. Once the plaudits began to come in years earlier, it was a battle for the praisers to find a spot in the sporting press in which their praise would be written and thus "heard."

Joe Paterno simply is an unusual football coach...and, an unusual person.

In an exceptional display of generosity and affection for Penn State, that the family was not keen on publicizing, Joe Paterno; his wife, Sue, and their five children announced a contribution of $3.5 million to the University in 1998. My father-in law, Smokey Piotroski, often said, "Treat people as they treat you." This was the Paterno credo.

This huge sum brought Paterno's lifetime giving total to more than $4 million. The gift was believed to be, Penn State Vice President for Development Rod Kirsch said, "the most generous ever made by a collegiate coach and his family to a university."

The Paterno gift endows faculty positions and scholarships in the College of the Liberal Arts, the School of Architecture and Landscape Architecture, the University Libraries and supported two building projects -- a new interfaith spiritual center and the Penn State All-Sports Museum, both on the University Park campus. The museum opened in 2002 and the spiritual center was dedicated in 2003. The Paterno family, long before issues interfered, enjoyed being part of a helping hand of benefactors to the University.

"Penn State has been very good to both Sue and me," Paterno said. "We have met some wonderful people here, we've known many students who have gone on to become outstanding leaders in their professions and in society, and all of our children have received a first-class education here. I've never felt better about Penn State and its future potential than I do right now. Sue and I want to do all we can to help the University reach that potential."

He and Sue have been actively involved with the Special Olympics Pennsylvania Summer Games, held each June on the University Park campus. In 2008, the Paternos were inducted into the Special Olympics Pennsylvania Hall of Fame. Even without a dime given to the University, the Paternos are first citizens of Penn State and hopefully for merit, shall always be recognized as such.

The Paternos announced another $1 million pledge in 2009 for the Mount Nittany Medical Center. Their gift is part of the most ambitious fundraising effort in the Medical Center's history and helped support a three-floor, 42,000-square foot expansion of Centre County's primary health facility, which was completed in 2010.

Also in 2009. the Paternos were honored by the Charcot-Marie-Tooth Association for a lifetime of achievement. Coach Paterno is a national spokesperson for CMTA.

The Paternos understand giving in all different forms as long as it helps a great cause. For example, a pair of Paterno's donated personal items recently have raised funds and awareness for Penn State Public Broadcasting. In 2011, the tie that JoePa wore in his 400th win was auctioned for $10,200. In 2010, a pair of Paterno's glasses made national headlines, as a Penn State couple bid $9,000 to purchase the donated, autographed specs. None of the proceeds in any way go to the Paternos. They just love helping people. It is their style.

In 2006, Paterno was bestowed a trio of diverse honors in addition to the Hall of Fame announcement and Gold Medal presentation. He was named a Free Spirit honoree and recognized by The Freedom Forum at the National Press Club in Washington, D.C. In April, Paterno received the Lifetime Achievement Award from the Dapper Dan Charities in Pittsburgh and received the History Makers

Award, presented by the Senator John Heinz Pittsburgh Regional History Center. I bet there are many other tributes and acknowledgments for good deeds but knowing Joe Paterno, his objective is not to fill such a platter of plaudits. He knows his help is appreciated and that is enough for the Paterno family.

Joe Paterno was recognized twice for his illustrious football and speaking career in 2004. He was selected the second-best college football coach of all-time by a panel of more than 300 media, current and former football coaches, Heisman Trophy winners and members of the College Football Hall of Fame. I would say if given the opportunity to state that Joe Paterno is #1; I would also state that I can find no other coach who comes close.

Paterno was, however, chosen the nation's best college football coach of the past 25 years by an ESPN25 expert panel. He finished No. 8 overall in the listing of college and professional coaches from all sports over the past 25 years.

The American Football Coaches Association presented Paterno with its highest honor in 2002, the Amos Alonzo Stagg Award. We began this book with a speech the immortal coach gave when receiving this award. The award honors those "whose services have been outstanding in the advancement of the best interests of football."

In 1998, the coach of whom we speak, was the initial winner of the Eddie Robinson Coach-of-the-Year Award. This award recognizes an active college coach who is a role model to students and players, an active member of the community and an accomplished coach. If there is somebody who would vote against Coach Paterno, I would like to hear and to publicize their rebuke as I feel it would be folly.

The wisdom of Paterno's "total person" approach to football -- which addresses academic and lifestyle matters in addition to athletic prowess -- has won almost universal endorsement from the "products of the system."

"He's putting together this winning program, but meanwhile he's teaching 17-, 18-, 19-year old's how not to screw their lives up, how important education is, how important it is to have social acumen," All-America linebacker Greg Buttle told the San Antonio Express-News in 2007.

"Forget what he's done for players. He's done more for a single university than anyone else. It transcends his coaching. No. 1 to him is what he's done for Penn State University, No. 2 is what he has done for players."

"I can tell you that virtually all of the players he's touched in 50 years as an assistant and head coach have been enriched by the experience," former quarterback Todd Blackledge said in the forward to Quotable Joe, a book of quotations by and about Paterno. "I consider myself, and I know my teammates and Penn State players past and present feel likewise, a better person for having played for Joe Paterno."

LaVar Arrington, one of the 32 NFL first-round draft choices to come through Paterno's Penn State program, was a two-time All-America selection and won the 1999 Butkus Award as the nation's top linebacker as well as the Maxwell Club's Chuck Bednarik Award, presented to the top collegiate defensive player.

"If you're not a man when you get there, you'll be a man before you leave," Arrington said of his Penn State experience. "Joe has his system so that you're prepared for life. Joe trains you more mentally than physically so that nothing will rattle you."

Joe and Sue Paterno had five children, all of whom are Penn State graduates. In 2010 we know they had 17 grandchildren and that is wonderful. God bless Joe Paterno in heaven and his family here on earth.

LETS GO PUBLISH! Books by Brian W. Kelly
(Sold at www.bookhawkers.com; Amazon.com, and Kindle.).

American College Football: The Beginning From before day one football was played.

Great Coaches in Alabama Football Challenging the coaches of every other program!

Great Coaches in Penn State Football the Best Coaches in PSU's football program

Great Players in Penn State Football The best players in PSU's football program

Great Players in Notre Dame Football The best players in ND's football program

Great Coaches in Notre Dame Football The best coaches in any football program

President Donald J. Trump, Master Builder: Solving the Student Debt Crisis!

President Donald J. Trump, Master Builder: It's Time for Seniors to Get a Break!

President Donald J. Trump, Master Builder: Healthcare & Welfare Accountability

President Donald J. Trump, Master Builder: "Make America Great Again"

President Donald J. Trump, Master Builder: The Annual Guest Plan

Great Players in Alabama Football from Quarterbacks to offensive Linemen Greats!

Great Moments in Alabama Football AU Football from the start. This is the book.

Great Moments in Penn State Football PSU Football, start--games, coaches, players,

Great Moments in Notre Dame Football ND Football, start, games, coaches, players

Four Dollars & Sixty-Two Cents—A Christmas Story That Will Warm Your Heart!

My Red Hat Keeps Me on The Ground. Darraggh's Red Hat is really magical

Seniors, Social Security & the Minimum Wage. Things seniors need to know.

How to Write Your First Book and Publish It with CreateSpace

The US Immigration Fix--It's all in here. Finally, an answer.

I had a Dream IBM Could be #1 Again The title is self-explanatory

WineDiets.Com Presents The Wine Diet Learn how to lose weight while having fun.

Wilkes-Barre, PA; Return to Glory Wilkes-Barre City's return to glory

Geoffrey Parsons' Epoch... The Land of Fair Play Better than the original.

The Bill of Rights 4 Dummmies! This is the best book to learn about your rights.

Sol Bloom's Epoch ...Story of the Constitution The best book to learn the Constitution

America 4 Dummmies! All Americans should read to learn about this great country.

The Electoral College 4 Dummmies! How does it really work?

The All-Everything Machine Story about IBM's finest computer server.

Brian has written 110 books. Others can be found at amazon.com/author/brianwkelly

www.ingramcontent.com/pod-product-compliance
Lightning Source LLC
Chambersburg PA
CBHW071658090426
42738CB00009B/1577